PENGUIN B

—

Preparing
for
Parenthood

—

Roy Ridgway is a medical journalist. He went straight from school
into journalism. He was co-editor with his brother, Athelstan, of
the *Wirral Magazine* and subsequently became assistant editor of
Hutchinson's Encyclopaedia. His interest in medical journalism
began in 1968 when he was appointed editor of *New Doctor*, a
monthly leisure magazine for general practitioners. This was
followed by three years as executive editor of *BMA News Review*.
He is now Editor-in-Chief of *Holistic Medicine*. He has contributed
articles to various medical publications, including *World Medicine*,
General Practitioner, *Doctor*, and *Current Practice*. He is the
author of *Aggression in Youth* (1974), *The Unborn Child: how to
recognise and overcome prenatal trauma* (1987) and *Caring for
Your Unborn Child* (1990). He is a member of the International
Society for Prenatal and Perinatal Psychology and Medicine and of
the Medical Journalists Association.

Dorothea Ridgway's main interest has been in group dynamics.
For over twenty years she has worked mainly with children.
Trained originally as an artist at Epsom and Wimbledon Art
Colleges, she went on to take a teacher training course at King
Alfred College, Winchester. She also took a two-year course with
the Association of Psychotherapists. She has worked mainly at
Rookwood School, Andover, and in Further Education, but has
also worked with disturbed children at Rosemary Portal School,
Shawford. She has designed children's toys for production at the
Broadvale Association for brain-damaged people.

Preparing
for
Parenthood

A COUPLE'S GUIDE

Roy and Dorothea Ridgway

PENGUIN BOOKS

PENGUIN BOOKS

Published by the Penguin Group
27 Wrights Lane, London W8 5TZ, England
Viking Penguin Inc., 40 West 23rd Street, New York, 10010, USA
Penguin Books Australia Ltd, Ringwood, Victoria, Australia
Penguin Books Canada Ltd, 2801 John Street, Markham, Ontario, Canada L3R 1B4
Penguin Books (NZ) Ltd, 182–190 Wairau Road, Auckland 10, New Zealand

Penguin Books Ltd, Registered Offices: Harmondsworth, Middlesex, England

First published 1990
1 3 5 7 9 10 8 6 4 2

Copyright © Roy and Dorothea Ridgway, 1990

The moral right of the authors has been asserted

All rights reserved

Filmset in 10/12 pt Sabon

Made and printed in Great Britain by
Richard Clay Ltd, Bungay, Suffolk

Contents

—

Parentage is a very important profession;
but no test of fitness for it
is ever imposed in the interest of children.

GEORGE BERNARD SHAW
Everybody's Political What's What

Acknowledgements

Our thanks go especially to Mrs Belinda Barnes who has worked extremely hard for the Foresight Association for the Promotion of Pre-conceptual Care, and has provided us with a great deal of the background material for this book. Thanks are also due to Colleen Norman for her help with the section on Natural Family Planning and particularly for her diagrams (pages 165–6) illustrating the Billings Method; Dr Barbara Pickard for various useful suggestions; Dr N. I. Ward of the Chemistry Department of the University of Surrey for help with information concerning environmental hazards to health; Tamsin Wilson, the Maternity Alliance and Thames Television for permission to use the illustrations on pages 36, 52 and 220; Dr Michael Elspir for help with the section on epilepsy; Professor Bob Williamson, of the Department of Biochemistry and Molecular Genetics, St Mary's Hospital Medical School, for his help with the section on cystic fibrosis; Toni Belfield, Medical Information Officer of the Family Planning Association, for her suggestions for the chapter on conception; and Mr Steve Rabson, National Health and Safety Officer of the General, Municipal, Boilermakers and Allied Trades Union (GMB) for his suggestions for the chapter on health at work. Many thanks also to the following organizations for providing us with valuable information: Blithe (the British Life Insurance Trust for Health Education); British Diabetic Association; Cystic Fibrosis Foundation Trust; the Haemophilia Society; Health Education Council (page 37); National Childbirth Trust; Miscarriage Association; and the Parent

ACKNOWLEDGEMENTS

Network. We should like to thank Dr Pat Crichley for checking the manuscript for medical accuracy, and Pam Dix of Penguin Books and Janet Law for their editorial skills in preparing the manuscript for publication.

Prelude

Pregnancy is one of those life events, like marriage or retirement, that can be both exhilarating and disturbing. Most women negotiate it successfully and without too much anxiety. But we tend to put up with things if we think they are inevitable and that is what women have been told: it is a difficult time, you will be anxious, the birth will be painful, and so on. One of the aims of pre-conceptual care is to change such attitudes so that couples are prepared physically and emotionally for a pregnancy that is as trouble-free as possible. It is a hitherto neglected but important part of preventive medicine. Why wait until a baby is on the way before you start taking care of yourself? Why wait until you know you are pregnant before you start reading the baby books and asking questions such as 'Will the VDU in the office harm my baby?' or 'How much alcohol can I drink?' or 'What extra vitamins will I need?' Why wait until you are told the pregnancy test is positive before worrying whether or not you are going to cope?

It is a common failing to treat doctors as miracle workers, expecting them to solve all our problems. When they fail us we say they are no good. We should stop kowtowing to medical authority and start sharing among ourselves the knowledge of parents and others with experience of childbirth; we need to be ready to discuss among ourselves all the problems that might arise and be willing to try new remedies or therapies, so long as they do not put us at risk, if the old ones fail.

Our subservience to doctors is partly the media's fault. Anne Karpf, in her book *Doctoring the Media: The Reporting of Health and Medicine*, writes about the uncritical reporting of medicine. Journalism is rarely innovative and reporters, in thrall to a deadline, need authoritative commentators. They all tend to get quotes from the same medical experts – mostly establishment doctors. If someone from the British Medical Association (BMA) makes a pronouncement, it is treated with tremendous respect – but he (it is usually a man) is probably someone who spends his time reading reports, and has not seen a patient in years. What we need is some kind of slogan like 'Patient power' or 'Prospective parents unite!'

However, although there is a need for a much more critical attitude towards medicine as a whole, we should acknowledge the tremendous achievements of modern technological medicine, especially in the areas of pregnancy and childbirth. There are times when you simply must put yourself in the hands of the experts.

This book sets out some of the options open to you about where and when and how to have a child and deals with some of the problems couples face. We also suggest common-sense ways in which you can get fit for pregnancy. We would like to emphasize that we are writing for couples, for the man as much as the woman. We believe that the responsibility of making the decision to have a child must be shared by both partners.

Today fathers are there at the birth – or can be if they wish. So why not take the same interest throughout the pregnancy and even before conception? That is the really crucial time, when any decision to have a child must be a joint one. We hope that this book will help to change attitudes. The father should have as much of a caring role as the mother. The majority of couples will probably find planning for pregnancy more rewarding than simply letting things happen without making any plans. We hope both of you will be able to feel that you did your best for your child.

ROY AND DOROTHEA RIDGWAY
September 1988

1

Timing the Birth

There are so many things to consider before starting a family, yet it is rare to hear people talking about whether or not they are ready to become parents. Most people feel that the mere fact that they are married or living together qualifies them to have a child. Many couples do not really begin to think about what it means to have a baby until one is actually on the way. Sadly, for some, by that stage it may be too late. In the early phase of pregnancy rapidly-growing cells can easily be damaged, even before the couple know that they are going to have a baby.

The best way of making sure that your baby negotiates the early stages satisfactorily and develops into a healthy newborn is for you and your partner to build up your own health before you decide on a family. As a National Childbirth Trust leaflet puts it: 'Healthy babies begin before you're pregnant.'

Of course, things sometimes go wrong that no one could possibly have anticipated or prevented. There are many environmental hazards which could affect the health of the developing child in the womb. Dr D. Bryce-Smith, of the Chemistry Department of Reading University, who is an expert on environmental influences on the life of the child before conception and birth points out that it is not just the mother's health that could damage the child; the father, too, could cause birth defects through the poor quality of his sperm. There could be damage to the sperm or gamete (that is, one of two cells, male and female, whose union is necessary in sexual reproduction) by industrial chemicals or other environmental toxins. At an international conference on environmental influences on prenatal development, Dr Bryce-Smith said: 'Environmentalists should always keep in mind that life begins before birth, and in a sense before conception. These prenatal periods may well be the most critical of all for proper human development, both physical and mental.'

However, we do not want to be alarmist about environmental hazards. If you look around you in parks and school playgrounds, most of the children you see are bright and frisky. In spite of all the environmental hazards and warnings from the experts, most babies continue to be born healthy. At the same time, we should point out that there is a great deal of hidden illness not included in the statistics, such as a predisposition to coughs and colds, behavioural problems, or learning difficulties in children that may go unnoticed and could have had a prenatal cause. Nevertheless, serious conditions occur more frequently than most of us realize. According to the Office of Population Censuses and Surveys (OPCS), in 1986 there were 6,372 perinatal deaths, 3,549 stillbirths and 47,848 low-birthweight babies in the UK. It is estimated that approximately one in seven pregnancies goes wrong. In the past three years the number of low-birthweight babies has been increasing, an indication that, in spite of health education concerning diet, there are still many pregnant women who are malnourished.

Very few people, apart from relatives and a few close friends, are interested in the fact that a couple are planning to start a family – not actually starting one, but discussing the idea. Very few of us think seriously about preparing for pregnancy even though we prepare for all sorts of other things in life – for marriage, holidays, birthdays, Christmas, or buying a house. For many people, pregnancy is something that just happens.

Whatever we make of our lives, whether or not we live a happy, fulfilled life and whether or not we live in peace, everything starts with the health and happiness of the child. And the child's well-being depends on how we, as parents, carry out our responsibilities and how seriously we take family planning.

As parents there are some simple first steps – elementary steps – you can take, before pregnancy, to make sure that at least *your* child will have the best possible start in life.

Lifestyle

There are many factors that contribute to a baby's health at birth, the main one being, as we have said, the parents' health which in turn depends on where the parents live and how they live. The people who suffer most, it seems, are those in lower income groups. In 1986 over 6,000 babies died before reaching their first birthday. These deaths occurred in clusters in and around areas where there were socially deprived and isolated groups (such as single-parent families), a great deal of unemployment and substandard housing.

Ill health in general is associated with a poor lifestyle. This is demonstrated in a study, published by the OPCS in 1988, which recognized that the unhealthy eating habits of lower income groups (plus other factors like smoking) made them particularly vulnerable to cancer. People in skilled or professional employment, the report emphasized, tend to eat more fruit and vegetables. Why do some people eat so much junk food? George Orwell said the poor wanted comfort food. You could never get them to eat grated carrots and wholemeal bread; they found comfort in the sort of food mum cooked for them – good old greasy meat pies and chips and suet puddings. Or could a preference for this sort of food have something to do with the fact that information about the damage fatty and sugary food does to your health has not yet reached everyone?

STRESS

Stress is also a contributory factor in a number of illnesses, such as nervous tension, ulcers, insomnia, migraine and high blood pressure. Stress implies some kind of psychological or economic pressure, but what some people find stressful, others find stimulating. This makes it difficult to describe what stress is precisely. It is not something new, a response to the pressures of modern life; Hippocrates knew about it in the fifth century BC and warned pregnant women to avoid unnecessary 'psychic stress'.

A number of studies show how maternal stress can create

difficulties and complications in childbirth and a variety of disturbances in infants. The part played by stress in child handicap was demonstrated in a study carried out in the 1970s by the sociologist Dr D. H. Stott in Glasgow and Lanarkshire, where there were histories of mental abnormalities, such as low IQ, feeblemindedness, maladjustment, delinquency in childhood and adolescence, in some families and not in others living in the same conditions.[1] No genetic method of transmitting social, biological and mental impairments from one generation to the next had been demonstrated, nor could it be shown that postnatal influences played a part. There remained only one area of explanation, said Stott: *what happened in the womb*.

Stott made a study of 153 children, collecting information about the health, happiness, experiences and circumstances of the mothers during their pregnancies and related this to the children's development during the first four years of their lives.

In his report Stott wrote:

What emerged with surprising significance was that the great majority of mothers who had suffered from interpersonal tensions during their pregnancies had exceedingly unhealthy children . . . when the pregnant woman was subjected to continuous or recurrent serious interpersonal tensions, to which she could find no solution, the child ran twice the usual risk of handicap in health, development or behaviour. It could not be explained by birth complications, prematurity or postnatal influences.

Stott later carried out a similar study in Canada, only this time the children were from middle-class homes. But once again he found that it was stressful interpersonal relationships, in particular marital discord, which had by far the most damaging effects on the children.

Similarly, Dr Monika Lukesch, a psychologist at Constantin University, Frankfurt, followed 2,000 women through pregnancy and birth and said that her investigation led her to the conclusion that the mother's attitude had the single greatest effect on how an infant turned out.[2] A positive attitude, therefore, is important in pregnancy.

Many doctors know intuitively who among their patients are

going to have a difficult pregnancy. In the USA one study showed that there were cases of doctors sending pregnant women to hospital as high risk patients, on non-objective grounds, and the patients then developing complications during labour which no clinical test could have predicted.

However, it should be noted that doctors themselves, who are constantly looking for what can go wrong, often produce negative feelings in the mother. Modern medicine, in fact, may sometimes produce a biology of hopelessness.

HOUSING

If you are planning to have a baby, you might start by thinking about where you live and if it is a good place in which to be pregnant. Is it really the sort of place you want your child to growly in? For instance, what condition are the walls in? Are they damp? Is the electric wiring safe? Is the kitchen large enough and have you got the right kind of utensils for a family of three? A slow-burning cooker, for example, might come in handy if both you and your partner are working during pregnancy, so that you can come home to a cooked meal in the evening.

Perhaps you live in a ground-floor flat on a busy thoroughfare with petrol fumes and dust drifting in through the window. Can that be a good place to have a baby? Do you know about lead in dust, in petrol fumes, in tap water and in flaking paint, and the effect this could have on the health of your child? If there is nowhere else you can live, there are foods you can eat that will protect you against the ill effects of lead and other environmental toxins. You should know about these (see Chapter 2).

There may be other problems, some small, some big, that must be faced. What are your heating costs? Will having a baby mean you must spend more on heating? Is your home draughty? Perhaps you share a house with someone who doesn't like children. That is going to be difficult and it is better to choose someone, if you have a choice, who will not mind doing a little baby-sitting. Or do you live in a bed-sitter? That may put a strain on your marriage when a baby arrives.

It might also be a good idea to take a closer look at your

neighbourhood. What are the other children like? What are the schools like? Is there a nursery school nearby? Is there a park? Are there playgroups?

Ages and Seasons

Is there a right time to have a child? The timing of course depends on a number of different factors – on your health, where you live or on whether you can afford to stop work and start looking after a child. But given the right circumstances, is there an ideal time – time of the year or ages of a couple – to have a child?

The experts say that reproductive efficiency is at its best in the young woman aged between seventeen and nineteen. But for various reasons, largely economic and psychological, it is not regarded as the best time to have a child. The best time, according to statistics, is between the ages of twenty-three and twenty-nine. After that, having a child becomes slightly more risky. The risk increases with the years until as you approach middle age, thirty-five to forty or more, there is a risk of serious things going wrong, including the possibility of having a baby with Down's syndrome. No one, of course, can be certain what will happen when an older woman has a child. Most have perfectly healthy babies nowadays. But it is best, if you can arrange it, to have your baby before the age of thirty-five and preferably between the ages of twenty-three and twenty-nine.

TEENAGE PREGNANCY

There are several big snags about having a child when you are a teenager. If you are sixteen, you are probably still at school. And if you are seventeen, eighteen or nineteen you may be at school, polytechnic, university or learning a trade or profession. You are probably entirely dependent on your parents and the young father of your child may be quite incapable of supporting you and the baby. So although from the point of view of the health of your child, the late teens may be quite a good time to become a mother, economically and psychologically it could be disastrous. Unless, of course, you have understanding parents who are in a position to take care of the child for you while you get on with your education or career. If you are quite happy to be a mother and have a partner who is loving and attentive and can support you, it really does not matter what age you are, so long as the reproductive system is fully mature. You will probably make a go of things together. You will have problems, but you will also have lots of fun, and solving the problems together is part of the joy of being parents.

Dr J. K. Russell, until retirement head of the Department of Obstetrics and Gynaecology at the University of Newcastle upon Tyne, was involved in the management of 317 single girls aged seventeen to nineteen who were referred to him with first preg- nancies.[3] Circumstances in the north-east of England – a fairly static population, the high standing of the two hospitals in the community and a long history of close collaboration, for research purposes, between the university, the teaching hospital and the community health services – helped Dr Russell to maintain contact with the majority of these girls and their families for up to ten years. One of his findings was that the medical and social problems of girls aged sixteen and under were rather different from those faced by older teenagers. There were, for instance, obstetric com- plications due to the immaturity of the girls' cervix. Girls in the younger age group tended to be unconcerned or careless about the use of contraceptives. Many of them had believed they were too young to become pregnant, or thought it impossible because they had intercourse infrequently. Another common difficulty was that certain forms of contraception increased the chance of their sexual activity being discovered by their parents.

By and large, Dr Russell found that teenage girls did relatively well in their first pregnancies and posed few obstetric problems. The greatest risk was in giving birth to a low-birthweight baby.

THE OLDER WOMAN

The 'baby-boom' children of the years immediately following World War II grew up to become the young adults of the 1960s and '70s, many of whom were responsible for the political and social upheaval of those years when the values of established society were profoundly called into question. Demonstrating against the bomb and the Vietnam War, they were a generation in revolt against almost everything that their parents stood for.

One of the consequences of this revolt was an awareness by many women that they had been treated as second-class citizens by previous generations. Many of them deserted the home, refused to go on spending their days doing the things that women were supposed to be good at, like cooking, shopping and having babies. They began to pursue careers that were previously reserved for men.

This generation was the first technically able to control fertility almost completely, first with the Pill and then with legal abortion. Many women decided not to marry until they were in their late twenties and thirties, and many remained childless at thirty-five. This is also becoming the pattern of the post-'baby-boom' generation who are deferring the age at which they have their first baby.

In fact, the number of older women who become pregnant for the first time is steadily increasing. In 1984, 166,000 women in their thirties had babies, compared with 119,000 ten years earlier. Many of these women who defer childbearing become excellent mothers. Dr Zena Stein, of the New York State Psychiatric Institute, who made a study (published in 1985) of a woman's age in relation to childbearing and child-rearing, wrote:

Women who have deferred childbearing beyond their twenties in order to attend to the other concerns of life do well in many aspects of founding a family, and often better than younger women. Thus they have an excellent record of conscientious prenatal attendance, corresponding to their education and economic advantage. Several health indices favour their offspring. For instance, the risks for infant mortality in general and sudden infant death syndrome (cot death) in particular are lower among them.[4]

Dr Stein also found (in a seven-year study of over 50,000 children) that the older the mother the higher the child's IQ. Dr Stein said that as an older woman herself she would like to believe 'that age-related attributes (such as wisdom, judgment, restraint, and perhaps economic security) make for better mothering'. It sounds right, though it is a hypothesis that hasn't been tested.

HAVING A CHILD AT FORTY PLUS

A pregnancy for those in their forties is usually regarded as 'high risk'. It is seen not so much as a risk to the mother as to her baby, though in the older woman there is always a risk of a prolonged and difficult labour. In the child, there are risks of chromosomal abnormalities (the main one being Down's syndrome), a premature birth and above average infant mortality. However, in a study of 174 women of forty years of age and over who gave birth at Oulu University Central Hospital in Northern Finland, it was found that modern diagnostic methods considerably reduced the risk of a baby dying at birth.

In this study the risk factors in the pregnant woman included high blood pressure, impaired glucose tolerance (a kind of diabetic condition) and the use of diuretics (drugs for stimulating the flow of urine). The doctors who carried out the study said:

From our results it can be stated that a pregnancy with modern antenatal follow-up at an advanced age does not endanger the mother's health or life. Furthermore, the risks to the newborns can be reduced almost to the level of the younger pregnant woman, with careful monitoring and active management of the pregnancy and labour.

Women in their mid-thirties and over, who are keen to start a family, can improve their chances of success with a healthy diet, stress-reduction exercises and, of course, by giving up smoking and alcohol. As the doctors who carried out the Finnish study pointed out, modern diagnostic methods have also improved the chances of a successful outcome to pregnancy for women of all ages, including those at risk from such conditions as diabetes or high blood pressure (see Chapter 5).

SPRING, SUMMER, AUTUMN OR WINTER?

It is a good idea to think about the advantages and disadvantages of having your baby during a particular season of the year. Do you want your baby to feel the warm summer breezes lapping around his half-naked body as he lies kicking and gurgling on the lawn? Well, maybe it will never be quite like that, but summer is a good time to give birth, even though the baby and the weather may not live up to your expectations. But what about that holiday you were planning to take? Of course you do not want him to be born far away from home, and you probably will not feel like going away soon after the birth. If you take him out in the heat of the day, the chances are he will feel uncomfortable and perspire, or be plagued by insects.

On the other hand, autumn and winter babies may object to all the additional layers of clothing you have to put on them. There is also the risk of catching colds in the winter. There is an increased incidence of asthma among susceptible babies in the last three months of the year, linked, it is said, to the life-cycle of the house dust mite. Having a baby in the autumn will also mean that you will be heavily pregnant in the hot weather and this can be most uncomfortable.

Spring is the most popular time for having a baby. You will certainly feel more comfortable in the months immediately preceding the birth and you will feel better about night-feeding too because the nights are shorter.

Cost is something you will want to consider before making a decision on when to have your baby. What with the expense of making the house a safe place – the fireguard, the socket covers, the safety gate – decorating the nursery, and purchasing a cot, nappies, baby clothes, car seat, nursery bag, baby walker, bouncing cradle, food, medicines, bibs, even a washing-machine and tumble drier, the cost of having a baby can be high. It may be as much as £1,800. If you include a mother's loss of earnings, the grand total could be as much as £10,000 for the first year. Indeed, it has been estimated that it costs £50,000 to raise a child from birth to the age of eighteen.

You will get some government help. Child benefit amounts to £7.25 per child per week which totals £377 a year. You may be entitled to maternity payment of £85 if you or your partner is claiming income support or family credit. Working women will also qualify for eighteen weeks' statutory maternity pay of at least £34.25 a week. It is all helpful, but it does not make much of a dent in the annual budget.

Is the time of the year you plan to have your baby right economically? It could add to the financial strain at Christmas time and babies born at Christmas do not receive the exclusive attention they usually get at other times. As children they may have to combine a birthday party with a Christmas party. Another consideration is the spacing of a family. It may be a good idea to space your family so that the children have birthdays at different times of the year. This could save you a few financial headaches in the years ahead. Birthday presents can be expensive – and remember, they get more expensive as children grow up: a bicycle, for instance, can cost you £100 or more. You should also bear in mind that children born in the summer can miss a term or two in infant school.

Birth Spacing

The spacing of children is an important consideration. Inadequate spacing can create health problems both for the mother and her children. The main problem is low birthweight because the mother usually suffers from nutritional deficiencies when one pregnancy is followed swiftly by another. Any deficiency in essential vitamins and minerals will have an effect on fetal brain development in the early stages of pregnancy and may lead to various neurological or mental disorders.

In poorer countries close spacing does seriously affect the survival chances of infants and children through an initial low birthweight and breast milk of inferior quality. But even in countries whose standard of nutrition is good, the risks of death for closely-spaced children is high: 30 to 50 per cent higher than in widely-spaced births.

From the psychological point of view, children often thrive in a family in which there is not too great a gap in their ages. However, the gap between pregnancies should not be less than twelve months and ideally should be at least eighteen months.

Women who have suffered some form of loss, such as a miscarriage, may space their pregnancies closely and may then suffer another loss. Smaller than average birthweight babies may be born to women who have suffered the loss of a premature baby. If parents have a miscarriage or lose their first child, they should seek pre-pregnancy counselling before trying again.

A big gap between siblings can put too great an intellectual and emotional distance between them. However, there are psychological gains. The older child is often very caring and protective towards a younger sister or brother, though the children are less likely to share the same interests as they grow up, and may drift apart. However, giving the older child a parental role may not be something that parents would necessarily want to do. Some younger children would perceive such a role as threatening: the parent demanding compliance; the child being projected into adulthood, which means obedience and 'good' (not spontaneous, child-like) behaviour. Such children are often 'parentalized' away from their own inner reality.

Children whose ages are too close often become cantankerous and quarrelsome because of their rivalry for parental affection and attention. A great deal of sibling rivalry can be channelled into games. In poorer countries this competition is not just psychological: it is competition for food and parental care, a matter of survival. The competition for food is a very strong drive in all of us but in wealthy societies it is kept under control through ritual – e.g. the planned meal, at which we are all offered equal helpings – or sublimated in play.

Becoming a Parent
THE 'GOOD ENOUGH' PARENT

Bruno Bettelheim, one of the most distinguished child psychologists of our time, is the author of *A Good Enough Parent* which every prospective parent should read.[5] The title is derived from D. W. Winnicott's concept of the 'good enough' mother: in order to raise a child well, one should not try too hard to be a perfect parent. As Bettelheim says, 'perfection is not in the grasp of ordinary human beings. But it is quite possible to be "a good enough" parent – that is, a person who raises his child well.' He goes on to say:

To be a good enough parent one must be able to feel secure in one's parenthood, and one's relation to one's child. So secure that while one is careful in what one does in relation to one's child, one is not over-anxious about it and does not feel guilty about not being a good enough parent. The security of the parent about *being* a parent will eventually become the child's feeling secure about himself.

Bringing up a child, Bettelheim believes, is a creative endeavour. It is a matter of responding to every individual child rather than following any particular set of rules. His main thesis is that parents must never give in to their desire to create the child *they* would like to have, but should instead help their child to develop into the person he or she wishes to be. The book deals with every aspect of child development from birth to adolescence: it is the distillation of the lessons learned in a lifetime's work among children.

The Parent Network (see p. 246) was established in 1986 with the aim of improving relationships between children and adults, and particularly between parents. It enables those who are parents to be of practical help to couples who are contemplating parenthood. 'There's a lot of resistance to the idea of learning anything about parenthood,' says Ivan Sokolov, founder of the Parent Network. 'We have to tread very carefully. We don't regard ourselves as therapists. The word "therapy" alienates millions.'

The Parent Network does not aim to help 'problem' families but rather ensures that situations are tackled before they turn into problems. Parent–child problems begin with expectations before birth. The time to start thinking about parenthood and the problems it can create is before conception as part of a programme of preparation for pregnancy. Many prospective parents are influenced by their own memories of childhood, which can be distorted. It is far better for them to learn from parents of their own age group, than to base their ideas of parenthood on their memories of the grievances or pleasures of their own childhood.

EXPECTATIONS

You may not be able to avoid the regression that takes place – flashbacks to your own childhood – when a child is on the way. This is not necessarily a bad thing. It is part of the process of adjusting to your new role.

A woman's role (as it has been perceived in the past, and still influences expectations today) as mother and housewife and her wish to succeed in a career outside the home may conflict. A woman can be very positive about wanting a child, but unconsciously she may be anxious about her career and about being forced into a situation in which she is entirely dependent on her partner. The conscious wish to have a child does not in any way exclude anxiety about the consequences.

A woman with a demanding and exciting career may find it difficult to make a decision about having a family. There is a theory that the so-called 'happy accident' sometimes solves her problem for her. For instance, she may switch from an effective contraceptive like the Pill to something a little riskier like a barrier method or withdrawal. To the surprise and delight of both mother and father, she becomes pregnant. They find they are both emotionally ready for a baby; nature, in the end, proves stronger than the practical considerations of career and money.

Paul Entwistle, a biochemist researching into infertility at Liverpool University, believes that many 'accidental' pregnancies are unconsciously planned. Also a trained hypnotherapist, he is interested in the workings of the unconscious, and believes that infertility problems are sometimes solved on an unconscious level. According to Entwistle, not only does the unconscious mind make you forget the usual contraceptive precautions, it can actually bring ovulation forward, or delay it.

He tells the story of a couple who had two boys and then decided they couldn't afford to have any more children. 'The husband had been working away from home,' he says, 'and when he came back they made love on day eight of the wife's menstrual cycle, which they assumed was quite safe – and lo and behold she got pregnant. Afterwards she told me that deep down she had been longing for a little girl.'

There are various theories about what motivates people to have children. If you ask yourself why you want a child, you will probably find it extremely difficult to give a straightforward answer. For many, having a child is simply a need, which they cannot explain, a strong biological urge. Life must go on producing life. There are some who recognize this need but reject it. They want to enjoy life without the responsibility of bringing up a child.

They see a child as an encroachment on their freedom, a financial burden and a constant source of anxiety for at least eighteen years. There are some who do not think about these things at all and simply do not realize what they are letting themselves in for when they have a child. This puts a terrible strain on their marriage.

Writing in the magazine *Bella*, Jane Bidder describes the reaction of one father to the birth of his first child:

When baby Andrew was born last Christmas, his father Kevin's personality suddenly changed. Instead of being a caring, loving husband he became moody, complaining that his wife, Marie, spent more time with the baby than with him.

'I couldn't understand it,' said Marie. 'He'd been looking forward so much to our first child. Yet it was almost as though he was jealous.'

In fact, that's just what it was. Kevin was jealous, even though he loved his baby. It's a common problem with new dads.

Suddenly, a father discovers he is no longer part of a cosy twosome and that three can be a crowd – especially if that third demands 24-hour attention.

A woman gets used to the idea of having a baby during pregnancy. She becomes aware of the baby's movements in the womb and will be psychologically prepared for the threesome; but to the husband it may come as a shock and it may take him some time to adjust to the presence of another person who demands so much attention at first. This happens less when planning for the baby is shared and both the father and mother feel a physical and psychological closeness to the growing child (see also Chapter 9).

BONDING

Planning a pregnancy helps prenatal bonding. For both parents to choose when and where to have a child is of enormous psychological importance. It is one of the biggest decisions you will ever have to make, and it is not easy: it would be easier just to let things happen.

Make sure you know why you want the baby. There are powerful pressures to procreate – from family and friends, for instance. Are you sure you are not just giving way to these pressures or do *both* of you really want the baby? Really wanting the baby is an important part of bonding.

Accepting the pregnancy helps bonding and involves the man in the whole process of childbearing. 'We're going to have a baby,' should perhaps be followed by 'Hello, there! Welcome!' It is important to recognize that from the moment of conception there is a child to be loved and protected. Thinking in terms of caring for the unborn child rather than just in dealing with the problems of pregnancy will make the next nine months more of an adventure and less of an ordeal. The father must cultivate good feelings for the child as well as for the mother.

So bonding is not something that suddenly happens at birth, though there is a sensitive period just after the baby is born when skin contact is important. Not all parents form close attachments with their children. There are some who can be extremely cruel; usually they are themselves the children of rejecting parents. So family background plays an important part in the bonding process – you learn about parenting from your own parents.

Bonding is a combination of many factors – physical, psychological and cultural. All these things should be discussed at the planning stage. Are there any cultural differences between you? Are there class differences? How do you feel about your own family and your partner's family? All these things will influence your attitude to your own children.

During pregnancy, and later when the child is born, what the mother will need most of all from the father is emotional back-up. She will be feeling a bit insecure and will depend on her partner to meet many of the expenses involved in childbirth, which is why it is so important that the decision to have a baby is a joint one. That commitment will be all the stronger if the father takes a close interest in everything that goes on from conception to birth.

Both parents should know the biological facts when starting a family. To remind you of them during pregnancy, you could put up a wall-chart in the bedroom, and perhaps some good pictures of embryonic and fetal development. More important is close physical contact between a couple during the whole of this period, so that, when the time comes, both can feel the unborn child's movements in the womb. In the later stages of pregnancy there can be some communication with the child whose hearing is very acute. He or she will respond to a wide range of sounds and has been known to move about to the rhythm of music. The child recognizes both parents' voices immediately after birth, but responds more to the mother's than the father's voice. The parents and the child are pulled together by various signals – by touch, scent and sound – and there is plenty of evidence now that this physical attachment starts before birth.

For most women the purely physical aspects of bonding are normal. Soon after birth she knows her own baby's smell and she usually knows what the baby's cries mean, whether he is hungry or if he has a pain. There is eye contact between them and there is also verbal communication of a kind. The mother will talk to her baby in a high-pitched voice because the baby's hearing is attuned to high-frequency sounds. There is evidence that the unborn baby is stimulated by these sounds in the womb. The mother is intuitively aware of this – but not the father, who will wonder why there is no response to his usual voice which he has to pitch a little higher to be heard.

So the father has a lot to learn. His role is changing, though it is still largely a supportive one, giving the mother emotional back-up. However, in recent years he has become more involved with what was once regarded as the maternal role: actually physically caring for the baby.

WHY CHILDREN?

Among the main reasons for wanting a child are:

1. *As a source of pleasure.* Allied to this is the feeling, when a marriage is becoming rather dull, that a child will bring fun, drama and excitement into the relationship. Having a child for others is the answer to the frustration of not having anything else to do. 'She hasn't got a job and is into the baby thing,' said one mother about her sixteen-year-old daughter who became pregnant. But treating a child as a plaything or distraction is never a good idea. The child may grow up feeling that he is (to quote Sartre) 'condemned to please'. He can never be himself; he must always fulfil his parents'

expectations, amusing and interesting them. This situation often comes to a head in adolescence when there is a family row and the child leaves home.

2. *To help to patch up a failing relationship.* Sheila Kitzinger writes about this in *Birth Over Thirty*.[6]

'If I had heard anyone else give this reason,' Geraldine confessed, 'I would have thought they were mad. It was quite irrational. I was very depressed, hated the house we live in, resented doing anything to it or buying anything for it . . . I knew I was drifting away and thought I could recapture some of the happiness we had earlier in our marriage.'

Babies cannot really be used to patch a failing relationship, or, at least, if they are conceived in this hope, other things have to happen between the couple before any fresh start can take place. Fortunately Geraldine and David both responded to the challenge and after a frightening first year or so following the birth, when she was depressed and living under a permanent black cloud, talked things through as they had never done before, and made radical adjustments in their life together.

He gave up his job which was a demanding one . . . and took another which allowed Geraldine to do a postgraduate degree and him to look after the family for one day a week.

Sheila Kitzinger describes Geraldine as a 'passive dependent'. She had believed herself indispensable in this passive role, but after the crisis in her relationship with David, realized that: 'There's nothing I do for my children that they cannot do for themselves or that someone else cannot do for them.' So many women want children because they feel it gives them some security; they have a strong sense of being needed. This may give some satisfaction, but it is a feeling that does not last for ever and, far from solving the boredom of a marriage, it can add to it.

3. *Children will eventually contribute to the family income.* That was certainly the expectation of many hard-working parents in the 1920s and '30s who found it difficult to make ends meet, and it is one of the main reasons why people in some poorer countries have large families. But in a Western urban society today children are less of an asset and more of an economic burden than in agricultural societies where there are no laws preventing children from working.

Laws restricting child labour make it difficult for children to make a contribution, as they once did, to the family income until they are adults and may be thinking of setting up home on their own. So it is a mistake for parents to imagine that children are going to be an economic asset and it is an expectation that could lead to family rows later on.

4. *As a source of security in old age.* This is another illusion. Children grow up and get married and have families of their own which they may find difficult to support. Sadly, old people in our society are often regarded as a nuisance and a burden. This is the reality. In many other countries old people are better cared for and respected. But that is another story.

So thinking about reasons for having children may not be very helpful. Someone once said, 'Lose your head and come to your senses.' He meant that 'gut feelings' or 'reasons of the heart' sometimes count more than intellectual analysis. If having a child has anything to do with making a painful sacrifice for the sake of your partner's wish for an heir or because your parents want grandchildren, you are not making a good decision. The best reason for having children is what your gut feeling tells you.

Doctors and Pre-conceptual Care

Nurse Sue Bradley spent eight childless years with her first husband. Their relationship was not very good and Sue says, 'My infertility was almost certainly due to stress.' She quickly became pregnant when she married again; but this time she had a series of miscarriages, usually in the first eight or nine weeks of pregnancy. Her husband was not infertile and had children by a previous marriage. Sue was very depressed. She had numerous tests in hospital and took infertility pills but no one could offer any explanation for her failure to bear children.

She had just about given up hope of ever having a child when she heard of a teach-in about pre-conceptual care and childbirth at

Aston University. She attended and heard Dr Patrick Kingsley, a physician, obstetrician and clinical ecologist, explain his approach to some of the problems of infertility. After hearing him talk Sue made an appointment with him.

Dr Kingsley carried out a number of tests, including blood tests and hair analysis, which revealed a deficiency in various essential trace elements. He told Sue that a lack of zinc was the main cause of her miscarriages. She was put on a gluten-free and milk-free diet, forbidden to eat pre-prepared food or food containing additives and told to eat plenty of vegetables and fruit. The couple were told not to try again to have a baby until they had followed Dr Kingsley's health-building regime for about nine months. But after six months Sue and her husband took a holiday in Greece, and they couldn't hold back any longer. 'I was very pleased,' says Sue, 'when I found I was pregnant after the first time of trying.'

The pregnancy was by no means an easy one. There were a couple of scares at eight and twenty-seven weeks. Charlotte, who weighed 6lb 3oz, was delivered by caesarean section at thirty-seven weeks. 'She was in very good condition,' says Sue. 'A good colour. And her weight was quite good considering she was born three weeks early.'

No doubt Sue's confidence in her doctor contributed a great deal to the successful outcome of the pregnancy. These days the medical ecologist has more to offer than the orthodox practitioner in cases such as Sue's which fail to respond to orthodox treatment. For one thing he can spend more time with his patient. NHS doctors are extremely busy people – on average, a consultation with a GP lasts little more than three minutes, which is hardly confidence-building. This is one of the main reasons why so many people are turning to alternative or complementary medicine for help with their health problems. Another reason is that there are so many illnesses nowadays that are caused by environmental pollution of one sort or another and orthodox medicine does not always take into account factors such as allergic responses to certain foods, dust and so on; nor does it always consider vitamin and mineral deficiencies brought about through an inadequate diet or smoking, alcohol or prescription drugs. Most important of all is what Michael Balint, a specialist in the doctor–patient relationship, describes as the doctor's *calculated* ability to listen – paying as much attention to non-verbal signals as to the patient's words. An understanding of body language is important in the consulting room, particularly when dealing with people who have difficulty expressing themselves verbally. There are still many doctors who talk down to patients because they are too busy, too tired or too bored with the sheer repetitiveness of problems they encounter.

Problems of pregnancy are no longer regarded as purely physical, but research in recent years has shown that the outcome of a pregnancy can depend to a significant extent on psycho-social factors: such as the inner and outer environments, attitudes of friends and relations, stress, your own fears and fantasies. Someone who has several miscarriages will be fearful that the same thing will happen again if she does not change her doctor or her treatment. She may become introspective and even afraid of her own thoughts. When the mind is at sea it needs a raft. Often the raft that seems to offer the best hope of a safe passage through the storm is some branch of complementary medicine which puts great emphasis on treating the whole person. A routine examination by an obstetrician, though necessary, is not enough. At a time of anxiety someone who teaches meditation or relaxation exercises may be more helpful than a doctor.

THE PRE-CONCEPTUAL CLINIC

To sum up, pre-conceptual care is mostly about doing commonsense things in preparation for pregnancy. You do not need to see a doctor to learn about what you should do. Having a baby is not an illness; you don't have to go to medical school to understand what it means to start a family. More than anything else, starting a family is concerned with relationships, and the outcome of a pregnancy is influenced more than many people realize by the attitudes of parents.

Pre-conceptual care should be discussed openly during our daily lives: in the family, at school, at youth centres or social clubs and at further education colleges – it should be part of a total education for living. However, there may be occasions when you need to get expert medical advice as well; for pre-conceptual care is also concerned with contraception, the spacing of children, the possible dangers of drugs, such as alcohol and tobacco, and certain prescription drugs.

A pre-conceptual clinic can be very helpful. It can identify risk factors and provide remedies for physical problems or anxieties you may have about being able to cope, or about illnesses in the family. It can help you cope with those influences, medical and social, that you cannot alter, including your genetic make-up. Your family history may indicate that certain precautions must be taken to lessen the risk of giving birth to a deformed or sick child.

On the other hand the pre-conceptual clinic can help you or refer you elsewhere for help with attitudes to pregnancy that *can* be changed. For example, lifestyles can be changed, bad eating habits, smoking and alcohol consumption, with all their dangers to the health of parent and child, can also be changed. Stress is another factor that may damage the unborn child. And there are ways of reducing stress; through relaxation exercises, yoga, massage, meditation and counselling, including co-counselling and other forms of psychotherapy. Mostly the clinic is used by people who have medical problems; but any couple planning a family would benefit by a thorough pre-conception check-up.

The clinic will assess the health of *both* partners. Ill health in the male can result in poor quality sperm which may prevent conception or lead to miscarriage. You will be offered advice about nutrition, smoking, alcohol, prescription drugs, contraception, sexually transmitted diseases, AIDS, illnesses in the family, such as diabetes or epilepsy, and illnesses that may be inherited.

If there is no pre-conceptual clinic in your area you will find names and addresses of organizations which can help with particular problems in the Further Information section of this book (see page 246). For example, Foresight, the Association for the Promotion of Pre-conceptual Care, has branch secretaries throughout the UK, who will be able to give names of publications or doctors who can help you with your problem, as well as directing you to your nearest clinic or Foresight GP. There are also a number of NHS pre-conceptual clinics in the UK attached to hospitals and health centres.

The Foresight GP and the clinic aim to detoxify prospective

parents from drugs and toxic trace elements such as lead and cadmium. A thorough physical examination involves blood pressure check, hair analysis and tests to detect the presence of toxic trace elements or a deficiency of essential trace elements such as zinc or manganese, tests on the thyroid gland, for rubella and for abnormal sperm. Foresight publishes pamphlets on various aspects of pre-conceptual care and is very keen on educating couples in nutrition, which plays such an important part in building health. All these aspects of pre-conceptual care are discussed in the chapters that follow.

2

Environmental Hazards

—

Among the main environmental risks to our reproductive systems are alcohol abuse, smoking, radiation, street drugs such as marijuana, cocaine and heroin, some prescription drugs, and exposure to toxic substances such as lead, aluminium or mercury. This chapter will suggest common-sense precautions that can be taken to avoid such risks before conception. When planning for parenthood, an intelligent individual response to external factors which can affect both male and female reproductive systems is crucial in preventing possible damage later on to the unborn child. Doctors cannot be held responsible for what may go wrong; a couple must practise their own preventive medicine and, in the case of illness, participate in the diagnosis and treatment.

There is a growing interest in ecological medicine, a new discipline which is examining, among other things, the way environmental pollutants, such as the so-called phenolic compounds used as colourings and preservatives in our foods, can damage our health. Research in the USA has identified some ninety chemicals of this kind which are responsible for food-sensitivity problems. One of these, for instance, is nicotine, which is not only found in tobacco but also in potatoes and tomatoes. Another is tyramine, which is a powerful migraine precipitant. Some migraine sufferers are deficient in the enzyme which metabolizes tyramine and if they take too much food containing this compound, it can trigger a migraine attack. One case reported in the medical press told of a three-year-old who had a disabling migraine with vomiting.

By excluding all tyramine from his diet his migraine was cured.

There are also industrial chemicals released into our environment that have been shown to damage the reproductive systems of some women, and to bring about changes in the quantity and quality of male sperm. We are just beginning to understand how all this is happening, which is why there is so much concern about pesticides, additives and other chemical agents that are involved in the production of foodstuffs.

Toxic Trace Elements

Trace elements such as manganese, copper, cobalt, zinc and iron are present in the body and are needed in extremely small amounts. They are crucial to the normal development of the unborn child. But there are some trace elements that are environmental pollutants. For example, lead, mercury and cadmium have been found in the placenta, and we now know they can be extremely damaging to the neurological or physical development of the fetus. The effects of some of these metals begin at conception and continue deleteriously throughout pregnancy.

Until quite recently medical researchers paid little attention to the wide range of differences in size, structure, growth rate, motor function and performance in so-called 'normal' infants. It is now believed that trace elements account for some of these differences and that some infants who at one time were described as 'normal' were, in fact, 'abnormal' – though perhaps not obviously so – having been damaged at conception and during pregnancy by chemical pollutants. In the past God or genetic variations were blamed for physical or behavioural differences in infants not pronounced enough to be described as abnormal.

One of the latest findings (reported in the *British Medical Journal* in February 1988) is an association between zinc deficiency, as revealed in sweat tests, and dyslexia. Less surprising was the fact, reported in the same paper, that higher concentrations of lead and other toxic metals were found in children with impaired learning. The effect of lead on children's learning ability has been known for some time; but apparently other metals are involved, including copper and cadmium. It is also believed that heavy metals, such as lead and cadmium, which are antagonistic to various essential minerals such as zinc, manganese and chromium, are among the contributory causes of hyperactivity in children.

LEAD

There is plenty of evidence to show that lead is one of the most dangerous of all environmental pollutants. It is mainly a problem in cities where research has linked high lead levels in children with behavioural problems and below average IQ. The young child is particularly vulnerable to lead exposure because there is evidence that excessive levels can injure the central nervous system before it is fully developed. High lead levels can also cross the placenta and damage the growing embryo or fetus.

Lead, however, tends to concentrate in the placenta, which probably accounts for the fact that it can induce miscarriages. This was recognized at the turn of the century when lead was used by back-street abortionists to terminate unwanted pregnancies with disastrous side-effects on mothers, including brain damage and blindness. If lead does cross the placenta, it will damage fetal bone and liver. Indeed, lead levels in the bones of stillborn babies have been found to be five to ten times higher than those in normal live births.

HOW TO AVOID LEAD POISONING

• If you live on a main road it is advisable to minimize the amount of lead absorbed into your system by eating foods rich in calcium. A pint of milk a day is a good idea. If you are worried about calories, choose skimmed milk which contains calcium but is low in fat.

• Check that any paint you buy is lead free. If you are stripping old white paint, mask your nose and mouth with some material with a fine mesh such as a handkerchief.

• If there are lead pipes in your house, use a good water filter. Draw off about a washbasinful of water, which could be contaminated, before using water for drinking or cooking.

There is lead in the dust we breathe in our cities. A high level of lead has been found in the playgrounds of some London schools. In 1982, sampling of lead in dust in school playgrounds in the London borough of Hammersmith and Fulham found only one school in twelve which had an acceptable dust lead level – i.e. below 500 ppm (parts per million). Others had dust lead levels ranging between 535 to a staggering 10,300.

Dr Claire Patterson of the California Institute of Technology claims that in industrialized societies lead emissions into the environment have been so excessive that people probably have 500 to 1,000 times more lead in their bodies than did their prehistoric ancestors. The extent of the exposure is so great, she says, that it is very probable that most people are suffering from its effects.[1]

There is lead in flaking paint, and in paint dust; and from the unlined seams of food cans. Lead is sometimes found in tap water where lead piping is still used or where copper piping joints contain lead alloys.

Hair analysis can reveal the presence of heavy metal toxicity. If lead or any other metal is found, it is important to trace the source. It may be in the drinking water or in household dust. Foresight clinicians like to see a lead level of below 2 or 3 ppm in a small child or in parents who are planning a family. If lead is found to be just 1–2 ppm, it may be possible to lower it through vitamin C supplemented with certain trace minerals.

MERCURY

Mercury poisoning is not considered directly harmful to pregnant women because, although large quantities of this trace element are highly toxic, the body can absorb as much as 2 milligrams of metallic or inorganic mercury a day without ill effect.

However, it is now believed that even small quantities of mercury in the mother could still be harmful to the unborn child. That the fetus is known to trap the mercury selectively was shown in a study following an outbreak of mercury poisoning in 1956 when a Japanese plastics plant released alkyl (including methyl) mercury into Minamata Bay, poisoning all the fish. People who ate the fish suffered from mercury poisoning. Among them were pregnant women whose children were born physically or mentally deformed, although they themselves were not affected. The study showed that the concentration of mercury in the fetal brain was four times higher than in the mother's brain, while the level in the fetal blood was about 28 per cent higher than that in the mother.

Because of what is now called the 'mercury trap', the fetus is regarded as being at extreme risk even when there is a low exposure of mercury to the mother. So it would be sensible to take certain precautions against the possibility of mercury poisoning, which can severely damage the fetal central nervous system. Your water supply should be checked for mercury. The use of weed-killers containing mercury should be avoided. Some dental amalgams also contain mercury and dentists and their assistants may be at risk. Dental patients usually have significant amounts of mercury in their urine following a filling, so a woman should either insist on fillings that don't contain mercury or avoid a filling around the time she is likely to conceive.

CADMIUM

Cadmium has a long biological half-life (that is, the time it takes to reduce the metal by half through decay) and therefore accumulates in the organs, especially the kidneys. Prolonged exposure to cadmium leads to kidney damage. The main source of this metal is cigarette smoke – your own and other people's. However, it is sometimes present in drinking water. Some plumbing amalgams contain cadmium. The metal has been shown to be teratogenic (that is, it causes physical defects in the developing embryo) in animals and it is reasonable to suppose that it may also damage the human embryo. One study has shown high levels of cadmium in stillborns and in placental tissue as the result of smoking during pregnancy.

COPPER

Although in small quantities copper is an essential trace element which has a part to play in the activity of a number of enzymes called metallo-enzymes, in large quantities it is toxic. Lead can raise copper tissue levels; and high levels of copper, like most heavy metals, can interfere with the activity of many enzymes. It is believed to be one of the contributory causes of lead encephalopathy, a serious disorder of the brain.

Copper tissue levels can also be raised by the contraceptive pill and the copper coil. There may be copper in drinking water in areas where the water is soft and acid – that is, in areas where there are pine trees, gorse and heather. Other sources of copper are, of course, copper pans and kettles.

ALUMINIUM

Following reports in the media about aluminium poisoning in February and March 1989, many people became extremely worried about the possible toxic effects of aluminium in drinking water and in some infant milk formulas. Aluminium has long been suspected of being a source of food contamination by practitioners of various alternative therapies who believe that it gets into food via aluminium kettles, saucepans and other cooking vessels and can do a great deal of harm; but scientists on the whole have not been impressed by the available evidence. However, as long ago as 1927 the first report of aluminium poisoning concluded that it was the cause of loss of memory and Parkinsonian-type tremors. Recent research has resulted in similar findings as far as loss of memory is concerned and points to the likelihood that aluminium is a neurotoxin that, if it accumulates in sufficient quantity in the brain, can do considerable harm. It is now widely believed to be the major cause of symptoms such as speech disorders or convulsions which sometimes occur in patients on kidney machines (renal dialysis). Questions are now being asked: who is at risk? Are we fully aware of the risks? Is aluminium another metal like lead that at one time was not regarded as a health hazard, but is now known to put a great number of people, particularly children, at risk? Are the scientists making the same mistake as they did with lead in putting safety levels too high?

Since the discovery of a probable connection between aluminium and Alzheimer's disease which causes senile dementia, it is believed that aluminium is more toxic than was previously thought.[2] The elderly and infants are known to be at risk, and there are now strong grounds for believing that the unborn child may also be at risk, because the central nervous system can so easily be damaged in its early stage of development. Precautions against any possibility of aluminium poisoning should be taken before as well as during pregnancy. Indigestion remedies which contain aluminium should be avoided and tap water should be tested for concentrations of aluminium.

In some water boards outside London aluminium is added during the purification process. The aluminium level in water may be safe for general use, but it is known that in districts where concentrations of aluminium exceed 0.11 mg/l (milligrams per litre) the risk of Alzheimer's disease is 1.5 times greater than in districts where concentrations are less than 0.01 mg/l. As further evidence of the connection between aluminium poisoning and Alzheimer's disease, traces of the metal have been detected in the brain cells of patients in districts with the higher concentration of aluminium in water. Water treatment plants cannot be relied upon to keep the residual concentration of aluminium as low as possible, but they are bound by a European Economic Community directive to limit the concentration of aluminium to below 0.2 mg/l, which is considered a safe level.

Aluminium from drinking water forms only a small part of the total daily intake, but a disproportionate amount of it is absorbed from the gastro-intestinal tract because it is 'uncomplexed', that is to say, it is present in water in its pure form.

In March 1989 a letter in the *Lancet* signed by a paediatrician, a nutritionist and a chemist, concerning aluminium in infant milk formulas, attracted a great deal of media attention. It was alarming to be told that infants were being put at risk by what have always been considered perfectly safe milk substitutes. There is not enough information available at the moment to give firm advice on levels of aluminium that may be harmful, but the American Committee on Nutrition suggested that it would be prudent to avoid feeding low-birthweight infants, including premature babies, with soy-based formulas (i.e. milk food derived from the soya bean), which contain higher aluminium levels than any other milk substitute given to newborns.

One of the risks of feeding milk formulas containing aluminium to infants is that traces of the metal may accumulate in the brain at a time of rapid growth (80 per cent of brain growth occurs in infancy) and can cause serious damage with long-term consequences. Zinc deficiency enhances the uptake and absorption of aluminium. This is an important factor to be considered when preparing for pregnancy, because infants at risk of zinc deficiency are those born to mothers who smoked or consumed alcohol before and during pregnancy.

In general our fears may be unfounded, but as a precaution it might be advisable for couples planning a pregnancy to avoid cooking food in aluminium saucepans or other cooking vessels. Aluminium is absorbed by foods cooked in aluminium pans, especially leaf vegetables, rhubarb and apples which take particles of the metal from the pan. Pressure cookers are the worst offenders in this respect. Kettles and aluminium teapots are also hazardous, especially if the tea is allowed to stand in the pot, because tea leaves contain a substance that removes aluminium from the pot. Other cooking vessels that may leave traces of aluminium in foods include cake and pie tins, roasting pans and patty pans. Baking sheets should also be avoided. Canned food can also be a source of contamination: particles of aluminium can get into the food when cans are being opened. Even if there is no harm in ingesting tiny amounts of aluminium in canned food, it is best avoided: fresh food is much better for you.

Alcohol

Alcohol taken in moderation can be enjoyable and enhance a meal, or it can act as a stimulant and remove inhibitions at parties and other social occasions. Used in this way, it has a lot to be said for it. But it is a drug. And, like most drugs, it can be abused.

Alcohol is, in fact, a very powerful drug and can be extremely dangerous if taken in excess. No one would risk intoxicating a newborn baby by flavouring his food with alcohol; but many mothers do unwittingly intoxicate their unborn children. Alcohol can cross the placenta and get into the bloodstream of the unborn child. So when you are considering what you can do to get yourself fit for pregnancy, you should regard alcohol as something to be avoided. Put it among the foods and drinks on the forbidden list.

In the woman, alcohol can interfere with the reproductive process; and in the man it can affect the quality and quantity of sperm, which is one of the main causes of birth defects. The woman's ovaries can be damaged by alcohol at that crucial time when there is chromosomal activity in preparation for fertilization. Then, during pregnancy, especially in the early weeks, it can have very damaging effects on the health of the developing baby.

The term Fetal Alcohol Syndrome (FAS) was coined to describe a range of symptoms and mental abnormalities observed in babies born to alcoholic mothers. The problem is an old one, recorded in Old Testament times: 'You are barren and have no child, but you shall conceive and give birth to a son,' says the Angel of the Lord to a childless woman in the Book of Judges (13:7). 'Now you must do as I say: be careful to drink no wine or strong drink.' The ancient Greeks also knew about FAS, though they didn't have a word for it. Aristotle, for instance, wrote about 'feeble children and drunken mothers' and both Carthage and Sparta had laws prohibiting newly married couples from drinking alcohol in order to prevent conception occurring when the mother was intoxicated.

In Britain FAS was recognized in *A New Treatise on Liquors* by James Sedgewick, published in 1725. Sedgewick had the same idea as the people of Carthage and Sparta, recommending that pregnant women should be brought under control: 'The regulation of the mother during pregnancy is an affair of the highest moment and consideration.'

There are now over 800 clinical and research papers dealing with the effects of drink on the fetus. Dr Ann Striessguth, a leading researcher into FAS at the University of Washington, listed the main risks to the fetus: mental retardation; retarded growth; central nervous system abnormalities; a variety of malformations; death of the fetus within the uterus.[3]

FAS symptoms include low body weight, a short head, drooping eyelids and crossed eyes, a short snub nose, and an underdeveloped upper lip. The baby is often irritable, tremulous and has a poor sucking response. Later in childhood the baby is likely to be hyperactive and a slow developer.

The plight of FAS children is described by Mrs May Holland, of the National Council of Women, in 'Alcohol and the Unborn Child'.

International research . . . suggests that seriously affected FAS babies never catch up physically or mentally with their normal counterparts, and that they are often hospitalized because of failure to thrive. If they are living with an alcoholic mother then it may be suspected that this failure is caused by neglect – yet those in hospitals and in foster care generally do no better. As they approach adolescence they may develop better weight to height ratio, and no longer give the appearance of being under-nourished or ill, but the IQ (which is reported to range from 16 to 105, with an average of about 65) does not apparently improve with age and the child is likely to remain mentally and socially backward.[4]

Individual symptoms may be caused by other conditions unrelated to drink, but taken together they almost certainly indicate FAS.

The time to tackle any alcohol problem is well before conception because of the damage it can do to the ovaries. There are couples who do go on drinking throughout pregnancy and have perfectly healthy babies, perhaps because they have other healthy habits, such as eating the right food, which may offer some protection against the effects of alcohol. However, whatever the reason, it was found in a study of 952 first-time pregnancies carried out in Dundee that alcohol consumption of less than 100g (ten standard drinks) a week produced no ill effects.[5] It is mothers who drink more than this amount who are most at risk.

It would seem, therefore, that moderate social drinkers have nothing much to worry about although there are many people today who exceed the amounts recognized as safe drinking. And Professor Matthew Kaufman, head of the Department of Anatomy at Edinburgh University's medical school and a world expert on early embryology, believes that the risks are so great that a woman thinking of having a baby should not touch a drop of alcohol until her child-bearing days are over. Failing that, she and her husband should stop or cut down on their drinking as soon as they decide they want to start a family.

Damage from alcohol can occur in a period of about forty-eight hours just before the egg leaves the ovary in the course of the monthly cycle. This is when the chromosomes become active in preparation for possible fusion with sperm.

Alcohol is believed to be the principal cause of tens of thousands of miscarriages every year in Britain, as well as being a contributory cause of some genetic defects. The risks are higher in older women. Although the Dundee study shows that there was no detectable effect on pregnancy of alcohol consumption below ten standard glasses a week, it is well known that there are differences in the amount of alcohol women can consume without being affected. What is 'moderate' for one is more than enough for another. A toxic level for one can be one glass of sherry while for another it can be half a bottle. And 'no detectable effect' does not rule out the differences in size, structure and growth rate in children mentioned earlier, or behavioural problems that could develop later. The only really safe thing to do is to cut down on alcohol about six months before trying to become pregnant and to give up drinking altogether before conception.

HOW TO STOP DRINKING

For most moderate or occasional drinkers, giving up will present no problem. But there are many social drinkers who have acquired the habit of drinking regularly and may find this difficult. Those with a serious alcohol problem should contact an organization such as Alcoholics Anonymous which has branches in most cities. The National Council on Alcoholism can provide information about other available services.

If it is just a matter of reducing social drinking, alcohol intake can be reduced gradually, as part of a six-month fitness for pregnancy programme. The aim should be to stop drinking altogether within three months, and allow another three months to clear the system of toxins. Both partners should follow the same programme. There are systems for reducing and controlling drinking. *How to Control Your Drinking* by Doctors W. Miller and R. Munoz is a practical guide, describing simple cutting down techniques although this is written mainly for people with an alcohol problem.

For the social drinker the first step is to *want* to give up. Being aware of the harmful effects of alcohol on the unborn child should provide sufficient motivation to stop. But if you want to cut down and cannot, then you must accept the fact that drinking has become a problem for you and you should consult your doctor or contact one of the organizations recommended earlier for advice.

The ill effects of alcohol on women are more severe than on men, because their bodies are usually smaller and tend to contain a higher proportion of fat to water. This means alcohol is more concentrated in their body fluids. Thus women are more likely to develop digestive and nutritional problems and run a higher risk of liver damage. So any limits set for cutting down alcohol consumption should probably be a little lower for women than men.

The following strategy may help you to reduce your alcohol consumption gradually over three months.

1 *Set yourself limits.* If you average two and a half to three pints of beer a day, or the equivalent in wine or spirits, you may be damaging your health. You should aim to cut down your alcohol intake to an average of no more than two pints of ordinary beer, or four ($\frac{1}{2}$-gill) measures of whisky or gin, or four small ($\frac{1}{2}$-ounce) glasses of sherry or port, or four (4 fluid ounce) glasses of table wine per week, as this is regarded as a safe limit. Make this your goal for the first month, and then reduce by half again during the second month, aiming to stop drinking altogether by the end of the third month.

2 *Learn to say no.* Many people find it difficult to decline a drink on social occasions. One way to say no is to explain your refusal as a couple: 'We're cutting down because we're planning a family.' If you do not want to bore your friends with your plans for getting fit – few things are more off-putting in a pub! – simply tell them you have been drinking too much lately and you have to cut down for the sake of your health or your waistline. It is to be hoped that there will come a time when such explanations will be quite unnecessary, and people get the message that drinking, like smoking, can seriously damage your health.

3 *Drink slowly.* Try to make one drink last a long time. Never gulp it down. Do not choose sweet wine which you may be

35

tempted to drink quickly because it tastes so good. Instead, go for a dry white wine which can be savoured and sipped slowly. Become a wine connoisseur on social occasions, not a gulper who drinks any old plonk merely for its effect.

4 *Dilute your drinks.* Dilute your drinks with spring water, sugar-free fruit juice or cordials. Turn a short drink into a long one by filling a whisky glass to the top with water. Experiment with mixtures – e.g. wine and lemonade or whisky with lime (a very pleasant drink).

5 *Do not drink on your own.* It may be tempting at the end of a busy day to unwind with a drink, but you have to be careful when you are drinking on your own. One small drink can lead to another small drink and then to another and another until you reach a point when it is the drink itself that demands another drink. It is more difficult to hit the bottle when you're with a friend who is a moderate drinker.

HOW MUCH DO YOU DRINK?

One unit of alcohol is ½ pint of ordinary beer or lager; one standard measure of spirits; one standard glass of wine; one standard small measure of sherry.

Work out how many units of alcohol you consumed last week. Don't just guess – begin with yesterday and work backwards a day at a time. Try to remember the whole day and not just the evening.

How many units is your drink?

BEERS AND LAGERS	Units
1 pint of Export beer	2½
1 can of Export beer	2
1 pint of ordinary beer or lager	2
1 can of ordinary beer or lager	1½
1 pint of strong ale or lager	4
1 can of strong ale or lager	3
1 pint of extra strong beer or lager	5
1 can of extra strong beer or lager	4
CIDERS	Units
1 pint of cider	3
1 quart bottle of cider	6
1 pint of strong cider	4
1 quart bottle of strong cider	8
SPIRITS	Units
1 bottle	30
1 standard single measure	1
1 standard single measure in Northern Ireland	1½
TABLE WINE	Units
1 standard glass	1
1 bottle	7
1 litre bottle	10
SHERRY	Units
1 standard small measure	1
1 bottle	12

What is your total in a week?

 MEN up to 20 units
WOMEN up to 13 units

Drinking at this level carries no long term health risk.

 MEN 21–36 units
WOMEN 14–24 units

If you spread your drinking throughout the week you're unlikely to have any long term health risk.

 MEN 37–50 units
WOMEN 25–35 units

You're creeping up to levels where damage is likely.

 MEN above 51 units
WOMEN above 36 units

You may already be doing yourself harm. A lot of damage occurs without you being aware of it. Try to bring your drinking down to a safer level.

The amount you are affected by drink will vary depending on your body weight.

Remember home measures are usually much more than standard measures.

6 *Always have a nibble with your drink*. A biscuit or some other snack will soak up some of the alcohol. But avoid salty snacks which will make you thirsty.

There are a variety of reasons why people drink, but many do so because they feel uncomfortable in certain situations or they cannot face a difficult emotional problem and need to switch off for a while. Drinking alcohol may be a way of dealing with tension in the office or at home. But most interpersonal or emotional problems can be dealt with more satisfactorily by other means such as exercise, co-counselling, relaxation techniques, massage, meditation or a healthy diet (see Chapter 3).

Smoking

Smoking is one of the principal contributory causes of such illnesses as bronchitis, emphysema, heart attacks and lung cancer. A quarter of all regular cigarette smokers will be killed early by their smoking. Some of these, if they had given up smoking, would have lived ten, twenty or even thirty years longer. Each year in the UK about 100,000 people die of diseases caused by smoking. This is the equivalent of a jumbo-jet crashing each day, killing all on board.

There is evidence that a combination of smoking and taking oral contraceptives increases the risk of heart disease and stroke. Some calculations in the *Journal of the American Medical Association* (11 September 1987) indicate just how dangerous the combination seems to be: the authors attribute 3,000 heart attacks a year in women aged thirty-five to forty-five to this cause. Heart attacks are five times more common in those women than in women who neither smoke nor take the Pill. It should be stressed, however, that the risk is related to the amount of oestrogen in the Pill: low-dose pills carry less risk.

Ever since the Royal College of Physicians' report on the connection between smoking and lung cancer in the 1950s the medical profession has regarded smoking as something to be discouraged.

In most surgeries, clinics, and health centres no-smoking signs are prominently displayed. But in spite of over twenty years of campaigning in several developed countries, tens of millions of people in these countries still smoke.

As it is obviously extremely difficult to kick the habit once you have acquired it, the wisest thing would be for young people not to start smoking. In October 1987 the British Medical Association (BMA) launched a campaign to help families to avoid or stop smoking. Official figures showed that 7 per cent of boys aged eleven to sixteen smoked regularly. Among girls the figure was higher still at 12 per cent.

The BMA decided to aim its campaign at newly-weds. They distributed half a million leaflets to churches and register offices with the message: 'You owe it to yourselves, your family and your future not to smoke.' Evidence was produced which showed that children whose parents smoked were more likely than other children to suffer from a range of diseases and health problems. Some of the earliest evidence was published in 1974 in a study of 10,672 infants who were admitted to hospital during the first year of life. Since then there have been various other studies showing an increased risk of respiratory problems among children of parents who smoke.

It may be argued that this does not prove any congenital weakness in the lungs of these children, but rather that they are being affected by the smoke in the environment. Whether this is true or not, it is certainly a fact that smokers do suffer from more respiratory problems than non-smokers.

There is, however, plenty of evidence to show that smoking is a major cause of physical abnormalities and avoidable ill health in the unborn child. The following are the main risks

● *Low birthweight*. This risk increases with the number of cigarettes smoked by parents.

● *Damage to the placenta*. The smoker's placenta tends to be thinner and larger than the non-smoker's. This is probably due to a decreased supply of oxygen. The placentas of heavy smokers also tend to age prematurely and have damaged blood vessels.

• *Miscarriages and stillbirths*. When heavy smoking is combined with drinking there is a risk of miscarriage. In one study carried out by a group of doctors in the USA in 1978, the risk of stillbirth was found to increase six times in heavy smokers and drinkers.

A report in August 1989 of a research project, funded by the charity Action Research for the Crippled Child, warned women smokers that they were risking damage to future babies even before conception. The study, carried out by doctors at Cambridge University, showed that the membranes of the placenta were thicker and the blood vessels smaller in the placentas of women who had smoked at any time during pregnancy, even if they subsequently gave up smoking. The membranes, which carry oxygen and vital nutrients to the unborn child, can be damaged quite early in pregnancy in mothers who smoked before conception. Dr Graham Burton, of the Department of Anatomy at Cambridge University, said the dangers should be pointed out to women before they become pregnant, rather than at the first antenatal appointment. 'By that time the damage to the placenta is already done,' he said (*Guardian*, 31 August 1989).

Smoking in men is also believed to put the unborn child at risk. Reports from the USA show that the quality of sperm in American males is under threat from various environmental poisons, some of which are undoubtedly derived from smoking. The toxins in tobacco smoke include carbon monoxide, hydrogen cyanide and, of course, nicotine. Small wonder that the sperm of a heavy smoker is of poor quality!

Various health-care and environmental groups have become alarmed at the risk posed by a combination of smoking, industrial chemicals, alcohol consumption and stress, on the health of young men. Friends of the Earth in the USA wrote to all members of Congress with a package of information gathered from various scientific papers showing that 80 per cent of birth defects are attributable to the male parent. A headline in one news magazine referred to what many Americans were calling the 'sperm scare'. The sperm count in American males has fallen significantly in recent years, and low sperm count is associated with birth defects.

Smoking cannot be blamed entirely for this, but it is probably a contributory factor. Men who are planning a family would be well advised to stop smoking long before conception.

HOW TO STOP SMOKING

The first step is to decide *when* you are going to stop. If you are planning to have a baby, you should stop six months before you become pregnant. Nicotine and carbon monoxide cross the placenta and pass into the baby's bloodstream. The nicotine makes the baby's heart beat faster; the carbon monoxide reduces the amount of oxygen getting to your baby.

Most people find that reducing the number of cigarettes they smoke during the day does not help them to stop. The best thing is to say to yourself: 'I am going to stop for good tomorrow.' Then let your family and friends know you have stopped. If you can persuade someone else to stop smoking at the same time, it will make it easier. You may find a stop-smoking group in your area or you could start one yourself with the help of your GP, who will put you in touch with other people in a similar situation.

Try and change your routine. If you are in the habit of smoking a cigarette as soon as you get up in the morning, do something different: drink a glass of orange juice; clean your teeth. Begin to establish a new, healthier kind of habit. Avoid those places, such as pubs, where you have been used to smoking. Travel in no-smoking compartments on trains and sit in no-smoking areas in restaurants and cinemas.

You will find it difficult to stop smoking while you are sitting at a desk searching for an answer to a problem. That is when you tend to light up a cigarette. There is no denying that it helps. In a report by the Independent Scientific Committee on Smoking and Health (1983) it was shown that nicotine enhances attention and concentration during prolonged tasks. In other words, it helps you to think; it fills a gap; it is an aid to concentration. But you could do something different. Stand up and set yourself some simple task, like tidying your desk. Or you could buy a chewy sweet or chewing-gum which last a long time.

The important thing is to have an incentive. What do I get out of it? What do we as a family get out of it? Prospective parents should have no difficulty in answering that question: they will have improved health and a child who is not at risk of any of the things that could go wrong as a result of smoking.

Most ex-smokers will tell you that they gave up entirely on their own. They may say, 'It was hell for three weeks, but OK afterwards and I'm glad I didn't give in to the terrible craving for a fag. I feel great now.' They will usually tell you there is no easy way to stop smoking: it requires determination, nothing else. However, you could try nicotine chewing-gum. This is available only on a doctor's prescription. It is not available on the NHS so you will have to pay about £8 for a week's supply (1989 prices). Chewing-gum is not a magic cure, but it will help to reduce the craving. It should be used instead of, not as well as, a cigarette. It is recommended for the first three to four months of withdrawal, never as a substitute for cigarettes during pregnancy.

There are other special chewing-gums or tablets which you can buy over the counter. Your chemist will recommend one. In addition, some people find acupuncture and hypnosis helpful.

Prescription Drugs

We have heard a lot in recent years about patients who have become hooked on tranquillizers and sleeping pills and who have found it very difficult indeed to take themselves off the drugs because the withdrawal symptoms are so unpleasant. Doctors are now being advised to be more circumspect in prescribing these drugs and not to give repeat prescriptions automatically, merely at the patient's request. These drugs, when taken regularly over a period of years, can be very damaging; and certainly in the case of a couple who are hoping to start a family, some prescription drugs can be as much of a problem as alcohol or cigarettes.

It is too simplistic to criticize the pharmaceutical industry and doctors for this state of affairs. Some drugs are in the nature of last-resort remedies, or should be regarded as such by doctors and patients alike. They are used when preventive or more gentle measures have failed; or because the patient has refused to take responsibility for his or her own health.

Some of the drugs we use, such as digitalis and aspirin, are derived from natural products, but switching to herbal remedies is not always advisable. Some medicines which are freely available over the counter without a prescription, including some herbal remedies, are not necessarily safe to take on all occasions. Some of them are known to have side-effects. There is no law regulating remedies on sale in health food shops to match that regulating the products of pharmaceutical companies which have to be tested for safety. The Committee on the Safety of Medicines are becoming alarmed about this and are in fact planning to review 700 herbal products. Those recommended for serious conditions, such as high blood pressure or depression, will have to show proof of efficacy.

We need to have a more critical approach to pills and potions of all kinds. The medical writer Dr Vernon Coleman said:

The simple fact is that if a drug is powerful enough to have a useful effect on the body it is likely to be powerful enough to have a dangerous effect as well. It is not what we know which should encourage us to reduce our total consumption of pills but what we do *not* know. For example, we do not know what effect the consumption of tranquillizers may have on genetic content. A woman who takes pills may be damaging her grandchildren rather than her children for all we know. The extent of our ignorance is truly daunting.[6]

Clioquinal is an example of a drug, prescribed for 'holiday tum', which was in use for forty years before side-effects were reported. Even then it took another eight years before the drug was withdrawn. It was thought to be a harmless bacteria-killing drug until it was discovered that thousands of Japanese men and women had been permanently disabled by it.

It is very important for a couple who are planning to have a baby to avoid all drugs that are known to be or suspected to be harmful. Iodides, for instance, which are used in some cough mixtures and asthma medications, can cause enlarged thyroid in the unborn baby. Anticoagulants, used for the prevention of blood clots, can cause birth defects, including mental retardation and blindness. In a study by Aubrey Milunsky of 224 women prescribed anticoagulants during the first three months of pregnancy, 14.7 per cent had miscarriages, 6.8 per cent had stillborn babies and 9 per cent had live infants with birth defects.[7] (It should be stressed here that varicose veins, which often occur in pregnancy, are not a cause for concern and will not be treated with anticoagulants.)

Table 1. DRUGS CAUSING BIRTH DEFECTS

Type of Drug	Use	Birth Defects and Consequences
Anticonvulsant	Treatment of epilepsy	Multiple and variable birth defects, including mental retardation.
Anticoagulant	Prevention of blood clots	Interferes with development of cartilage and bone, especially in the nose. There is a possibility of fetal or newborn bleeding.
Anti-cancer	Treatment of cancer	The consequences are so serious, with multiple and variable birth defects and possibility of fetal death, that if cancer is treated during pregnancy, termination must be considered.
Antithyroid preparation	Treatment of overactive thyroid	Enlargement or destruction of fetal thyroid gland.
Local anaesthetics	Used by dentists and surgeons	Slowing of fetal heart rate and possibly death.
Anti-malarial	Treatment of malaria	Miscarriage and possible deafness or blindness of fetus.
Drugs used in treatment of tuberculosis, particularly streptomycin	Treatment of tuberculosis	Hearing impairment and possibly deafness in the newborn.
Iodides	Cough mixtures and asthma preparations	Enlarged fetal thyroid gland.

At least sixty-two babies with birth defects have been born in the USA to women taking isotretinoin, the vitamin A derivative prescribed to treat severe acne. The manufacturers of the drug did give clear warnings that it could cause birth defects, but it is believed that in the USA more than 250,000 women have been prescribed the drug. In Britain it can be prescribed only by hospital dermatologists. The obvious lesson is: always ask your doctor about the side-effects of a drug. Some drugs that are normally safe can be damaging during pregnancy (see Table 1, page 44) so tell your doctor if you are planning to become pregnant. A drug can damage the early embryonic cells before you are aware that you are pregnant. The best plan is to keep off all drugs, if you possibly can, before and during pregnancy. All drugs cross the placenta and enter the fetal circulation. Some women, of course, need to take drugs to maintain normal health: for example, those suffering from diabetes or high blood pressure (see pages 115 and 118). These women should make sure that they are taking the right doses and their condition is properly controlled before becoming pregnant.

Street Drugs

Drug addiction is a serious social problem, particularly among teenagers and people in their twenties who seem to be unaware of the risks they take in their craving for excitement. Drugs are glamorized and easily obtainable – though at a high price, both in terms of money and human misery and degradation – on the street corner and in some clubs and pubs. Such a devil-may-care attitude may result in unwanted pregnancies; tragically, children are born suffering from drug addiction and undergo the same kind of unpleasant withdrawal symptoms as adults. It is bad enough seeing an adult going through the torment of drug withdrawal, but it is horrifying when this happens to a newborn. The infant suffers from diarrhoea, convulsions, rapid breathing and vomiting. Young people must be told the possible consequences of having a child while taking drugs.

Heroin is one of the commonest narcotic drugs and its quality and price vary. About half the babies born to heroin addicts have low birthweights and the risk of stillbirth is considerably increased. Drug withdrawal is hardly ever fatal for the mother but it may result in miscarriage or death of the fetus. There is also the risk of catching AIDS and hepatitis through contaminated needles and children are being born with hepatitis and HIV infection which may develop into full-blown AIDS.

Marijuana is a fairly innocuous drug compared with hard drugs like heroin, and there are women who are not unduly worried when they become pregnant while taking it. Indeed, it has been reported that about 13 per cent of pregnant women in the USA use the drug. However, mothers who take marijuana during pregnancy tend to have low-birthweight babies with associated complications. It is known that when marijuana is taken with alcohol it increases the risk of FAS (see p. 32) in the baby.

Paternal drug users have been shown to be at risk of fathering children with health problems. In one experiment with rats, methadone or morphine was put in the drinking water of male rats caged for mating with female rats. The litters these males later sired with drug-free females showed much higher pre-weaning mortality rates. A decline in paternal fertility has been found in heroin users. One suspects that other powerful drugs, such as cocaine or crack, which have come on to the market in recent years, may have equally devastating effects. It has been shown that some of the powerful mood-changing prescription drugs, such as the benzodiazepines, taken in the first three months of pregnancy have caused abnormalities of fetal development. It would be surprising therefore if cocaine or crack or any other powerful street drug did not damage the health of an unborn child.

Obviously, all such risks are entirely avoidable, and it cannot be over-emphasized that no one should consider starting a family until they are free of drugs.

Caffeine

There is no conclusive evidence that caffeine causes birth defects, but it is generally thought that consuming large quantities may lead to the delivery of a low-birthweight baby. Caffeine is a stimulant that will raise the blood pressure and this in itself could put the mother and her baby at risk. Your daily intake should not exceed 600 mg (five cups), but preferably you should give up coffee and other drinks containing caffeine in the period before conception and stay off caffeine until after the baby is weaned.

Besides coffee, caffeine is present in tea, cola drinks, cocoa and chocolate. As well as raising your blood pressure, large amounts of caffeine can lead to insomnia, irritability, headaches, palpitations, nausea and diarrhoea.

Radiation

Ionizing radiation is recognized as a cause of fetal abnormality. Although there is no evidence that the small doses of radiation involved in diagnostic X-rays not affecting the abdomen – for example dental X-rays – can cause fetal abnormality, it would be wise to consider the possibility of pregnancy before having an X-ray. The potential certainly exists for X-rays to cause fetal abnormality particularly in the early stages of pregnancy and X-rays should never be used on the abdomen during pregnancy.

There is, since the Chernobyl disaster, an increasing fear that radiation from nuclear reactors and reprocessing plants may be responsible for the clusters of childhood leukaemias and other cancers found in their vicinity. Although there is no conclusive evidence that these leukaemias are the result of radiation emanating from these plants, it would be a wise precaution for couples of child-producing years to avoid setting up home in their vicinity.*

Electro-magnetic fields

It is feared that overhead electricity power lines create electro-magnetic fields that could be harmful to human beings, because

* The results of a case-control study of leukaemia in very young people in the area of the Sellafield nuclear plant suggest that the disease could be passed on to children by fathers who are exposed to ionizing radiation at the plant. (Martin J. Gardner et al., 'Results of Case-control Study of Leukaemia and Lymphoma among Young People near Sellafield Nuclear Plant in West Cumbria, *British Medical Journal*, 17 February 1990.

high-frequency electro-magnetic fields have been shown to be dangerous in animal experiments. Long exposure to the high-frequency electro-magnetic waves from microwave ovens could be dangerous; but the ordinary domestic ovens are regarded as safe because they are used only for short spells and no longer leak as did some of the earlier models.

A Soviet study carried out by T. Sazonova, in the 1960s, showed that the incidence of depression and other psychological problems was much higher in workers exposed to electro-magnetic fields.[8] In the USSR there are now strict regulations limiting the time spent, either at home or at work, exposed to electro-magnetic fields.

There is also evidence of a greater than average incidence of leukaemia and migraine occurring in an area between Bournemouth and Poole where there are high-voltage electric power lines over people's homes. Dr David Dowson, when he was working in the area as a general practitioner, did a small study in which he found that out of sixteen people who came to him complaining of head-aches ten lived within 60–80 metres of a power line, whereas those who complained of depression lived less than 20 metres from the line.

This, of course, is not very impressive evidence if taken on its own, but there is a large body of research in America dealing with the problem of power lines. A weighty document, the *New York Power Line Report*, published in 1987, indisputably links high-voltage power lines with cancer and certain behaviour patterns. Other studies, not regarded as conclusive, link power lines with problems of reproduction and cell biology. Prospective parents should be aware of these possible dangers and at least try to avoid living too close to power lines.

We have mentioned some of the main risks to health that a couple planning to start a family should bear in mind. There are other potential risks, such as illnesses caused wholly or in part by allergic reactions to food or environmental chemicals. Most people are aware of hayfever which is triggered off by a high pollen count; but there are many other allergic illnesses, some quite serious, that are not so well known, such as the reactions to phenolic compounds (colourings and preservatives in food) mentioned at the beginning of this chapter. It is believed by some researchers that there is a link between many allergies and nutritional deficiencies. A conference of the British Association of Allergists in 1975 discussed allergy-prone families and put forward the theory that their way of life and the deficiencies in the foods they ate were the cause of such commonly-found disorders as dyslexia, hyperactivity, epilepsy and mental breakdown as well as the more easily recognized allergies such as migraine, asthma, eczema, hayfever and so on. Since then the theory that food allergy is the source of a great deal of physical and mental illness has gained increasing acceptance.

Dr David Dowson, a clinical ecologist working at the Centre for the Study of Complementary Medicine in Southampton, said (in a talk to the Medical Journalists Association in September 1987) that his interest in the subject developed when, as a GP practising in Hampshire, he had a patient who happened to be his own son who, at the age of one, was thought to have celiac disease with profuse diarrhoea and failure to thrive. A hospital biopsy failed to confirm the diagnosis. 'Somewhat in desperation,' said Dr Dowson, 'and against much criticism by my colleagues I removed him from cows' milk and within forty-eight hours he was better. Nowadays cows' milk intolerance is recognized by all paediatricians and most GPs.'

The best way to counteract some of the possible hazards in our environment, apart from avoiding them altogether if they are well recognized, as for instance smoking is, is to pay more attention to our diet and to make sure that we are getting all the nutrients we need. This is the subject of the next chapter.

3

Eating for Health
Before Pregnancy

In spite of the large sums of money spent on health education and the media coverage of medical reports on diet and exercise, we go on behaving in the same old unhealthy ways. We seem to be impervious to good advice and continue to suffer from diseases we could so easily avoid by a change of lifestyle. Probably one of the reasons for this is that what our doctors say does nothing but make us feel guilty.

What the doctors do not stress is the joy of eating well. And they neglect the psychology of eating which involves the need (which George Orwell recognized) for 'comfort food' which people are not prepared to give up. Nor do they tell us that you can get your weight down without going hungry – that, in fact, slimming can be fun.

Couples who are planning a family should try to make their 'countdown to conception' programme as pleasurable as possible, a kind of adventure they will, in years to come, look back on with a great deal of satisfaction and pride. There is no need to adopt a hair-shirt attitude to pre-pregnancy planning. There are a number of cookbooks concentrating on healthy diets, including vegetarian or diabetic cookbooks, that are full of the most mouth-watering ideas for meals that everyone will find delicious.

As a matter of fact, the kind of diet that is good for you is one that has been enjoyed for centuries by families: it includes dairy products, meat, fish, fruit and vegetables. The important thing is to eat enough of the right foods – that is to say, a balanced diet which contains the right amount of the essential nutrients and enough calories (not too many) to sustain you through the day.

A balanced diet is one which contains about 10 per cent high protein foods, 20 per cent natural wholegrains, 60 per cent vegetables, fruits and salads, 3–5 per cent fats (including the polyunsaturates from vegetable oils) and 5–7 per cent natural sugars (from fresh and dried fruits). This sort of diet would mean, for most people, eating more vegetables and fruit; cutting down on eggs, cheese, meat and other high protein foods; and cutting out refined sugar altogether. But this diet can still be very enjoyable – more enjoyable, in fact, because you will not suffer the usual after-effects of an unbalanced diet.

A couple should aim to plan meals that are not only good for them but are acceptable to everyone in the family and to visitors. A healthy diet does not mean a tasteless one; it should mean a diet that everyone can share and enjoy.

Although the sort of food that is good for you has been enjoyed for centuries, there are other foods that have become part of our staple diet: fatty food, for instance, like pork chops or sausages can do a great deal of damage if you over-indulge. And we have learned new eating habits that are just as unhealthy, such as the consumption of vast quantities of junk foods that have no nutritional value. The pleasure of eating such food is short-lived. It is frequently followed by indigestion, or some other bodily discomfort and the illnesses that come from vitamin and mineral deficiencies. When you shop at the supermarket spend more time at the fresh food counters and less at the shelves that are piled high with convenience foods, cakes, biscuits and sweets.

Many people, not only the old and those on the poverty line, suffer from varying degrees of malnutrition. Not so long ago the newspapers were full of stories about schoolchildren whose performance in the classroom was affected by the junk food they ate. We heard how they left home in the morning without a proper breakfast, and in order to boost their energy they bought sweets, crisps and ice-cream on the way to school. Then in the school cafeteria they chose food which, though tasty and satisfying, had little nutritional value. The result was their overall diet lacked essential nutrients and this, it was believed, affected their learning ability.

Busy parents tend to give their children the same kind of convenience food that they give themselves. It looks good, tastes good, is

filling and easy to prepare. But it may not contain essential nutrients.

In planning for pregnancy you are planning your family's future.
It is worth taking the trouble to create a healthy lifestyle for
yourself before your baby's conception and, among other things, to
learn something about the food you need for a healthy life.

Good Eating Habits

To cultivate good eating habits you may need to abandon some of
the things you were taught as a child: For example:

- You need a 'square meal' once a day.

- You can't live without meat – meat puts muscle into you.

- Bread and potatoes make you fat.

- Eat up all the fat – you need a lot of fat in cold weather.

In cultivating good eating habits the basic rules are:

- Whatever you eat, avoid over-eating.

- Cut down on sugar in all its forms including honey, but especially in its refined forms: in biscuits and cakes or puddings made of white flour. There is sugar in bread, canned soup, many breakfast cereals, tomato ketchup and baked beans. Sugar contains no vitamins, no minerals, no fibre – it is pure calories. Always look at the ingredients on the labels of pre-packed foods to check for sugar and additives (see page 67).

- Reduce the proportion of animal (saturated) to vegetable (polyunsaturated) fats. Their proportion in your diet should be under 30 per cent of the calories taken. The oil in oily fish, such as sardines and mackerel, is polyunsaturated

- Eat wholefoods, fresh foods and raw foods where possible.

- Cook with wholemeal (also called wholewheat) flours and pastas; brown rice and pulses and eat wholemeal bread. When buying wholemeal make sure it is 100 per cent – i.e. unrefined.

- Avoid eating too much fried food. Grill, bake, steam or boil instead of frying.

- When baking large pieces of meat and some vegetables use roasting bags or cover with foil to retain the juices and keep the food tender.

- If you grow your own food, do so in compost. Try to avoid using chemical pesticides and fertilizers if you have any suspicion of their toxicity. There are alternative ways of enriching the soil and keeping pests away. Soap and water, for instance, was once used effectively to get rid of greenfly.

- Avoid junk foods (empty calorie convenience foods) but, if you are tempted, use them with discretion, combining them with more nutritious foods.

• Watch the calories. This is the best way to keep your weight down. You should aim at getting your weight right before you become pregnant. When you do become pregnant, you will need extra calories, and unless you are very much overweight, you should not be too concerned about it. Wait until after the child is born before slimming.

• Be aware that different cooking methods alter the calories in food. For example, potatoes vary as follows: boiled potatoes: 21 calories per ounce; chips (thick cut): 39 calories per ounce; chips (crinkle cut): 87 calories per ounce; crisps: 159 calories per ounce. The nutritional value is not increased with the calories. The best way to eat potatoes is baked in their jackets. They retain the goodness: the nutrients are just under the skin, and the skin itself, which is high in fibre, can be eaten.

• A lot of the goodness in vegetables is often lost in boiling. Up to 80 per cent of vitamin C can be lost and up to 90 per cent of the vitamin B group and minerals. When boiling vegetables use very little water and save it afterwards to use in soups or gravy, or drink it neat.

• To preserve nutrients, cook vegetables rapidly, e.g. pressure cooking (though this must be done carefully), steaming or dicing and tossing in oil. Chinese stir-frying is a good way of preserving nutrients. Use a heavy skillet or a wok.

• Valuable unsaturated fatty acids can be turned into the more harmful saturated ones when heated. This happens in deep frying. Chips fried in vegetable oil are no better for you than chips fried in animal fat.

BREAD

Bread is our main source of dietary fibre and provides a quarter of our daily intake. At one time bread was on the list of forbidden food for slimmers because of its high carbohydrate content, but it is now regarded as essential to a well-balanced diet, being low in

---

TIPS FOR REDUCING PESTICIDES

1 Wash fruit and vegetables thoroughly before cooking or using in salads.

2 Remove the outer leaves of leafy vegetables such as cabbages or lettuces. This should get rid of the worst-affected parts. When vegetables are sprayed with chemicals, any residue will tend to concentrate on the outer surface. It is estimated that about 90 per cent of lettuces are treated in this way.

3 Scrubbing fruit and vegetables should get rid of residues, but you should skin fruit, if you are unable to wash it beforehand. Always wash fruit that you buy from a stall or shop, especially if it is on a main road where there are petrol fumes and other pollutants in the environment. The skin should not be discarded if you can possibly help it because it contains valuable nutrients.

4 Grow your own food without chemical treatments. You are not subject to the same controls as farmers and food shops and will not know what constitutes 'safe' levels of residues. However, this will not necessarily mean that your vegetables are residue-free because there may be chemical treatments in your soil. The same applies to 'organic' food grown without chemicals: there is no agreed definition of 'organic'. Wash *all* vegetables thoroughly whether you grow them yourself or they are described as organic.

---

fat and containing protein, calcium, vitamins and minerals. The problem for slimmers is not the slice of bread but what they put on it. The American Heart Association is encouraging Americans to reduce their fat and sugar consumption by substituting them with complex carbohydrates – the starch found in all grain products.

Bread can be used effectively in a calorie-controlled diet while at the same time giving you the feeling that you have eaten well. Unlike other fatty foods, such as chips, it is good for you as well as being satisfying. An average slice of bread has about 60 kilocalories, so if you keep to salads and other low-calorie fillings in a sandwich it makes only a small hole in a 1,000–1,500 calories a day diet.

Many of us these days eat on the move and tend to choose snacks which provide us with a lot of calories, but which are not necessarily nutritious. Wholemeal bread makes an ideal base for what the baker calls 'morning goods', which are things like baps, rolls, crumpets and various buns.

There is a lot of nonsense talked about bread. Most bread, whatever its colour, contains virtually the same nutritional and calorific value, there is simply more fibre in wholemeal bread than in brown or white bread. This has been recognized by the Committee on Medical Aspects of Food Policy (COMA) which recommends that 'consumption of bread, whether white, brown or wholemeal, should be promoted and bread should replace some of the fat and sugar in our diet'.

White flour must by law contain the three nutrients – vitamin B, nicotonic acid and iron – at the same levels as high extraction flour milled from the wheat grain. It is often said that white bread contains no dietary fibre. This is not so: it contains 2.7 per cent dietary fibre, which is more than half the concentration in brown bread and nearly one-third that in wholemeal bread. So don't feel guilty if you like white bread and tend to eat more of it than wholemeal. Just watch the calories and make sure that you make up what you need in dietary fibre from other foods: e.g. wholegrain breakfast cereals. Fibre in food slows the absorption of sugar so that the body is better able to cope with it. It is also one of the best measures against constipation and many diseases of the bowel. One possible harmful effect of dietary fibre is that it is believed to immobilize zinc and calcium which are essential minerals, especially during pregnancy.

The following gives you some idea of what happens when wheat is made into flour.

White flour. The pure, starchy endosperm (containing about 10 per cent protein) is separated from the wheatgerm and bran which are removed during milling to give a 70–75 per cent extraction rate from the wheat (i.e. contents extracted from wheat – the wheatgerm and bran – 25–30 per cent – and not used in the white loaf).

Brown flour. This represents 85–90 per cent of the wholegrain with only the coarse bran particles removed (it contains wheatgerm).

Wholemeal flour. By law this includes the whole wheat grain with nothing removed.

PROTEIN

Proteins are the chemical compounds that form the basis of the structural framework of living matter. A regular daily intake of protein is needed for the repair, replacement and growth of body tissues. Too much protein – more than is needed by your body tissues to provide extra energy – is converted to fat and is stored. There are people who eat as much as 50 per cent more protein than the body needs. This puts a strain on the liver and kidneys and can lead to various health problems, including a tendency to rheumatism and arthritis.

Protein requirements vary according to the number of body cells being built up, repaired or replaced. Among those most in need of more than the minimum recommended intake of protein (about 10 to 20 per cent high protein foods) are expectant mothers, nursing mothers and babies, who are growing fast.

Ruth Jervis (in *The Foresight Wholefood Cookbook*, Aurum, 1986) suggests combining selected groups of protein foods, each lacking in different amino acids. She suggests the following complementary groups:

● Animal protein (milk, yoghurt, cheese, eggs, meat, fish, poultry, dried milk powder) with wholegrain cereal or vegetable protein.

● Wholegrain cereal protein (wheat, bread, pasta, wheatgerm, flour, rice corn, barley, oats) with animal or pulse protein.

● Nut and seed protein (brazil nuts, almonds, sunflower seeds, sesame seeds, pumpkin seeds) with pulse and animal proteins.

Some of the popular traditional meals provide the best complementary protein foods, such as fish and chips, roast beef and Yorkshire pudding, macaroni cheese, and spaghetti bolognaise. Vegetarians will be pleased to know that bread and beans, or bread and cheese, eaten together, provide a better kind of protein than meat. Vegetarians, however, risk zinc deficiency.

While it is as well to warn people of the risks attendant on a high protein diet, it should be pointed out that there are many who need to increase their protein intake. Pregnant women, for instance, may eat food that is satisfying because of its bulk, but is low in protein content.

FATS AND OILS

Some fifteen years or so ago you might have heard a mother say to her child, 'Eat up all the fat. It's good for you.' She was right in the sense that fat is absolutely necessary in a healthy diet, but wrong because too much of one kind of fat, described as *saturated*, is bad for you.

Fats (technically known as *lipids*) provide energy, and small quantities are required for growth and body repair. It is now thought that high levels of fat in the blood lead to the condition known as atheroma, in which fatty plaques build up on artery walls. The plaques, combined with clotted blood, can block the arteries and this causes serious diseases such as atherosclerosis, coronary thrombosis and strokes.

Saturated fats, which are the ones that clog up the arteries, are found in meat – even lean meat – dairy products, pastry, cakes, biscuits, ice-cream and in some vegetable oils such as coconut and palm oils, which are sometimes used in margarines.

This doesn't mean that you must cut down your consumption of meat and dairy products too drastically. Meat is a valuable source of many essential nutrients. Liver and kidney, for instance, are rich in iron which, in pregnancy, is needed to make healthy blood for a baby. (Vegetarians will get their iron from pulses, dried fruit and leafy vegetables.) And milk and eggs provide a high quality protein and are rich in vitamins and minerals.

The trouble with whole milk, however, is that it contains butterfat and this can add to the accumulation of fatty plaques which build up on artery walls, so people in sedentary jobs or who need to lose weight should be careful about drinking too much rich, creamy milk and would be well advised to use more skimmed milk on cereals and in cooking. Whole milk, however, is good for the pregnant woman, who needs the extra calories.

Like other dairy products, butter has come under attack in recent years because of its high saturated fat content. The polyunsaturated margarines have taken the place of butter in many homes.

But completely cutting out butter is quite unnecessary, so long as your diet as a whole does not exceed the daily intake of 25–30 per cent of dietary fat recommended by Foresight nutritionists.

CARBOHYDRATES

These are chemicals containing carbon, hydrogen and oxygen. They are the foods we call 'starchy' or 'sugary', such as biscuits, bread and potatoes. They are good sources of energy, and in their natural state contain vitamin B which is needed for their absorption. Vitamin B is extracted from refined foods so that their consumption puts a strain on the body, particularly on the pancreas which produces insulin, a protein hormone involved in carbohydrate metabolism. If you think of the body as a wood-burning stove, eating refined food is like putting petrol into the stove. It burns up too quickly. The wood, or the natural carbohydrate, is slow-burning: i.e. it produces energy as it is required over a period of time. The natural carbohydrates, such as wholemeal or wholegrain cereals, bread, biscuits, and cakes, slow down the absorption of sugar.

Ruth Jarvis gives a good example of how a natural carbohydrate works:

Consider: a whole yard of succulent sugar-cane would take about half an hour to chew, leaving you well satisfied from a good snack containing many vitamins and minerals, good natural energizing carbohydrate with a little protein and fat, and lots of fibre. This yard of sugar-cane, in processing, is stripped of all its nutrients, leaving only pure sucrose – one white lump. Truly a junk food which contains nothing other than energy.

Everyone should avoid junk food from which all the goodness has been removed during processing and which may contain additives which could damage your health. Apart from this, the important thing is for couples to be sensible about what they eat and to keep asking themselves, 'Is this helping us to get fit for pregnancy?'

There are no universal hard and fast rules about diet. Different people need different diets. Obviously, manual workers do not have the same requirements as office workers. But this is mainly a problem of how many calories they need. There are, however, those whose diet consists mainly of foods from which some essential nutrients have been removed. You should try to obtain adequate amounts of all the essential vitamins and minerals from the food you eat. The following tables will give you some idea of what you need.

Table 2. **VITAMINS**

Nutrient	Uses	Sources
Vitamin A	Important for healthy eyes, hair, skin, teeth and for good bone structure. In the fetus a deficiency can lead to eye defects or heart problems. Your diet should supply you with adequate amounts of this vitamin. Excessive amounts can lead to headaches, vomiting, an enlarged liver and spleen.	Cheese, butter, margarine enriched with vitamin A, milk, yoghurt; liver, kidney; cod liver oil
Vitamin B1 (Thiamine)	Converts glucose to energy or fat. Lack of vitamin B1 can lead to muscle weakness, headaches, back pain, lumbago, fatigue and depression.	Wholemeal/granary bread/rolls; peas, lentils, soya beans; liver, kidney. Buy high fibre or wholegrain breakfast cereals if possible for extra fibre
Vitamin B2 (Riboflavin)	Works in combination with other B-complex vitamins, some amino acids and vitamin A. B2 deficiency leads to bloodshot eyes and the 'grog-blossom' cheeks of alcoholics. It has also been found to cause sterility and stillbirth.	Brewer's yeast; wholemeal/granary bread/rolls; milk, butter, yoghurt, cheese; eggs, peas, beans
Vitamin B6 (Pyridoxine)	Needed by the body to make use of the essential fatty acids and many of the amino acids. Deficiency can lead to a host of unpleasant symptoms, including anaemia, diarrhoea, haemorrhoids and insomnia. Zinc and B6 are removed from the body by the contraceptive pill, cigarettes and alcohol.	Wholemeal/granary bread/rolls; molasses; liver, heart, kidney; peanuts; wheatgerm; mushrooms, potatoes

Vitamin B12 (Cynocobalain)	The only B-complex vitamin found, in the main, in animal products. Most diets contain adequate amounts, but there are only insignificant traces of the vitamin in vegetables. Vegans may therefore need to supplement their diet with small amounts – this vitamin is stored in the body – 50 mcg once a week has been recommended as adequate. B12 is used in the treatment of pernicious anaemia.	Milk; cheese; eggs; red meat (i.e. beef, lamb, mince); fish
Nicotinic acid	Needed for tissue oxidation. Deficiency leads to pellagra-type diseases, characterized by the three Ds – dermatitis, diarrhoea and dementia. Pellagra is a complication of chronic alcoholism. It was once prevalent in British asylums which were notorious for their poor diet. There is very little nicotinic acid in white flour.	Meat, especially organs such as kidneys and liver; wholemeal bread/rolls; peas, beans, lentils
Folic acid	Another member of the vitamin B group, folic acid plays a part in the formation of red blood cells in the bone marrow. Essential for the utilization of sugar and amino acids and for the production of antibodies. The need for folic acid increases by at least two-thirds during pregnancy. It is advisable before pregnancy to start increasing intake. Failure to have enough folic acid will prevent baby's new tissue and blood supply from forming properly, and could cause other complications such as cleft palate and hare-lip. Some research suggests that deficiency of folic acid may lead to neural tube defects, including spina bifida.	Liver, kidney; green leafy vegetables; nuts; wholemeal/granary bread/rolls or wholemeal pitta breads; milk; wheatgerm; Brewer's yeast

Choline	Needed for cell formation. Lack of it can be serious, causing, for example, high blood pressure, swelling and strokes. Most diets contain adequate amounts, but insecticides in common use inactivate choline-containing enzymes – so wash all vegetables and fruit thoroughly or, if possible, take care to buy vegetables and fruit that are not subjected to constant spraying with insecticides. Many health food stores now sell compost-grown vegetables, which are safe.	Wholemeal/granary bread/rolls; green leafy vegetables; meat
Vitamin C (ascorbic acid)	Many varied roles, in respiration, growth, ensuring the body's efficiency in the absorption of iron from food, promoting a healthy supply of blood and protecting against infection, toxins like lead, harmful social or prescription drugs. The need for vitamin C virtually doubles during pregnancy, so it would be as well to get into the habit of eating foods rich in this vitamin when preparing for pregnancy.	Fresh/frozen vegetables or salad are rich sources of vitamin C when quickly cooked or eaten raw. Vitamin C-containing fruits include oranges, tangerines, lemons, grapefruits, guavas, blackcurrants, blackberries, rose-hips
Vitamin D	Essential for the absorption of calcium to make strong teeth and bones. Normal exposure to sunlight (even in Britain!) provides all the vitamin D we need. But extra vitamin D is needed in pregnancy, so you should make sure you are getting enough at the start, though excess should be avoided because it can cause headaches, nausea, vomiting and diarrhoea.	Try and get some sun every day but don't overdo it. No more than twenty minutes a day sunbathing in bright sunshine. Mackerel and kippers are an excellent source, as are tuna and pilchards – choose those in brine or tomato sauce

| Vitamin E | Needed for the utilization of fatty acids. Helps to protect cells from damage or degeneration. Protects from scarring after burns. Some authorities say that you are unlikely to suffer from vitamin E deficiency, but others say that a mother who has a prolonged and difficult labour could be in need of this vitamin. | Wheatgerm; milk; egg yolk; nuts; green leafy vegetables |

Table 3. **MINERALS**

Nutrient	Uses	Sources
Calcium	Essential for the formation of strong bones and teeth. During pregnancy a woman may lose calcium from her bones and teeth, which are prone to decay. It is advisable to make sure your teeth are in good condition before you become pregnant or at the start of pregnancy and to get treatment (which is free during pregnancy and for one year after the birth) for any dental decay.	Cheese (preferably medium or low fat), milk (semi-skimmed or evaporated); eggs; nuts; mackerel, sardines or kippers; bone broth
	Calcium deficiency can cause rickets, once a fairly common complaint among children in smog-bound city areas. The cause of the deficiency was lack of vitamin D combined with a poor diet.	
	Today rickets is rare; but it is thought calcium may be lost from the bones during bed-rest, or while on a high protein diet, and this can cause back pain, cramping of the uterus and premenstrual tension.	

During pregnancy the need for calcium increases dramatically to more than double that of the non-pregnant woman.

Iron	Needed to make haemoglobin, a component of the red blood cells, which combines with oxygen in the lungs and carries it through the circulation to all tissues in the body. Iron deficiency causes anaemia, a condition where the haemoglobin falls below the level needed to carry adequate amounts of oxygen to the tissues. This is not uncommon in women (about one woman in ten) because heavy periods can drain their reserves of iron. Iron-deficiency anaemia weakens the body's resistance to illness, causing tiredness, weakness and breathlessness. The disorder must be treated by a doctor, but you can help yourself by eating foods rich in iron. If you are prone to attacks of anaemia, you should tackle the problem before becoming pregnant, at least by increasing your intake of foods rich in iron.	Red lean meats, e.g. beef, lamb, mince; liver, kidneys; peas, beans, lentils; molasses, shellfish; dried fruits, especially dried apricots; leafy vegetables, parsley
	The pregnant woman needs a great deal of iron to help the baby to form his own blood and to maintain the health of the placenta. Anaemia can easily develop during pregnancy and iron supplements are often prescribed routinely.	
Magnesium	Necessary for the production and transfer of energy, muscle contraction, protein synthesis.	Milk; eggs; green vegetables; sea foods; whole grains
	Deficiency of magnesium causes tremors, confusion, depression and irritability. Lack of	

magnesium in the fetus causes cardiac abnormalities, convulsions and death at birth or soon after.

Chromium	Needed in glucose metabolism. Lack of chromium reduces insulin activity and results in impaired glucose tolerance, which is a characteristic of late onset diabetes mellitus.	Fruits; vegetables; beef, liver; beets, mushrooms
Selenium	Integral part of an enzyme found in red blood cells which functions as an antioxidant: i.e. it inhibits the combination of other substances with oxygen. Dietary selenium has been shown to prevent chemically induced cancers in animals, a finding which is being investigated in humans. One research group has reported low blood selenium level in almost all types of cancer patients. There is also some evidence that selenium combines with toxic metals such as lead and helps to get rid of them from the body. Selenium itself is toxic if large amounts are ingested. It is an example of a substance where a balance between excess and deficiency is crucial. Operators of some photocopying machines are at risk of inhaling large amounts of selenium. Excessive amounts of selenium have also been found in people using anti-dandruff shampoos containing the metal.	Eggs; liver; garlic; whole grains
Zinc	Essential for the health and maintenance of bones, muscles, eyes and organs. It is an important component of sperm and of many	Fruit; vegetables; nuts; meat, poultry; fish

different enzymes. It is needed in the liver for conversion of carotene (the yellow-brown pigment found in carrots, tomatoes, egg yolks) into vitamin A.

Zinc deficiency in women can cause problems during childbirth. In the fetus zinc deficiency can cause growth retardation, and various other defects in kidneys, bones and brain. Pregnant women are said to need 20 mg daily and lactating women 25 mg.

Alcohol and cigarettes can have the effect of removing zinc from the system. Zinc depletion is a contributing cause of FAS (see page 32). Zinc is required for the absorption of some vitamins, a deficiency of which is believed to play a part in causing spina bifida.

This mineral is so important in the reproductive process and in many other bodily functions that if a deficiency is found in either partner it should be put right before conception. There is evidence to suggest that zinc supplements may be of benefit before, during and after pregnancy. Certainly vegetarians, who tend to eat food that is not rich in this mineral, should consider taking extra zinc in the form of tablets.

Signs of zinc deficiency include: white spots on the fingernails, lank, lifeless hair, painful knee and hip joints, no periods, stretch marks on the skin.

Manganese	Important in the building and breakdown cycles of protein and nucleic acid (the main carrier of genetic information). Acting through certain enzymes it affects glandular secretions underlying maternal instinct. It is said to nourish a mother's love and protective instinct, though there is no convincing medical evidence for this.	Eggs; liver; onions, green beans, parsley; bananas, strawberries, apples
	Manganese deficiency in the fetus causes malformation of the inner ear, irregularity of bodily movements and malformation of bones.	
	Choline, a vitamin involved in the formation of cell constituents, helps the uptake of manganese; and it is a matter of concern that some common insecticides destroy choline. As a precaution, it would be advisable not to use insecticides in the garden in the pre-pregnancy period as well as during pregnancy. Use non-chemical alternatives, if possible.	

Food Additives

There has been a great deal of concern in recent years about the increasing number of additives used in our food. A law was passed in 1986 making it compulsory to identify additives on food labels, and making us more aware of 'E' numbers. 'E' stands for EEC, the European Economic Community, which requires that all additives other than flavours and one or two exempt categories be declared either with E numbers or the full name of the substance used and the use to which it is put. For some 'E' stands for poison and an absence of E numbers indicates purity. One advertiser found that sales increased when they promoted their product with the words, 'It's never clapped eyes on an E number.' Pregnant women in particular are concerned that some foods with E numbers may damage their health and the health of their developing babies. There have been reports that some artificial colours (dyes) used in certain foods, such as gelatine desserts and some fruit yoghurts and coloured ice-cream, have been shown to cause cancer in experimental animals. As a result the use of some of these dyes has been forbidden in the USA and other countries.

Public concern has led supermarkets and other food retailers to pay particular attention to E numbers in the packaged foods and drinks sold in their shops. Boots, for instance, issued a pamphlet describing their policy concerning food additives. They have eliminated fifty commonly used additives, such as monosodium glutamate (used to enhance flavour), some anti-oxidants (used to prevent decay in food exposed to oxygen) and the colour caramel from concentrated fruit drinks and squashes, crisps and sugar confectionery.

Additives have been in general use for many years, though there are a great number that have been recently introduced for the first time in convenience foods, such as instant soup mixes. Additives have been commonly used in the curing process to prevent meat from developing harmful bacteria that could cause food poisoning, and there are additives that have been used in the kitchen for the preparation of food since grandmother's day, though only now would we describe them as additives. Such traditional ingredients as sodium bicarbonate, pectin and cream of tartar are now included in lists of additives and have been given E numbers.

The sort of foods that rely mostly on additives for their flavour and colour are convenience foods that have no nutritional value and should be avoided. As many as thirteen additives have been used in some snack products which cannot possibly contribute anything to a healthy diet, but they may look good and taste good. Do not, however, be kidded into believing that everything that tastes good is necessarily good for you, except perhaps in the psychological sense.

Some additives are extracted from natural foods for use in other products. For example, anthocyanin in grape skins is used to colour soft drinks. There are also artificial colours made to the same formula as natural colours. For example, β-carotene, which is used as a colouring agent in the food industry, is the natural orange colour that occurs in carrots. Artificial colours are made mostly from coal tar, although artificial caramel (banned by Boots) is produced by burning sugar in the presence of certain chemicals.

Different countries have different policies concerning additives. Some additives that may be potentially harmful are allowed in some countries when used in small quantities, but not allowed in others as a precaution or to allay public concern. The levels allowed vary in different countries. In the UK, which is bound by the EEC directive, a watchful eye is kept on the use of all additives by the Food Advisory Committee (FAC), an independent body advising the Ministry of Agriculture, Fisheries and Food (MAFF), which draws up regulations to control the use of additives.

Some additives are believed to have a deleterious effect on people with certain allergies. For instance, there are some experts who say that lutein (E161b) or sodium sorbate (E201) may bring on an attack of asthma. Sodium propionate (E281), calcium propionate (E282) and potassium propionate (E283) may bring on migraine. There are others that are unsuitable for children under six months, so it is thought they could also be harmful to a developing baby. Lactic acid (E270) is one of these. A list of additives that, as a precaution, should be avoided in pregnancy, is published by the Foresight Association.

What Should Your Weight Be?

Provided you eat a balanced diet over a period of three months or more, and you are feeling fit, your actual weight at conception is not so important. However, it is better not to be too fat or too thin.

If you become too thin through dieting you may find that you are temporarily infertile. Underweight women usually give birth to smaller babies and these often have more health problems. If, on the other hand, you are grossly overweight, you will be at risk and may have problems during pregnancy such as diabetes or high blood pressure. However, you do not have to worry if you are slightly overweight: the problems of overweight women during pregnancy have been exaggerated. Whatever your weight, a severe reducing diet is not a desirable preparation for pregnancy. You should eat a normal, healthy, balanced diet and be content to lose weight gradually. If you do become pregnant without getting down to a reasonable weight, remember that a fat woman who is eating wholesome, nutritious food will be less at risk than a fat woman who eats poor quality, processed foods.

There is a range of ideal weights for women of different heights. This is shown in Table 4. The figures given are for women between twenty and thirty years of age. Older women would be well advised to try to come within the same range if they are planning a pregnancy.

Table 4. IDEAL WEIGHTS

Height	Weight Range	Average
4 ft 10 in (145 cm)	6 st 4 lb–7 st 12 lb 40.0 kg–49.9 kg	7 st 2 lb 45.3 kg
5 ft (150 cm)	6 st 10 lb–8 st 6 lb 42.6 kg–53.5 kg	7 st 8 lb 48.1 kg
5 ft 2 in (155 cm)	7 st 2 lb–9 st 1 lb 45.3 kg–57.6 kg	8 st 2 lb 51.7 kg
5 ft 4 in (160 cm)	7 st 9 lb–9 st 9 lb 48.5 kg–61.2 kg	8 st 9 lb 54.9 kg
5 ft 6 in (165 cm)	8 st 2 lb–10 st 3 lb 51.7 kg–64.8 kg	9 st 3 lb 58.5 kg
5 ft 8 in (170 cm)	8 st 9 lb–10 st 12 lb 54.9 kg–68.9 kg	9 st 11 lb 62.1 kg
5 ft 10 in (175 cm)	9 st 2 lb–11 st 7 lb 58.0 kg–73.0 kg	10 st 5 lb 65.8 kg
6 ft (180 cm)	9 st 9 lb–12 st 3 lb 61.2 kg–77.5 kg	10 st 13 lb 69.4 kg

4

Exercising for
Fitness at Conception

In a healthy body there is free and spontaneous movement all the time and everything as it moves affects everything else; legs, arms, heart, lungs, brain, nerves, muscles, are all functionally related to one another. All these and other parts of the body make up an incredibly complicated pattern of energy and movement. It is like a balancing act with many participants. If someone is weak, the others have to try to adjust their movements to restore the balance. Medically, this way of maintaining a balance, where everything in the body tends to move towards a state of stability, is called 'homeostasis'.

The body never achieves a perfect balance. Homeostasis is a state, one might say, of travelling hopefully but never actually arriving. The important thing is the way one travels, the way one moves; the continuing effort, hardly noticed, which is made to maintain the balance between opposing forces, inner and outer, good and bad, sickness and health.

Ill health occurs when the balance becomes difficult to maintain. There is a collapse when movement in some part of the body becomes seriously blocked or paralysed. Then more than the usual effort is required to restore the body to a state of balance or stability. And it is this effort that produces pain. Sometimes systems break down altogether, and there is chronic or fatal illness when the restorative powers of the body (the immune system) are weakened or destroyed. This happens naturally in old age; but it can also happen at any time in life when we neglect or overwork our bodies or do not provide ourselves with the nutrients that are needed for energy.

One of the reasons why many of us are not fit is that we live in an industrialized society and are constantly under a great deal of pressure, performing tasks which require more brain than body power. So our bodies are neglected. Hence the need for exercise.

Many of our health problems, in fact, have probably arisen because of our failure to adapt to an industrialized society. This is not surprising when you consider that the human species has lived in industrialized societies for only the last 200 years.

Dr Marshall Klaus, professor of paediatrics and human development at Michigan University in the USA, believes that anthropological data on the physiological processes of the human species, which have not changed in a million years, may provide vital clues to some of the medical mysteries of childbirth and early infancy (e.g. the so-called cot death). The Stone Age diet is, in fact, one clue. The sort of food that prehistoric people ate, which provided them with their energy, was totally different from the sort of refined or processed food we eat a lot of today.

We have changed in many different ways. Our ways of behaving, of living together, the way we work with machines and move about in cars and trains and planes, not exercising very much, and all our relationships, our sense of family, and the way we feed and bring up our children have changed. We have not noticed the changes over the years, although they have been very sudden in terms of the evolution of homo sapiens.

'Behavioural patterns,' says Dr Klaus, 'have changed radically in industrialized societies, particularly in childbirth practices and the rearing of infants. One has only to look at the mother–infant relationship in agricultural societies to appreciate the extent of the changes. There, mothers had close bodily contact with their infants for a year after birth and breast-fed them for four years.'

Men and women knew how to move – their lives depended on maintaining an ease of movement – and they did not need to exercise. You see them today, in agricultural communities, doing ordinary tasks, their limbs functioning beautifully with an economy of effort. Watch the way women walk, with such grace and poise, as they carry pitchers of water on their heads.

In the West we work to earn money so that we can enjoy life when we are not working. Much of the time we are competing for work, anxious about our status, keen to acquire possessions of one sort or another, cars and houses, and this is the way we live most of our lives. We push and shove and fight for seats in the rush-hour train, we sit tensed up behind the steering wheel of a car, or hunched up at an office desk, pounding a typewriter or word processor. Sadly, many of us have forgotten how to move, how to walk and how to relax.

Health is mainly a matter of living in harmony with nature, which means harmonious movement or activity, keeping muscles in trim, and this should happen spontaneously without conscious effort or thought.

So what can you do about it? What relevance has all this to pre-conceptual care? Well, pregnancy can be very uncomfortable if you have not even learned how to stand, walk or sit properly (or, more correctly, you have forgotten how to do these things), all the elementary movements of everyday living. Your body knows what to do, but you do not listen to it. If you are full of tension, and have lost the art of natural movement, as many of us have, you will find that the later stages of pregnancy can be a pretty miserable time. On the other hand, if you have learnt to move in a natural, spontaneous way, the chances are your pregnancy will be free of some of the back problems and pelvic troubles that some women experience. Your movements will be more spontaneous and not so clumsy. And your breathing will improve, which will help you during labour.

Why Exercise?

Since most of us are not engaged in the sort of activities that keep all our muscles in good condition, it is essential that we exercise regularly. Exercise should be an important part of the programme to achieve a healthy physical and mental state before starting a family.

One of the objects of all kinds of exercise is to remind you of what you are capable of doing or being. Exercise helps you to become the healthy, active person you truly are. Exercise makes you aware of your body. It makes you aware of any breathing problems or neck or back problems, or any other muscular problems you may have. In fact, all your problems of movement are related in some way to the muscles.

We have different types of muscles. There are, for instance, those in the back or head that are designed for sustained activity. They enable us to keep the back straight and the head raised from the chest. When we are fit, they perform well without our noticing them. There are other muscles designed for sudden bursts of activity such as the leg muscles, which, besides enabling us to move about, are part of an animal's fight/flight mechanism which we have inherited: that is, for chasing a prey or running away from a predator. In a normal state of health, they perform well in accordance with our needs. We become aware of these muscles when we use them in a sudden burst of energy because of the increased activity of the heart and lungs, which feed the muscles with oxygen and fuel. There is at least a tingling in the muscles as they are stretched.

Without exercise muscles grow weak. We neglect our muscles and they become stiff and do not function very efficiently. Anyone who has spent time in bed because of an illness or injury will have noticed how the legs become weaker and thinner. In hospital the physiotherapist slows this process by helping the patient to exercise in bed.

Exercise helps people in various ways.

• It has important effects on heart and lungs, improving their efficiency and capacity. This is measured by VO: that is, the volume of oxygen that can be transported to the muscles in a minute. VO is at its peak (in people who are physically fit) around the age of twenty, and then gradually declines until around eighty to ninety years when the maximum oxygen volume is too small to sustain life. Exercise can help to maintain or improve oxygen supply throughout life.

• It improves circulation, both from the heart end with its pumping action and from the muscle end by increasing oxygen uptake.

• It improves mobility and agility.

- It lowers blood pressure.

- It provides more energy and the ability to keep going for long periods of activity.

- It improves reserves for coping with stress. It makes people feel good because it releases endorphins, the morphine-like chemicals in the brain. Long-distance runners often talk of the 'internal fix' they get after an hour or so.

CAN EXERCISE DO ANY HARM?

The answer is yes: you *can* exercise too vigorously and this can be damaging. Judith Lumley, a senior lecturer in the Department of Obstetrics and Gynaecology at Monash University, Melbourne, gives a list of possible hazards which is enough to scare off any woman who wants a baby from becoming addicted to strenuous exercise.[1] They include infertility, reduced birthweight, pre-term labour, joint or ligament damage. Among those most at risk are ballet dancers, athletes, including marathon runners, and those who practise such sports as scuba-diving or water skiing. Many highly trained athletes have to give up training or train less rigorously during pregnancy because of nausea and vomiting and joint and ligament pain. However, the Alexander Technique, yoga and walking are perfectly safe if practised correctly without too much muscular effort.

It has been suggested that some exercises may not be helpful in late pregnancy because exercise tends to direct cardiac output to priority organs, which does not include the pregnant uterus. This may be why there is a slight faltering of fetal growth towards term. Some experts recommend bed-rest in late pregnancy and the avoidance of work that involves a lot of standing. This should be borne in mind by those who establish a habit of regular exercise before conception. Some exercises may not be appropriate later on in pregnancy.

Stepping Your Way to Health

Walking is one of the best ways of keeping fit. It improves lung function and increases the supply of oxygen to the skin and muscles.

It thus builds up the body's capacity to work and to use energy more efficiently. It is one of the least strenuous and safest kinds of pre-conception exercise. When walking, the force of the body on the knees and hips is one and a half times your body weight and on the ankles two and a half times your weight. When you run this force is much greater, so that there is a risk of damaging weak muscles in the legs.

Walking is just as good for you as running provided you walk more often and for longer periods. For slimmers, it burns up calories as well as decreasing the appetite (see Table 5). There are several reasons for this.

● Exercise regulates your appestat (the brain centre that controls appetite).

● It redirects the blood flow away from the digestive tract.

● It stimulates the utilization of blood fats, instead of blood sugar, by the muscles.

The best way of walking is the heel-and-toe method because it uses the calf muscles more productively. You should walk regularly for at least forty-five minutes three or four times a week. At the beginning, however, for those who are unaccustomed to exercise, it would be advisable to get into training with a short fifteen-minute walk every other day for about two weeks. Then increase this by thirty minutes every two weeks until you are able to walk up to four forty-five to sixty-minute sessions.

Here are some more tips:

1. When walking never hurry. If you hurry you could build up tension and make the heart beat too rapidly. When walking

Table 5. **CALORIES BURNED WHILE WALKING**

Walking pace	Calories/Minute	Calories/Hour
Slow (2 mph)	4–5	240–300
Moderate (3 mph)	5–6	300–360
Fast (4 mph)	6–7	360–420

Heel-and-toe Walking

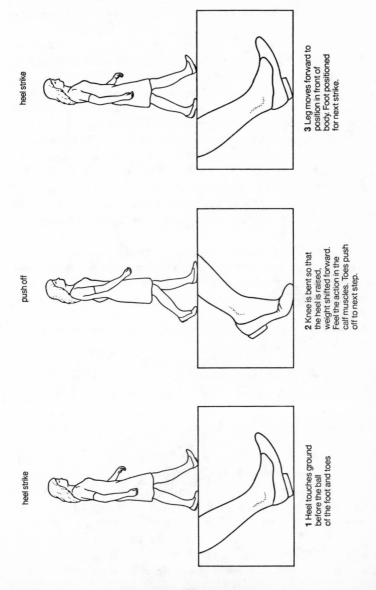

heel strike

push off

heel strike

1 Heel touches ground before the ball of the foot and toes

2 Knee is bent so that the heel is raised, weight shifted forward. Feel the action in the calf muscles. Toes push off to next step.

3 Leg moves forward to position in front of body. Foot positioned for next strike.

77

trate on the legs, leaving the mind alert and at peace. Walk with complete attention to what you are doing. Walk at a constant speed, not too fast and not too slow. What is important is an easy rhythm. If you move correctly, you will feel light, as if you are walking on a cloud. Give yourself a goal – a circular walk of say three miles; or a walk to some beauty spot or museum or zoo or restaurant (where you will eat and drink sensibly, of course).

2. Walk with your partner, hand in hand or arm in arm. Keep in step. If you find you start thinking of problems, try turning your attention to your breathing as you walk. Imagine you are breathing in peace, breathing out tension. Always use your imagination to dispel unpleasant thoughts. Don't try fighting them. Just allow good feelings to wash them away. Try to keep your attention focused on your legs and the accompanying movement of your body and limbs. Let the energy flow between you.

3. Do not go walking immediately after meals or when it is bitterly cold or very hot or windy.

4. Even though walking is a gentle exercise, if you have any respiratory or heart problems, it would be wise to consult your doctor before starting on a walking programme. Walking will probably be very good for you; but it is best to get professional advice.

The Alexander Technique

The Alexander Technique is not so much an exercise as a way of living – a way of getting rid of bad habits and restoring the body to its natural way of moving. It is mainly a matter of discovering how you are preventing yourself from moving freely and naturally. F. M. Alexander, the Australian who invented the technique, said: 'When you stop doing the wrong thing, the right thing does itself.'

For instance, when a person is sitting at a table writing, some of the most peculiar ways of treating the body can be seen. The person sits bent over the desk, shoulders up, the neck very often tense. People lean heavily on one elbow and their legs are often twisted. The result may be symptoms such as headaches, writer's cramp, backache, stomach pain and so on. If you know what you

are doing wrong, you can stop doing it and start sitting at a desk or table in an easy relaxed way.

Practitioners of the Alexander Technique insist that you need an experienced teacher to show you where you are going wrong; your particular needs and difficulties cannot be dealt with in a general way. By using his hands, the practitioner can show you what changes are needed in the way you sit, stand, walk or lie down. Then you need to know about what Alexander called 'inhibition'. This word is used in its physiological sense to mean the suppression of unwanted reactions in the body. You are taught to acquire 'primary control over your actions' by stopping before performing simple activities.

As well as curing many of the aches and pains that come from bad posture and movement the Alexander Technique can, like many other forms of exercise, help to lower blood pressure, improve breathing and solve digestive troubles. The way you move your arms and legs, the way you stand and walk can affect internal movement, the functioning of the lungs and heart and your digestive system.

ALEXANDER TECHNIQUE RELAXATION EXERCISE

Relaxing the body and allowing it to be free of tension is the object of this simple exercise. This is all-important in preparing for pregnancy when there will be unfamiliar strains in the body. The exercise can be continued throughout pregnancy.

Lie on a hard surface – a carpeted floor is best – with the legs apart at shoulder width, knees bent, and the head resting on two or three paperback books, not a pillow. The bony bump at the back of the head (the occiput) – not the neck – should be resting on the books, as in the illustration. The arms should be placed with the elbows on the floor and the palms of the hands across the midriff.

Maintain this position for about twenty minutes. As you lie there imagine your shoulders spreading, your spine being pulled down and straightened by gravity, your head growing upwards and outwards. If you keep this up every day, you will find that your spine *will* straighten, and all the bones and muscles in your body will feel right. Tensions will go, including feelings of discomfort in the stomach or other internal organs of the body.

Yoga

A lot of exercise leaves you feeling tired, aching all over and discouraged. This, however, is not true of the oldest system of exercise there is, yoga. Yoga, like the Alexander Technique, is a way of life. In the East there are many different yogas concerned with different levels of reality, and there is said to be a yoga for every event in life.

The yoga that has been taken up so enthusiastically by people of all ages in the West is called Hatha Yoga, a physical discipline aimed at raising consciousness. It consists of a series of exercises designed to help you become aware of your body and every part of it. The goal is complete control of all bodily activities, including your breathing and heart-rate.

Yoga is considered to be the joining of the inner and outer self or body and spirit. Spirit is positive; body is negative. The spirit provides energy and the body receives it. Yoga is also concerned with joining or relating the parts to the whole: the functioning of individual parts of the body to the efficient functioning of the whole body.

More than anything else, yoga is about achieving balance. In every exercise or posture (asana) it is the quality of movement that counts more than the effort that is put into achieving a particular posture. Mind, body and spirit must be totally involved in every exercise and this must be accomplished with a minimum of muscular effort. It is believed that when there is perfect harmony between body and spirit there is perfect health.

Many people find that the exercises are exhilarating and at the same time relaxing, and that they have a kind of spiritual content to them: a feeling of uplift. One student who had tried many other forms of exercise, said that yoga increased the confidence in her body, which the other exercises failed to achieve: 'Far from being the stiff ungainly object that was forever letting me down, I found that my body was strong, dynamic, capable of far more than I ever imagined. It was just a matter of working *with* it rather than pitting myself *against* it.'

Yoga helps people of all ages and there are exercises to help you through all kinds of problems, physical and mental. The exercises tone muscles, increase strength and suppleness and give a sense of freedom from the tensions of daily life. They are just about the best kind of exercises for pre-conception because they are as much about relaxation as loosening and stretching the muscles. They will help to prepare your mind and body for the months of pregnancy. If you are used to practising yoga exercises before you become pregnant, you will have a head start because you will know about the benefits of good posture and a balanced programme of exercise and relaxation. During pregnancy yoga will help to give you a sense of what is happening to your body when a baby starts growing inside you. The exercises will relax you and help you to cope with some of the swings of mood that you may experience.

A few simple exercises are given here, but your best plan would be to join a yoga class, making sure you explain to the instructor why you need to exercise. He/she will help with stretching and muscle-toning exercises and others that will benefit you during pregnancy. The shoulder stand, for instance, has been described by one teacher as giving a tremendous sense of well-being during pregnancy, and giving greater space to the developing child. Your partner could accompany you to the yoga class. He may learn something about a woman's physical needs during pregnancy and labour, which a good instructor will explain, besides feeling exhilarated and relaxed himself.

YOGA SITTING POSTURES

Sit cross-legged on the floor in what is called the lotus position: put the right foot on the left thigh and the left foot crossing the right one on to the right thigh. Your hands should rest lightly on your knees. If you find this difficult, there are several other positions you may find more comfortable; but all yoga sitting postures are difficult at first when your body has lost its suppleness. It is worth practising a yoga position regularly until you find you can achieve it without effort. In the end, when your spine and limbs become more supple, you will find the lotus position is the most comfortable.

The lotus position is given that name because in India the white lotus flower is a symbol of purity and effortless power. In its natural habitat the flower floats serenely over a swamp and maintains perfect equilibrium. When you are sitting in the lotus position there is an equal distribution of power to all parts of the body. It is recommended as the best position for meditation. The 'swamp' habitat represents all the things in our daily life that drag us down or disturb us; the lotus flower represents the empty but attentive mind that is achieved in meditation, maintaining its equilibrium above the 'swamp'.

You can, however, sit down on your crossed ankles (called the heroic posture); or bring the soles of your feet together (cobbler posture), releasing your knees down to the floor; or simply sit with your feet away from you and your knees flopping outwards.

In the cobbler position your thighs may feel very tight at first, but gradually they begin to stretch and open out. This posture will help to stretch the pelvic muscles. It has also been described as an exercise for stimulating the ovaries.

STRETCHING THE SPINE

Besides loosening the vertebrae, stretching your spine is said to have a beneficial effect on the central nervous system. This will help you when your baby starts to develop in the uterus and your balance is altered.

You begin the spine-stretching by stretching your neck as much

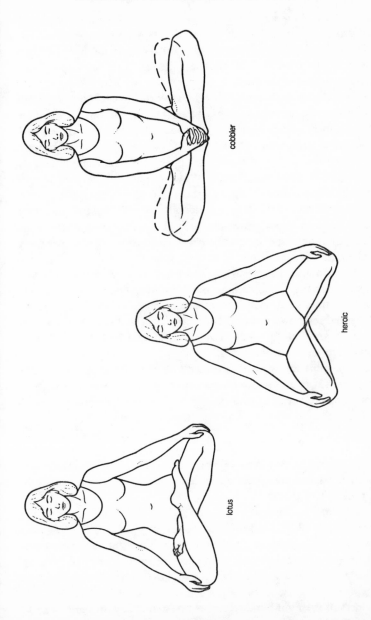

cobbler

heroic

lotus

as you can. Breathe in; then focus all your attention on the spine and try to lift it up. Breathing out, slowly drop your chin on your chest. Then link your hands and place them on the back of your neck, your arms resting on the sides of your forehead. Keep breathing rhythmically.

After about 30 seconds, while breathing in release your hold and drop your hands to your knees. Stretch your head upwards until it feels as if it is floating above your body; and then as you breathe out stretch the crown of your head backwards towards the floor.

Move your lower lip over your upper lip several times to stretch your throat. While breathing in allow your head to move back into the upright position. Then, breathing out, stretch your right ear to your right shoulder. After 15 seconds, as you breathe in, allow your head to float upwards; then, breathing out, allow your head to come down and your left ear to move towards your left shoulder.

After another 15 seconds, as you breathe in, allow your head to float up again. On breathing out look over your right shoulder. Breathe in, breathe out, look a little further. Breathe in, and then, as you breathe out, come back to the centre. Now repeat the exercise on the other side. Your spine should be lifting and your shoulders should feel relaxed.

This spine-lifting will be difficult at first, but it will gradually become easier and you will feel your spine moving upwards from its base in the back of your pelvis.

SIDEWAYS STRETCHES (Triangle)

This exercise strengthens the dorsal muscles, which hold the vertebrae in place, and the pelvic muscles, which need to be stretchy and strong for pregnancy.

Standing up, with the feet 3 to 3½ feet apart, slowly lift your arms to shoulder height, breathing in as you do this. Hold this position for a moment, and hold your breath at the same time; then, as you breathe out, stretch your fingers as far as they will go. Relax your fingers as you breathe in. Finally, as you breathe out, swing your body to the right, touching the right toes with the fingers of the right hand (1). Note position of left arm and head in

diagram and the position of the feet: left foot turned in, right foot out; your right heel should be in line with your left instep.

Return to the standing position, legs apart, arms at your sides. Slowly raise arms to shoulder height, taking a deep breath in, holding it, and then breathing out as you stretch your fingers. Breathe in again, and as you do so relax your fingers. Then as you breathe out, swing your body to the right side, touching the right toes with the fingers of your left hand (2). Note the positions of right arm and head in diagram and the position of the feet, as before, left foot turned in, right foot turned out.

Now repeat this movement after returning to the standing position, with arms resting at your sides. Slowly lift arms to shoulder height, breathing in and out as you stretch and relax fingers. Then as you breathe out, swing your body to the right, but this time bending your right knee and placing the palm of your left hand on the floor (3).

Return to the standing position, your arms resting at your sides. Repeat the exercise, this time bending your right knee with the palm of your right hand placed on the floor (4).

Your movements and breathing should be in harmony. Generally speaking, you should breathe out with a stretch and in when you relax your posture or come up out of a posture. Practise these exercises until you achieve a rhythmical movement, going slowly from one exercise to the next. The exercises will strengthen the dorsal and pelvic muscles, which need to be stretchy and strong for pregnancy.

ARCHING THE BACK (Bridge)

Lie on your back, absolutely flat, with your legs slightly apart and arms flung wide. Palms of the hand should be upwards. Do not stretch out the fingers; leave them loose. Keep your eyes closed. It is important in this and all yoga exercises not to wear anything tight around the neck or waist. Stay in this position, lying flat on your back, for a minute or two or until you feel perfectly relaxed.

Very, very slowly, raise your legs, moving your hands under the hips (1). Your hands should help to push the legs upwards. Breathe in deeply as your legs are raised. Then keep your position (2) for a

few seconds and hold your breath at the same time. Then gently lower yourself to the arched position (3) and breathe out completely as you do so. Hold this position for a few seconds at first. This exercise will help to tone the abdominal organs.

Ta'i Chi Chuan

Another ancient system of exercise which has been taken up in the West is Ta'i Chi Chuan, which also improves posture. Like yoga, it is concerned with the whole person and does not treat bad posture or physical stiffness or disability symptomatically. Instead, it offers gentle, flowing movements (called 'forms') that are relaxing and restorative, giving the sensation that all parts of the body are connected 'like a string of pearls'. In the Chinese language *T'ai* means great or original, *Chi* means life force or energy and *Chuan* means fist, but also implies way. Taken together they mean 'the great, restorative way of nature'.

Ta'i chi (as it is popularly known) aims at releasing the *chi* in the body. The state of mind of the person who practises the movements is important. Total attention must be given to every movement, which can never be automatic. The mind governs the way the *chi* circulates through the body. The mind leads and the *chi* follows. When the mind is calm and attentive the body is filled with energy.

It is beautiful to watch and for those who practise the slow and graceful movements it produces a feeling of tranquillity which most Western exercises do not give. Ta'i chi is often described as a healing art and has been found to be effective in the treatment of high blood pressure.

In the first place it is important to practise the 'forms' under the guidance of a trained Ta'i chi teacher. Ta'i chi forms have, however, been adapted in the West as individual exercises. The exercise on page 89 is a variation of a form called 'White stork flaps its wings'.

SWINGING ARMS

This is done as a warming up exercise in Ta'i chi class. It is a very simple exercise, which everyone can do. It has enormous benefits: arm swinging improves lung function; it strengthens the back; gets the blood flowing around the body; and helps your breathing.

Stand with feet apart at shoulder width, swinging your arms up, just to above shoulder height, without straining, and then down and back, as far as you can manage. Do this rhythmically, up and down 300 times every day, preferably in the morning soon after getting up. It should take about seven minutes. It is a good idea to do the exercise to music: something with a distinctive but gentle beat (nothing too strident) which will help to establish a rhythm. Try to do the exercise in a clean atmosphere, standing at an open window in warm weather or outside in the garden. If you do this regularly every morning, you will notice the difference it makes to your general feeling of fitness in about fourteen days.

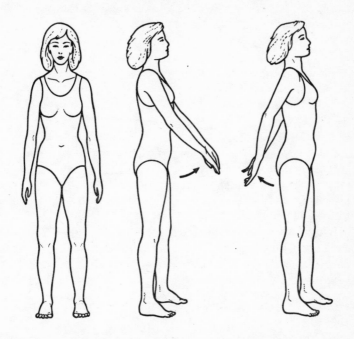

T'AI CHI EXERCISE FOR RELAXATION

This T'ai chi exercise, besides toning you up physically, should help you to achieve a state of mind that is receptive to and goes along happily with the changes that occur during pregnancy.

Stand with your feet about shoulder-width apart (1). While breathing in, slowly raise your right hand, palm down, forwards and upwards, until it is straight above your head.

As you raise your arm, filling your lungs with air, rise on to your toes, so that you find yourself stretching slightly (2).

Hold this position – and at the same time hold your breath – just for a moment. Then slowly lower the arm in an arc (2) while breathing out.

Repeat with the right arm.

Repeat the actions using both arms together (3 and 4).

Try to coordinate your arm and ankle movements with your breathing.

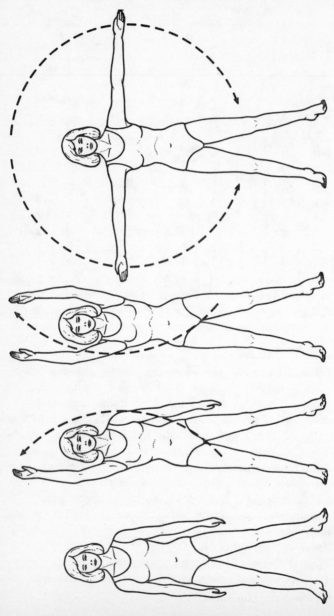

Focus your attention on each movement, so that you feel you are not doing the moving yourself, but are being moved. In the East they would say, 'It moves my arm', *not* 'I am moving my arm'. Similarly, 'It breathes me', *not* 'I am breathing'. Thinking in this way may sound a bit strange to you at first, but it works; the use of the word 'it' dampens down the will, and therefore any straining. 'It' acknowledges a force or energy that is always there apart from yourself – apart from the 'I' or self-image.

Stress and Relaxation

No one doubts that stress is something to be avoided, particularly during pregnancy. It is as much a health hazard as smoking or alcohol. In fact, all these things go together. Smoking and alcohol are unhealthy ways of coping with stress, making the situation worse, not better.

Stress is an endogenous condition that can change the chemistry of the brain and affect individual behaviour. It also changes the way cortisone, adrenalin and zinc are used by the body and converted into energy. Take adrenalin, just one of the substances involved in stress, which provides energy for the flight/fight mechanism. When someone has psychological fears, their pituitary gland behaves in the same way as it does in response to an imminent physical threat and stimulates their adrenal glands to release hormones to help the body to cope with the threat. When this response is inappropriate because of an imaginary danger we call it stress. In effect, more adrenalin is released into the body than is actually needed. This can affect the whole chemistry of the body leading to rapid heartbeat, high blood pressure and the secretion of more acid in the stomach which can cause ulcers.

For the pregnant woman, an overload of anxiety and the release of too much adrenalin can harm her child. The adrenalin crosses the placenta and produces symptoms in the child such as rapid heartbeat. So it is important to understand what is going on in our bodies and to remove the causes and symptoms of stress. This can be done in several ways: through relaxation exercises or through a healthy diet or counselling.

It should be emphasized, however, that many women are anxious at times during pregnancy and this normal anxiety cannot harm the baby. For most pregnant women there is absolutely no reason to be anxious about being anxious. It is prolonged emotional stress or what the psychologist sometimes calls 'trait' anxiety – a nagging fear of imagined dangers or threats to safety, or health or peace of mind; an inbuilt attitude of mind – that may lead to complications in labour and the possibility of harming the child.

If you are, in fact, emotionally disturbed about anything in your life – your relationship with your husband, for instance – or you are the kind of person who is neurotically anxious about all sorts of things, obviously you are not going to do very well in pregnancy, and you should consult your doctor before becoming pregnant. He should be able to refer you to a counsellor or qualified psychotherapist, who will be able to help.

Whether it is normal or not, the effect of a mother's anxiety on her unborn child is now well recognized. A paper by Dr H. B. Valman, a consultant paediatrician at Northwick Park Hospital, and Dr J. F. Pearson, a senior lecturer and consultant obstetrician and gynaecologist, published in the *British Medical Journal* described how the level of activity of the fetus, including sharp kicks and squirming movements, increased when the mother was under emotional stress.[2] If the stress was prolonged, there was a corresponding increase in fetal movements – up to ten times their normal level. Anxiety in the mother results in a hyperactive fetus.

Understanding stress and working out healthy ways of coping with it should be an important part of pre-conceptual care. Stress is infectious: it builds up at work and then it is taken home where it poisons the atmosphere. There are four conditions which are stressful and can lead to illness.

1 *People poisoning*. Pressures exerted by other people from which there is no escape – e.g. people at work, neighbours, relatives. You can have too much of them!

2 *Unacceptable time pressures*. Not being given enough time to do a job; not having time to stand and stare; working round the clock to meet a deadline. These are all right occasionally, but not all the time. We all know people who say, 'There aren't enough hours in the day!' They – the over-achievers – are the people most

likely to get ulcers or heart attacks. And however much we tell ourselves we mustn't be like them, we often find ourselves ruled by the clock.

3 *Sleep deprivation.*

4 *Too many important lifestyle changes happening at the same time.*

Becoming pregnant is one of those lifestyle changes that can be stressful. Like puberty or the menopause, it is a point of no return, involving irreversible profound endocrinal and somatic changes. Once an adult, you can never be a child again; once menopausal, you can never bear children again; once pregnant, you can never be a single unit again except, of course, through an abortion or the death of the child.

So how do we manage stress? The key to good health is to use stress to your advantage. We need a certain amount of stress, or stimulation, to keep us interested and alive. But it can become like a drug: we crave excitement all the time. We have lost the ability – in the pursuit of a career or money – to step to one side and say, enough is enough.

There are many stress-reducing exercises and strategies. The simplest are to go for a swim, have a bath, go to the theatre, talk to a friend, dig the garden, listen to music, and so on. These are all worthwhile activities, but if they are done on the spur of the moment as a reaction to something that is bothering you, they do not have a lasting effect. The best way of controlling stress is to create a balanced way of living. This means cultivating a programme of regular balanced meals, moderation in drinking, daily exercise, adequate sleep and putting aside some time every day for relaxation exercises, such as yoga. Massage is also very relaxing and has the added merit of being an activity in which a couple can feel a physical closeness and the release of tensions. At home you should always relax together. It is no use one person relaxing while the other remains tense.

MEDITATION

Relaxation is a letting go psychologically as well as physically. It enables you to let go of your hopes and fears, all the things that are bothering you, including all your attachments, your worries about people, especially relatives. Relaxation calms the mind by stopping the endless internal chatter. Meditation is a technique for doing this (for example, reciting a mantra to empty the mind of problems) or it can become simply a way of living.

Meditation is the basis of various systems of physical relaxation. The following is an example.

Lie on the floor flat on your back with your legs apart, your arms lying loosely at your side, but away from your body, your fingers curling naturally. Gently close your eyes. This is the resting pose (sometimes called the corpse pose).

Now release the tension from every part of your body, moving upwards from the feet to the head.

Focus your attention on your feet. Do you feel any tension there? Don't think about it. Just try to feel your feet. Merely by focusing your attention on the feet, you will find they will gradually become relaxed. Don't move up your body until your feet feel completely relaxed. Now pay attention to your right leg, then your left leg. Feel them relax, the tension going out of the muscles. Then move your attention up to the knees, the left knee, the right knee, to your thighs, your arms, your stomach, your shoulders, your neck, your head.

Do this in your own time. Don't hurry. And don't worry if the tension doesn't go away so easily. Don't try to *make* it happen. Keep your attention fixed on a particular part of the body. If your attention strays, let that happen too. Pay attention to how it is happening. Just let everything wash over you, and bring your attention gently back to where it was. Move your attention gradually up your body as you feel the tension going away.

The most familiar form of meditation, which is designed to get rid of all the chattering that goes on in the mind, can be practised by choosing a word that has no emotional overtones for you – any word, like 'wood' or 'cup'. Then without moving your lips, repeat the word silently to yourself, giving your full attention to the sound of the word, not to its meaning. If any problem or thought enters your mind, do not actively try to banish it. Without thinking about thinking, give your full attention to whatever the thought is and in this way allow it to drift away and gently replace it with the sound of your word. Instead of a word, you could light a candle and concentrate on that or you could hold something in your hands and use that as the focus of your attention.

Meditate steadily for five minutes twice a day for a week – or until you have become adept at emptying your mind of all thoughts. Then gradually increase the meditation period until you can manage a twenty-minute session every day.

Meditation has proven physiological benefits. Besides getting rid of unwelcome thoughts, it can, for instance, help to reduce high blood pressure.

BREATHING THE YOGA WAY

The quality of your relaxation improves with correct breathing which is essential to health. It is important to approach pregnancy with an understanding of the function of breathing. When you breathe rhythmically and easily your body is supplied with all the oxygen it needs for energy production, and it is able to get rid of carbon dioxide (a waste product of energy production) from the blood. When this exchange process is functioning efficiently, you enjoy good health and are able to cope when your body is called upon to make a special effort, for example, during labour and childbirth. Lungs that are full of tobacco smoke or damaged by disease will affect the functioning of your limbs, muscles and heart, and will deplete the supply of oxygen to the brain. Your body is then under an extra strain to perform all its functions.

When you breathe in, your diaphragm, which is a dome-shaped sheet of muscle underneath the thorax, is pulled flat. This has the effect of pulling your rib-cage upwards and outwards, causing your lungs to expand and air to be sucked into them. The stronger the muscle action the more air enters your lungs.

Your breathing function is related to your state of mind and when you are relaxed your breathing becomes deeper and slower and your lungs get all the oxygen they require. But much of the time we breathe fairly rapidly and shallowly from the chest and this upsets the delicate balance of oxygen and carbon dioxide in the body. Your breathing goes wrong at times of stress. Many people have breathing problems, though they may not be aware of it.

To check if you are breathing properly, place one hand on your

Breathing

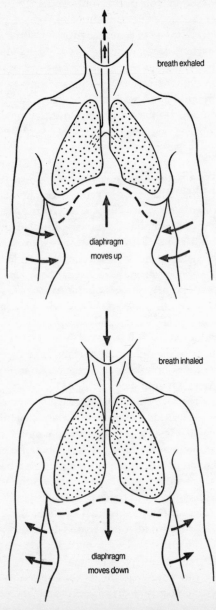

breath exhaled

diaphragm
moves up

breath inhaled

diaphragm
moves down

chest and the other on your stomach, and breathe normally. Which hand moves? It should be the hand on your stomach.

Much of our breathing is haphazard and changes as our moods change. We do not notice this because we have become accustomed to breathing in this irregular way. There are those who go so far as to say that, for many of us, our breathing went wrong at the start of our lives: we were born under bright lights and thrown into a panic when we were forced to breathe through mouth and nasal passages still clogged with amniotic fluid. Leboyer's *Birth Without Violence* first drew our attention to this kind of birth. His theory is that the memory of that gigantic struggle remains in our system as body tensions and feelings of insecurity. 'We learned to breathe in the middle of pain,' says Leonard Orr, a psychotherapist with a large following in the USA who practises a form of therapy called 'healing the breath'. This is more or less the purpose of yoga breathing exercises. They aim at making us aware of our breathing in order to bring it back to its natural rhythm, and they increase vitality and strengthen the muscles of the chest. Along with other yoga exercises, these are a good preparation for pregnancy. All yoga breathing exercises are powerful, so you should practise the ones described below for short periods only. But keep doing breathing exercises every day.

The basis of yoga breathing, known as 'complete breathing', consists of three parts: 'abdominal', '(middle (rib-cage)', and 'upper chest' breathing.

Abdominal breathing. This is done standing, sitting or lying. It is best at first to practise the exercise lying down with knees bent, because then you can really feel what is happening. Your attention is directed to the region of the navel. You place the palms of your hands over this region while exhaling and emptying your lungs completely. The abdominal wall is drawn in tightly, forcing air out of the lungs through the nose. Then you breathe in slowly through the nose, relaxing the diaphragm. The abdominal wall curves outwards and the lower part of the lungs fills with air.

Middle (rib-cage) breathing. This time your attention is directed to the ribs. Rest the palms of your hands on the lower rib-cage. After exhaling and emptying the lungs completely, you inhale slowly through the nose and the ribs expand. When exhaling, the ribs contract and squeeze the air out through the nose. In middle breathing the middle part of the lung is filled with air. The abdomen and shoulders do not move.

Upper chest breathing. Your attention is directed to the top of the chest where you place the palms of your hands with fingertips touching. Exhale, emptying your lungs completely. Then breathe in slowly lifting the collar bone and shoulders, allowing the air to flow in through the nose and fill the upper part of the lungs. Your fingertips should be pushed apart. You exhale by slowly lowering the shoulders and squeezing the air out through the nose.

Complete breathing. Your attention is directed to the whole of your trunk as you follow the wave-like movements of your breathing. Begin with palms placed on the stomach and exhale to empty the lungs. Slowly breathe in through the nose, counting up to eight, sliding the hands upwards as the diaphragm moves down and the rib-cage expands as the lungs fill with air. Exhale, relaxing the diaphragm and sliding hands down to the stomach. Repeat the exercise with your arms resting at your side. The whole exercise should be experienced as a single movement.

Many claims are made for this exercise: it is supposed to aid digestion, help reduce blood pressure and slow the heart-rate, as well as producing a feeling of peace, quiet and security. Western teachers recommend trying to attune the breathing in 'complete breathing' to your own natural rhythm. This means that you observe your own natural breathing reflex and breathe only when it demands. Exhale and do not inhale until your body demands it. Then inhale really deeply. Exhale again when your body is ready. Do not attempt to force your breathing into any particular rhythm. Concentrate on making sure all the air goes out of your lungs, which will then fill up automatically.

If you cannot manage the yoga breathing exercises, it would be helpful merely to do some deep breathing regularly every day. To develop the habit, sit or lie in a comfortable position and breathe deeply and slowly, timing the breaths with the aim of taking half as many as usual in a minute. Continue breathing rhythmically in this way for about five minutes, but stop if you feel dizzy. You should plan to do this exercise twice a day, every day.

BREATHING AND SWIMMING

Swimming is an excellent exercise for anyone, but especially as a way of getting physically fit for pregnancy. For one thing, it helps you to control your breathing. It is recommended to anyone who lacks the patience to practise yoga breathing exercises.

While swimming the breast stroke, for example, you cannot breathe haphazardly. When making the first stroke with the arms, you must take in a big breath of air through the nose, and then plunge your face into the water. You then hold your breath under water and as you come out of the water you let it out. If you swim rhythmically without exertion, you will establish a rhythmical way of deep breathing which is one of the best ways of releasing tension in the muscles.

Besides teaching you to breathe deeply, swimming helps to strengthen and relax the muscles and regular swimming can do as much for you as any exercise. It is also an excellent form of exercise during pregnancy because the baby's weight is supported by the water. Swimming too vigorously is not recommended.

Be careful where you swim. Many UK waters are polluted. Anne Scott, pollution control officer of the Marine Conservation Society, which produces *The Good Beach Guide* (Ebury Press, 1989) says that out of 150 or so accessible beaches in Britain, one in three monitored does not meet water quality standards set out by a European Directive in 1976.

Pelvic Floor Muscles

It is very important to keep the pelvic floor muscles in good condition both before and during pregnancy. These muscles are attached to the sides and back of the pelvis and form a sheet-like mass at the bottom of the abdomen. The muscles control urinary flow, vaginal contractions and the sphincter which controls the bowel. If the muscles are slack, they may cause problems during labour, lack of feeling during sex and difficulty achieving orgasm.

You can check how strong they are the next time you go to the loo. While sitting with your legs apart try to stop and restart the flow of urine several times. If this is no problem, you can rest assured that they are in good shape. If, however, you find you leak urine when trying to stop the flow, there must be a weakness there that needs to be corrected with exercise. However, even if the muscles are in good condition now, it is a good idea to exercise them regularly to keep them firm. They will need to be in peak condition during pregnancy and labour.

The simple, most effective exercise is to imagine that you desperately want to go to the loo, but find it occupied and there's nowhere else to go. Hold back as you would in a real situation by contracting the pelvic muscles. Hold the contraction for ten seconds, then let go; then immediately contract the muscles again for ten seconds. Do this several times. Don't hold your breath during the exercise and don't make the mistake of contracting your stomach, thigh or back muscles. Exercise every day, gradually building up the contractions to fifty. Eventually you should be able to do this four times a day, achieving 200 contractions altogether. Once you have mastered this technique you will find that you can do the exercise invisibly at your desk, waiting for a bus, sitting in the train, watching television. After a few months, you will find an improvement of muscle tone in the vagina which will enhance your enjoyment of sex. During pregnancy there will be an increase of pressure on the pelvic muscles, so the earlier you start exercising them, the better.

It may sound paradoxical, but the muscles need to be firm and at the same time relaxed. There should be no tension in the area and no difficulty in letting go completely after tightening the muscles. There are relaxation exercises which will be helpful in relieving pressure during pregnancy. If you practise them before pregnancy, they will become second nature to you when pressure on the pelvic floor increases and learning a new exercise may be difficult. A number of pelvic floor exercises, of Chinese origin, are described in *The Chinese Exercise Book*.[3] You may find the squatting exercise helpful in relaxing the pelvic floor.

PELVIC FLOOR SQUATTING EXERCISE
Bend down in a squatting position with feet flat on the floor and

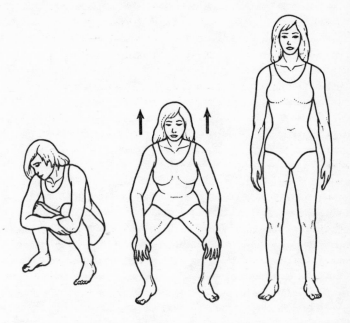

hands folded across the knees (1). Then, using the hands pressed firmly on the knees, slowly move up to a standing position (2). Stand for a few moments with feet apart and hands resting at your sides (3); then repeat the exercise. Pay attention to your breathing. Keep it rhythmical and unstrained. This may be difficult at first, but will not bother you after a while. At each session repeat the exercise six to eight times.

5

Infections, Illnesses and Genetic Disorders

A mere forty years ago pregnancy itself was regarded as a life-threatening condition. In the days before antibiotics, infections put both mother and baby at risk. Not a lot was known about preventive medicine and next to nothing about environmental hazards, such as smoking. At that time infections and other illnesses claimed the lives of many mothers and their babies or produced what are now preventable birth defects.

With pre-conceptual care the risks of pregnancy can be reduced still further. The important thing is to know before conception about what can go wrong, what the risks are, and how to build up your health so that you are better able to resist infections or can avoid them through immunization.

This chapter describes some of the main illnesses, infections and genetic disorders that can damage the health of the pregnant mother and her baby. There are some virus infections that are still a serious risk to the baby, though not necessarily to the mother. Rubella is one of these, and it can be prevented through immunization.

The unborn baby is sometimes put at risk by the drugs necessary to treat a feverish condition in the mother. Fever alone, if it occurs at a critical time in the baby's development, can result in miscarriage or stillbirth as well as birth defects. Thus, although most maternal infections do not spread to the unborn baby, they can put its life at risk. Experiments on animals have shown that merely raising their body temperature can cause serious birth defects in their offspring.

There are also a number of metabolic illnesses, such as diabetes and high blood pressure, which present risks that can be greatly reduced through proper control. At present little can be done about genetic illnesses, but genetic counsellors can advise parents about the risks and there are serious inherited conditions that can be diagnosed before birth so that parents now have the option of terminating a pregnancy.

Infections

RUBELLA (GERMAN MEASLES)

A common infection that is a serious threat to the unborn child is rubella or German measles. Rubella in children, or even in adults, is a relatively harmless infection, causing no more inconvenience than a common cold; but it is teratogenic (that is, it can cause deformities) in the first three months of pregnancy, producing severe birth defects or death. During the 1964 world-wide rubella epidemic more than 20,000 children were born with serious birth defects.

The effects of rubella on the unborn child are so serious that it would be advisable for all women planning a family to be vaccinated at least three months before contraception is discontinued. All girls in the UK are, in fact, offered immunization at the age of thirteen or fourteen, to prevent them from catching the disease later on, during pregnancy. The newly-introduced triple MMR vaccine (mumps, measles and rubella) which is being offered to babies of both sexes may help to eradicate rubella altogether.

TOXOPLASMOSIS

This is a very infectious disease caused by the organism *Toxoplasma gondii*, which lives in the intestines of dogs and cats and is excreted in their faeces. It is present in some 20 to 30 per cent of all American women and even more western Europeans. In Paris, it is believed that as many as 80 per cent of all women have been infected by the organism.

The unborn child can be infected only when the mother contracts the disease around the time of conception or during pregnancy. An earlier bout of toxoplasmosis presents no risk and, in fact, may produce antibodies in the mother's blood which will protect her when she conceives. Toxoplasmosis is most dangerous in the first three months of pregnancy. It can cause abnormalities such as hydrocephalus ('water on the brain') or brain malformation.

Some women who are infected may not know it because the symptoms – vague abdominal pains, a flushed feeling and swollen lymph glands – occur only in 10 to 20 per cent of those infected. The best protection against the disease is to get a friend or relative to look after your pets, especially your dogs and cats, from the time you plan to conceive until your child is born. But, if this is not possible, and you feel you want your pets around you, it's important to observe all the normal rules of hygiene very strictly, to keep your pets clean and not allow them to lick you.

Toxoplasmosis can be present in the street and in the soil in your garden, as a result of animal excretions. It is spread by flies, cockroaches, mice, rats and birds. You should always wear gloves when gardening.

Because raw animal products – especially lamb or pork – could be infected, they should be well and truly cooked before eating. Never eat rare meat at the time you are hoping to conceive or during pregnancy. Take care when preparing meat for cooking.

Keep your pets indoors as much as possible. If you suspect that a pet may be suffering from an infection which could be Toxoplasmosis take it to a vet, who will treat it with a course of drugs. Feed pets only prepared food and always wash animal and human eating utensils separately. Do not handle litter boxes.

TOXOCARIASIS

This is caused by the common roundworm called *Toxocara*, which lives in the intestines of dogs and cats. The eggs are excreted in their faeces. In two or three weeks they can mature into larvae which can survive in the soil for two or more years. Only burning or digging up the soil can destroy them. Though toxocara infection is rare in adults, there is an increasing number of children who are being infected through playing in parks. This has led some authorities to forbid pets from being exercised there.

Toxocariasis is caused by the larvae being swallowed – through touching the mouth with dirty fingers or eating unwashed vegetables. In humans the larvae do not develop into adult worms but pass through the stomach wall into other parts of the body. The effects vary from a minor stomach upset to serious liver damage and blindness. As with many other infections, personal hygiene is the best protection. Wear gloves when gardening, wash your hands after fondling or stroking pets and always before eating meals or snacks. Pets should be wormed, but make sure you dispose of their faeces safely – bury or burn them.

CYSTITIS

Cystitis is a bacterial infection of the urinary tract or bladder. It is a very common ailment and most women suffer from it at some time in their lives. It is one of the commonest types of infection to occur during pregnancy. The main symptom is a frequent urge to urinate, but when you try to do so only a small amount of urine is passed. Though it can be very distressing, it does not usually present a serious health risk, and does not have any effect on a pregnancy or on the fetus. About 20 per cent of women have bacteria normally present in their urine, which some experts blame on a poor diet. These women are particularly liable to urinary tract infection during pregnancy.

Severe attacks of cystitis will be treated with antibiotics by your doctor, but in the pre-pregnancy period it is best to avoid any powerful drug. If you act quickly when symptoms occur, you may be able to clear up the cystitis yourself. Drink plenty of fluids to flush out the germs. Take a teaspoon of bicarbonate of soda in water and repeat this dose every hour for the next three hours. This makes the urine less acid and prevents bacteria from multiplying. If, however, you have high blood pressure, you should consult your doctor before taking bicarbonate of soda.

Allergic reactions to certain chemical substances can affect the bladder. Vaginal deodorants, talcum powders, scented soaps and bath oils should be avoided. The naturopathic practitioner believes that foodstuffs may well cause cystitis – and not just those containing chemical additives. Raw carrots and beetroot can have an irritating effect on the bladder and urethra. Alcohol should be avoided because it raises the urinary acidity.

Hygiene is, of course, of the utmost importance in the treatment of cystitis. The organisms that cause cystitis are 'anaerobic', that is, they are killed by fresh air. They thrive in the anal and vaginal areas because they are usually warm and airless. It is important, therefore to wear loose-fitting clothes, preferably made of cotton or another natural fibre, and to avoid tights and nylon briefs. Hosing down with cold water will wash away the germs, but take extra care when washing the genital area because the skin there is delicate and easily broken. Damaged pores will be quickly invaded by bacteria.

PYELONEPHRITIS (also called pyelitis)

This is a urinary infection which affects the kidneys and can come on suddenly (acute) or can persist in a mild form over a number of years (chronic). There is usually a severe pain in the back just above the waist. Although both kidneys are normally affected, the pain is more severe on one side of the body, spreading down into the groin. There is a sharp rise in temperature, often reaching 40 C (104 F), and you may feel cold and shivery. There may also be nausea and vomiting. The symptoms of cystitis – such as the feeling of constantly needing to urinate although your bladder is empty – are often present.

The infection usually enters the urethra (the tube that leads from the bladder to the outside) and spreads up through the ureter to the kidney. With prompt treatment, complications are unlikely. After a course of antibiotics and bed-rest the attack usually subsides in a day or two. Your doctor may require blood and urine tests, but for most healthy adults this is not necessary after a single attack.

Chronic pyelonephritis seldom produces symptoms until the condition is well established when early signs of kidney failure (for example, increased urination and tiredness) may appear; but because the condition progresses so slowly there are many who go on to a ripe old age without even realizing that they have the infection.

As with all urinary infections, attention to personal hygiene is the best way of preventing pyelonephritis. All clothing must be kept scrupulously clean and it is best not to use detergent washing powders. The infection has no effect on pregnancy itself.

URETHRITIS

This is the name given to inflammation of the urethra which, in women, is usually caused by bruising during sexual intercourse. The symptoms of chronic urethritis are similar to those of cystitis except that they last for only a few days after intercourse. It is common in women who have just started intercourse, which is why it is sometimes known as 'honeymoon cystitis'. It can be avoided by using a vaginal lubricant before intercourse. Tension can cause the bruising, so being relaxed during intercourse is important. If the urethritis persists it may be necessary to have an operation to stretch the urethra or vagina.

VAGINAL THRUSH (*CANDIDA ALBICANS*)

Vaginal thrush is caused by the fungus *Candida albicans*, which produces irritation in and around the vagina, and may be accompanied by a white, curdy discharge and some pain or soreness during sexual intercourse. The fungus thrives in the moist, warm conditions of the vagina during pregnancy.

Candida albicans is very common and many women may harbour small amounts of it, but it is normally prevented from growing by harmless bacteria in the vagina. The fungus resides mainly in the intestines, but establishes itself in the vagina. The usual treatment is an anti-fungal drug given in the form of a pessary or cream, but this just removes the symptoms and the trouble may recur if the underlying cause is not tackled. Complementary medical practitioners see the main problem as the destruction of the 'friendly' bacteria by a poor diet, consisting of too many sweet foods, including alcohol, or by chemicals, food additives and antibiotics. They recommend cutting out yeast products from your diet, including sugar, alcohol, smoked fish, cheese, mushrooms, sausages, hamburgers and hot dogs. Natural live yoghurt contains the *acidophilus* bacillus which kills *Candida albicans*, so eat a generous helping every morning with your breakfast cereal and dab it on the affected parts. Garlic is also effective against thrush. Take three perles of garlic (which, in this form, are deodorized) twice a day. They can usually be bought at a health food shop. Your sexual partner may pass on the infection without being affected by it himself, so make sure that he pays attention to his diet and refrains from sugary food and alcohol.

HERPES SIMPLEX VIRUS

Herpes simplex infections can never be cured; the virus hides in the tissues and is there for the whole of an individual's life. The infection comes and goes: it may not bother you for long periods, or not at all after the first attack, but it can suddenly flare up, usually when you feel run down.

There are two main types of herpes simplex virus: HSV 1, which appears as cold sores, usually on the lips and mouth; and HSV 2 or herpes genitalis, which mainly infects the genital area and appears as small blisters which burst to leave small, red, painful ulcers. Herpes genitalis affects both sexes and is transmitted during sexual intercourse with a person whose genitals are infected or after oral sex with someone who has cold sores.

In what almost amounts to an epidemic of herpes simplex in the USA people have become unduly alarmed and in the general panic a lot of false information has been distributed. Many pregnant women with the disease have had unnecessary abortions and caesarean sections and some have been advised never to have children. The virus can be transmitted to the baby before birth, but in the majority of cases it happens at delivery through contact with the mother's infected genital tract. Then, in fact, the only reliable treatment is caesarean section.

If you are subject to herpes simplex infections, it should not stop you from having a baby, but you must look after yourself extremely well and not allow yourself to become run down. A wholesome, balanced diet (including plenty of fresh vegetables and fruit) and exercise will help. When you or your partner become infected, obviously you should not have intercourse. An attack usually lasts about two weeks. Many people are not troubled again, but there are many who have recurrent attacks, although these tend to become progressively milder and less frequent.

GONORRHOEA

This common venereal disease (popularly known as the 'clap') may have no obvious symptoms in women, but there could be fever, an increase in vaginal discharge, painful joints and lower abdominal pain. In men, symptoms first appear a week or two after they have become infected. At first there will be a little discomfort on passing urine. This will be followed by a slight discharge from the tip of the penis, which, if left untreated, will become thicker and more profuse.

In the majority of cases gonorrhoea does not directly attack the fetus. Usually a baby contracts the disease on delivery, as it passes through the vagina. Sometimes, however, gonorrhoea inflames the membranes surrounding the fetus causing them to rupture prematurely. The infection then spreads up from the vagina through the cervix to the uterus. An infected child will often have serious eye infections and there is a risk of blindness.

Fallopian tubes are very susceptible to gonorrhoeal infection. It is estimated that about 25 per cent of women who suffer from gonorrhoea will have significant tube damage resulting in infertility. It is not, however, a cause of infertility in men.

Obviously, if you or your partner have gonorrhoea or have had the disease in the past, you should see a doctor or you should go to a clinic specializing in sexually transmitted diseases before you start a family. It is important not to have any sexual relations until the infection has completely cleared up. Rapid treatment can prevent damage to the fallopian tubes. The most effective treatment is a course of antibiotics; but it cannot be emphasized too often that powerful drugs, although useful in emergencies, may leave the immune system somewhat battered and bruised. Treatment should be followed by healthy living, including a balanced diet with plenty of vegetables and fruit, and regular exercise, which will help to repair any damage to your immune system. This programme should be continued for at least six months before starting a family.

SYPHILIS

The symptoms of this sexually transmitted disease are usually more pronounced than those of gonorrhoea and more serious. The first sign (known as the primary stage) is a sore, called a chancre, that develops on the penis, vulva, vagina, cervix, or on other parts of the body where there has been intimate contact such as the lips, nipples or the anus. The chancre appears three to six weeks after infection and then heals spontaneously.

Several weeks after the development of the chancre, a rash appears all over the body. This secondary stage may be accompanied by a painless swelling of lymph glands and moist wart-like lumps around the anus. After several weeks the rash disappears spontaneously and the disease 'goes underground' in what is called the latent phase.

Ten or twenty years later the disease breaks out again with a complete breakdown of body functions, including heart disease and brain disruptions leading to insanity. Fortunately, antibiotics have made it extremely rare for the disease to develop to this tertiary stage.

In pregnancy syphilis in its first two stages will lead to premature birth, stillbirth or death of the newborn. In its third stage it will have devastating effects on all the organ systems of the unborn child.

Because syphilis hides for so long and is symptomless after the second stage, couples who have any doubts about their health past or present, should be tested for syphilis before conceiving.

As regards antibiotic treatment, as with gonorrhoea this should be followed by an intense health-building programme. Even though the serious effects are prevented by antibiotics, syphilis can still lead to a lifetime of ill health, through a weakening of the immune system.

AIDS (Acquired Immune Deficiency Syndrome)

The diagnosis of the Acquired Immune Deficiency Syndrome, or AIDS as it is usually called, is made when a person develops a variety of 'opportunistic infections' (and/or a rare cancer called Kaposi's sarcoma) and general ill health, including enlarged glands, and he or she is found to have antibodies to the AIDS virus. Antibodies are proteins produced in the body in response to stimulation by an antigen or foreign body. A particular foreign body such as HIV produces its characteristic antibody. It is nature's way of throwing off unwanted intruders, but it is not always successful. Once established, an antibody remains in the system. An opportunistic infection is one caused by a germ that is relatively harmless in healthy people. In AIDS patients a number of different illnesses can occur because the underlying disease has damaged their immune system.

AIDS is caused by a virus called Human Immunodeficiency Virus or HIV for short. However, not all those infected with the virus go on to develop AIDS, which suggests that other factors are involved. Alcohol, high stress levels and frequent exposure to other diseases, especially sexually transmitted diseases, have been suggested as possibilities.

With the world-wide epidemic of AIDS many couples are deeply worried about the possibility of becoming infected and of passing on the disease to their children. One hears of women mistakenly being afraid of becoming infected through close contact with AIDS carriers or even from lavatory seats. Having a baby then becomes to them a very hazardous undertaking. This is understandable because HIV infection cannot be cured and there is as yet no prophylactic vaccine, so for most people even a small but avoidable risk of becoming infected is unacceptable.

Some health workers, such as midwives and ambulance crews, who come in close contact with patients' blood and body fluids, may feel particularly vulnerable, and they need to take special precautions when handling people with AIDS. For midwives and obstetricians working with pregnant women who have the infection, the Royal College of Obstetricians and Gynaecologists have published a special report with recommendations about protection against infection. Pregnant women themselves may fear examination by doctors or midwives who are in contact with people with AIDS but they can rest assured that these professionals are carefully trained and have had years of practice in guarding against infections of all kinds.

It is important for couples to be completely honest with each other about previous sexual liaisons or drug abuse and, if they have any doubts or fears, they should be tested for HIV. For more information, health education pamphlets about HIV and AIDS are readily available and cost nothing.

CHLAMYDIA

Chlamydia is said to be the most common sexually transmitted infection in the western world. It is an infection of the urethra, the passage through which urine is discharged from the bladder, and is caused by the organism *Chlamydia trachomatis*, which is present in the genital tracts of some 4 or 5 per cent of all sexually-active women. In men the first noticeable symptom is a tingling at the tip of the penis, especially when urinating. This may be accompanied by a slight discharge first thing in the morning. If it is not treated, the discomfort may become worse and the discharge slightly heavier and thicker. In a woman chlamydia may produce a slight increase in vaginal discharge, but usually there are no symptoms. Pregnant women who have chlamydia have higher risks of stillbirth and prematurity. In the long term, chlamydia can cause pelvic inflammatory disease (PID), a more serious condition which may result in infertility, ectopic pregnancy and chronic pelvic pain (see below).

About 60 to 70 per cent of babies born to infected women contract the disease during delivery. The main effects on the child are conjunctivitis and pneumonia.

Both you and your partner should be screened for chlamydia before starting a family. If you have the disease, the treatment is relatively simple. You will be given a course of antibiotics which should clear up the condition. You should not, however, have sex until the course is completed, and you should defer any plan you may have of starting a family until you are restored to full health. Any kind of sexually transmitted disease can be very depressing and debilitating; and it is not a good idea to conceive when you are feeling run down.

PELVIC INFLAMMATORY DISEASE (PID)

Pelvic inflammatory disease (PID) is a condition caused by microbes which invade the uterus and spread to the fallopian tubes, ovaries and surrounding tissues. The symptoms include pain and tenderness in the lower abdomen and fever. You may have pain during intercourse (called *dyspareunia*), abnormally heavy periods and a smelly vaginal discharge.

PID is, however, an umbrella term for a number of different infections and is sometimes called the 'silent' epidemic because early signs may not be obvious, especially if the condition is mild. The most common form is salpingitis, which is inflammation of one or both fallopian tubes. The other two main infections are oophoritis, which is inflammation of one or both ovaries, and endometritis, which is inflammation of the uterus.

PID is often found in sexually active young women – genital infections are rare in women who are not sexually active – and is one of a new generation of sexually transmitted diseases which is causing considerable concern because it is spreading so rapidly throughout the world. One of the main reasons for the spread of this disease is undoubtedly the more liberal attitude to sex over the past two decades. At the same time, in spite of the fact that people talk much more openly about sex, sexual education, particularly concerning sexually transmitted diseases, is inadequate. The general public does not appreciate the magnitude of the problem; doctors themselves are still much too reticent about the subject, and there are still a number of medical schools which do not include tuition on sexually transmitted diseases in their curriculum (in the USA it is virtually non-existent).

It should, however, be emphasized that PID does not in all cases imply promiscuity on the part of the sufferer. It sometimes occurs after childbirth, miscarriage or the insertion of the coil (IUD). Diagnosis takes the form of swabs taken from the cervix, blood tests and urine tests.

The reason for infection travelling upwards to the uterus is the destruction of the normally tough barrier of mucus in the cervix, which protects the pelvic cavity. A common form of bacterial infection such as streptococcus can cause damage through travelling freely through the uterus into the fallopian tubes. Any bacteria in the right circumstances can cause PID. The invasion of bacteria can cause scar tissue as a result of white blood cells (part of the body's immune system) releasing a collagen protein which is said to resemble steel mesh. This can damage the cilia, which are the tiny hairs in the fallopian tubes responsible for wafting an egg down the tube to the uterus. Damage to the cilia can cause infertility (see Chapter 6).

As with all venereal diseases, rapid treatment must be given to prevent serious damage. It is important to identify which kind of organism is doing the damage, since different antibiotics are used to destroy them. Most women with PID have a number of invading organisms at the same time, the most dangerous being chlamydia (see page 112). An acute attack will be treated by a two- to three-week course of antibiotics. For chronic PID antibiotics may have to be taken for up to three months.

Prevention, of course, is better than cure and the best form of prevention is for both partners to observe a high standard of genital cleanliness. The man may pass on an infection to his partner. Microbes can breed in dirt under the foreskin without necessarily harming the man but harming his partner. In all cases of PID both parties should be tested for infection. If there is recurrent infection in the woman it might be worth considering using a condom in preference to the Pill or coil. Microbes flourish when the body's defences are weakened by an unhealthy lifestyle, including a poor diet, stress, smoking and drinking. Pre-conceptual care should help to prevent infections occurring during pregnancy.

PUBIC LICE

Pubic lice, also known as crab lice (popularly as 'crabs') are blood-sucking lice usually found in the pubic hair and hair around the anus, but they may also appear in other parts of the body in very hairy people. Pubic lice can be cleared up with a lotion or cream prescribed by a doctor.

This is a demoralizing condition which is almost always caught after sexual contact with someone who already has the infestation. For established couples, the problem is not so much the disease itself, as the fact that a partner has been unfaithful. For those who are infested, obviously this would not be the right time to start a family.

LISTERIOSIS

Listeriosis first came into prominence in 1988 as one of the latest of a number of health hazards caused by the contamination of food. The bacteria *Listeria monocytogenes*, which causes the disease, was found in pre-cooked, chilled food (especially chicken) and soft cheeses sold in some supermarkets. There are those who believe that the infection can be caused through sexual contact or close contact with animals or through handling raw meat. There are documented cases of veterinary surgeons and people handling poultry contracting the infection.

Its main symptom is a flu-like illness. If diagnosed early it is easy to clear up with antibiotics, but left untreated it can be extremely dangerous, leading to miscarriage, stillbirth and a wide range of complications in the newborn, from rashes and swollen glands to respiratory problems and meningitis.

The best way to prevent the disease is to cook all food thoroughly, to avoid eating pre-cooked food (unless it is cooked a second time very well), wearing gloves when handling raw meat, avoiding close contact with animals other than your own pets, and always washing your hands well before and after preparing food (see Chapter 8).

Metabolic and Chronic Disorders

Metabolic disorders are caused by flaws in the body's chemistry.

DIABETES

'My family said I was an absolute fool and an idiot to become pregnant,' said a diabetic mother. 'How could I do it and was I so stupid that I didn't know about contraception, and did I know what a trial I was being to them all with all the worry and everything?' This is quoted in a National Childbirth Trust book dealing with the emotions and experiences of some disabled mothers, including diabetics. In the case of diabetic women, the fears, in fact, are understandable because it was not so long ago that the babies of diabetics usually died. But things are different now. With proper antenatal care, a diabetic woman has a good chance of having a live healthy baby. The diabetic woman who becomes pregnant needs to be very careful about keeping her blood sugar level under control for the sake of her baby. In fact, Dr David Hadden of the Royal Victoria Hospital, Belfast, tells his medical students that they will find the best controlled diabetic patients in the antenatal clinic.

There are, however, potential problems and, if you are diabetic, it is as well to know what they are. The main one is that the child can easily become overweight. This is because sugar (glucose) crosses the placenta, but insulin does not, and when the mother has high blood sugar, the child gets too much sugar and his pancreas produces more insulin than he would otherwise need. The baby grows big and fat and this not only leads to problems during labour, but the high insulin level sometimes delays development of the baby's lungs, leading to breathing complications. The child could be born at term, but have some of the same problems as a premature baby. The child is also born hypoglycaemic (low blood sugar), which, however, is just the temporary effect of being inside a diabetic mother.

If a diabetic woman's glucose level is very high early in pregnancy, there is a much greater chance of her baby being born with some abnormality, the two most common being a congenital heart disorder and an abnormality of the spine.

It is important, therefore, for a diabetic mother to achieve really good diabetic control well before she considers having a baby. For her more than most a pregnancy must be planned, because in the early stages of embryonic development (when a woman may not even know she is pregnant) a lot of damage can occur. Do not wait until you are sure you are going to have a baby: that may be too late. Good diabetic control must be your main concern before you start trying to conceive. Then, if control is near-perfect at the start of pregnancy, the chance of any abnormality occurring in the child is very small.

If you are a prospective father who has diabetes you can rest assured that, if your partner does not have diabetes, there is no increased risk to your baby during pregnancy. There may, however, be a slight chance that the baby will carry a diabetes gene – this risk is greater for diabetic fathers than for diabetic mothers.

A pre-conceptual clinic will help diabetic women to achieve a good level of blood sugar control. One such clinic is held at the Edinburgh Royal Infirmary and gives advice to couples on family planning and the use of safe, effective contraceptives. It assesses diabetic women to make sure they are fit enough to become pregnant. Most diabetic women can be reassured on this point, but there may be some with, say, severe kidney disease or high blood pressure, who are advised against pregnancy. Women are asked to check their blood glucose four times daily. Sometimes it may be necessary to change their insulin levels.

High-fibre diet for diabetics

If there is no pre-pregnancy clinic in your area, your doctor should be able to give you advice. If, however, you have difficulty in obtaining advice, you can tighten up your control through diet. The high-fibre programme worked out by the Oxford Dietetic Group, in which starchy carbohydrate provides 50–60 per cent of total daily calorie intake, is now recommended by leading diabetic organizations around the world.

Dr Hugh Trowell was the first to suggest (in a paper published in the journal *Diabetes* in 1975) that fibre might protect against diabetes. He pointed out that during the war years and immediately afterwards there were half the number of diabetic deaths in Britain than before the war and this fall coincided with the compulsory use of high-fibre national flour which contained much more dietary fibre than white flour. Although sugar and fat consumption rose appreciably during the 1950s the diabetic death-rate continued to fall until 1954 when the so-called 'national loaf' was no longer compulsory. This suggested that a lack of fibre in the diet was more significant than an excess of sugar as a contributory cause of diabetes.

The good thing about the Oxford diet is that it is not only helpful in the control of blood sugar levels, but it is a healthy and enjoyable eating programme that will suit everyone, whether diabetic or not. This diet is recommended by the British Diabetic Association. It is described in *The Diabetic Diet Book*, by Dr Jim Mann and the Oxford Dietetic Group (Martin Dunitz, 1982).

HIGH BLOOD PRESSURE

High blood pressure in pregnancy calls for the most careful supervision. It can reduce the supply of blood to the placenta and can deprive the baby of oxygen – a life-threatening condition. If you have high blood pressure before you become pregnant, everything possible must be done to try and get this under control and to pay particular attention to your diet. The sort of healthy diet that is good for you anyway, whether you have high blood pressure or not, is likely to help to lower blood pressure. Not only diet, but relaxation exercises will help where there are emotional problems at home or at work.

Medical researchers who have been looking for a cause or causes of high blood pressure for many years say that they do not believe there is any single factor, but rather a combination of factors that are responsible for high blood pressure. Causes may include heredity, diet, lifestyle generally, staying up late, not getting enough sleep, drinking and smoking, working at some stressful job and so on. A bereavement, retirement, loss of a job can also have an effect on your blood pressure.

Blood pressure is constantly changing. A visit to a doctor can send it shooting up. A study of forty-eight patients reported in the *Lancet* showed that in every case their blood pressure rose sharply at the beginning of each visit. Because blood pressure is influenced by so many emotional and environmental factors, and can vary at different times of the day, it is difficult to get a true measurement. A more accurate picture can be obtained by measuring blood pressure every day over a period of weeks or even months. If you feel you have a blood pressure problem, you should ask your doctor if he thinks home recording would help you. Taking your own blood pressure is something that can be learned with help.

Out-patients at the Rosie Maternity Hospital in Cambridge are taught to operate an automated blood pressure monitor. The pressures are memorized on a micro-processor and then telephonically transmitted to a hospital computer and displayed on a VDU two or three times each day. Thus a check is kept on the patient's blood pressure and the obstetrician can decide if and when it is necessary to admit the patient to hospital. These are usually 'high risk' cases who would normally be admitted to hospital for 'rest and assessment'. Telemedicine of this kind is a thing of the future; it is not widely available at present.

Management of blood pressure is becoming highly sophisticated. Treatment with drugs depends on the level of hypertension and the age of the patient, but drugs are not usually recommended these days for mild or moderate cases and anti-hypertensive drugs can cause infertility (see Chapter 6). However, a young person with high blood pressure should certainly follow the advice of a doctor, who may in fact prescribe drugs in some cases. In any event, there is a certain amount of controversy about the value of any treatment and the US National Heart, Lung and Blood Institute recommend non-pharmacological approaches to the treatment of mild or moderate hypertension. In other words, diet and exercise.

THYROID DISEASE

The thyroid gland undergoes various changes during pregnancy and any existing thyroid problem will be magnified. It is therefore important that the risks are fully understood if you have a thyroid problem and are wanting to have a baby. Hypothyroidism, or under-active thyroid gland, has been associated with infertility and miscarriages. Symptoms of hypothyroidism build up over a period of months or even years. Your whole body slows down; you become tired and jaded, the simplest mental tasks take longer; you are intolerant of the cold; your skin becomes cool and dry, your hair coarse and you may have feelings of 'pins and needles' in the fingers. Women have heavy, prolonged periods and both men and women lose interest in sex.

Treatment is straightforward, consisting of thyroid hormone supplements which can be taken safely during pregnancy and will not harm the baby.

Hyperthyroidism, or over-active thyroid, is fairly common, occurring in about one in every 500 pregnancies. It does not affect fertility or bring about miscarriages, but it can lead to low-birth-weight babies and treatment for the condition during pregnancy can harm the baby. It is not easy to diagnose during pregnancy because its symptoms, such as over-sensitivity to heat, mimic some of the changes that take place in the body after conception. The symptoms of hyperthyroidism include a fast pulse, palpitations, breathlessness, scanty or absent periods, and a feeling of grittiness in the eyes, which may appear staring and protruding.

Anti-thyroid drugs can usually bring the disorder under control in about eight weeks, though tablets may have to be continued for a year. About 20 to 30 per cent of sufferers do not respond to this sort of treatment. The condition, however, can be treated surgically by removing a nodule or the whole of the gland if it is overactive. Hyperthyroidism can also be treated with radioactive iodine taken in the form of a clear, slightly salty drink.

Hyperthyroidism should be cleared up well before conception because treatment during pregnancy can damage the fetus.

EPILEPSY

Epilepsy is a breakdown or misfiring of the brain's communication system: electrical signals from a group of nerve cells become so strong that they overwhelm neighbouring parts of the brain. The sudden, excessive electrical discharge leads to a convulsion or seizure which we know as an epileptic fit. There are various forms of epilepsy – some inherited, some caused by injuries or diseases of the brain, such as a brain tumour, and some that have no identifiable origins.

A woman with epilepsy who becomes pregnant will be justifiably concerned that pregnancy might aggravate her condition and injure her baby. And she will probably be concerned about the possibility that her baby might inherit the disorder. The risks are low for women who have infrequent seizures. But fits do sometimes recur during pregnancy, even after an absence of years, and they may then increase as the pregnancy advances. Seizures during pregnancy may harm the brain of the developing baby by cutting off its supply of oxygen; so careful control and medical supervision are always necessary, even in low-risk women.

Women with epilepsy are, with proper care, perfectly capable of bearing a healthy child, but in some epilepsy conditions the risks are too great and it would be advisable either to postpone pregnancy or to avoid it altogether.

It is essential for all women with epilepsy, before they become pregnant, to seek advice from their GP, who will probably refer them to a neurologist and obstetrician, and, if they are worried about genetic factors, to a genetic counsellor. Pre-conception counselling should greatly improve the prospects for women with epilepsy and their babies.

In most cases of epilepsy, there is a low risk of passing on the condition to a child. Generally speaking, a child born to a couple, one of whom has epilepsy, carries an increased risk of 3 to 6 per cent of having epilepsy. However, if both parents have epilepsy, the risk is greater, up to one in four.

It is fairly common for an unwanted or unplanned pregnancy to occur because of an interaction between oral contraceptives and anti-epileptic drugs. It is believed that 'Pill failure' in these cases is caused by an acceleration of the metabolism of sex hormones induced by the combination of the drugs. This can be prevented and a woman with epilepsy should seek contraceptive advice from her doctor if she wishes to avoid pregnancy.

If pregnancy is planned when fits are infrequent, the anti-epileptic drug treatment may be withheld during the first three months. Certain drugs used to control epilepsy are believed to be among the contributory causes of birth defects in babies of mothers with epilepsy, such as hare lip and cleft palate. It is not thought that on their own they can cause these defects: usually there must be other environmental or genetic risks present, such as the age of the mother, smoking, alcohol or a family history of malformations. It is most important for both partners, if either of them has epilepsy, to abstain from smoking and alcohol for at least three months before conception. Weight gain should be restricted and iron and folic acid supplements (100 to 1,000 micrograms daily) should be taken. Other pharmaceutical drugs, including aspirin, are best avoided.

SYSTEMIC LUPUS ERYTHEMATOSUS (SLE)

SLE is a chronic disease which is believed to affect as many as one in 1,000 people. It is difficult to diagnose because it has a wide range of symptoms. It causes inflammation of many of the body's organ systems and also affects the skin, joints, kidneys and nervous system. It usually affects women in their second to fourth decades. Among the main symptoms are facial rash, fevers of unknown cause, swelling of the joints and nervous breakdown.

If you have active SLE, you should not try to conceive but should wait until the disease is in its inactive phase. Consult your doctor in case some of the medicines you have been taking could damage embryonic or fetal development. SLE does not affect fertility, but may cause a miscarriage. Usually, it does not lead to birth defects.

KIDNEY DISEASE

Pregnancy is not considered dangerous except for women with the most severe kidney diseases, but even if you have a mild kidney condition with no symptoms, you should consult a doctor before conception; pregnancy could worsen the condition.

Polycystic disease of the kidneys is symptomless unless it leads to kidney failure (usually late in life) when the cysts multiply to such an extent that they prevent kidney function. It is an inherited condition. It is unlikely that pregnancy will make the condition any worse.

Kidney transplants are becoming fairly common and there may be women whose fertility was once impaired by a severe kidney condition who, after a transplant, would like to have a baby. The transplant should solve the problem of the infertility, but most authorities advise an interval of two or three years following a transplant before planning a pregnancy. In any case, you should consult your doctor before pregnancy.

Genetic Disorders

Most families can tell you about some physical feature, character trait or disposition that keeps on turning up in generation after generation. It may be a snub nose or light blue eyes or ginger hair, or it may be a weak chest, a 'dicky' heart or a predisposition to coughs and colds or stomach troubles; or it may be a particular disorder like haemophilia or polycystic kidneys. There are the character traits which may or may not be inherited: they may be expectations or philosophies that are handed down, not genetic messages or flaws. Mothers, however, often say that a child is born with a certain unmistakable personality. It is there at the start, they say, and remains unchanged through the years. There are families whose members live long because of 'something in the genes' and others whose members never reach three score years and ten. There are families with strong constitutions, others with weak constitutions. There are families whose lives are beset with problems, others who seem to live charmed lives. It is partly nature, partly nurture.

Our ancestors live in us in different ways: we may have their illnesses, their virtues, their vices; and some of the illnesses can be predicted in our children. There are genetic disorders, some minor, some major ones, that will put your unborn child at risk; and there are some risks that you may consider worth taking if you are planning a pregnancy, others not worth taking.

It is essential for a doctor, and certainly for a genetic counsellor, to know your family history when you ask his advice about pregnancy. You should tell him everything that you feel is medically important. Sometimes there are skeletons in the cupboard – tuberculosis, for instance, at one time was regarded by some as something shameful; today a member of the family may be addicted to heroin or have a venereal disease or HIV – which your doctor should know about so that your fears can either be dispelled or the risks defined.

Genetics, which is the study of inherited conditions, is a rapidly developing science and can be a great help to couples who are planning a pregnancy. Family histories are of immense importance and it is as well to ask questions about possible inherited disorders before conception, rather than after.

Dr Elizabeth Thompson, who is a genetic counsellor at the Mothercare Institute of Paediatric Genetics in London, says:

With one child in thirty born with a mild handicap and one in fifty with a serious handicap which will show up at birth or later in childhood, the prospect of a handicapped child can be a worry for any parent. Of course no one can guarantee that a child will be born without a disability but we may be able to reassure some parents that a disability is not hereditary. Removing that worry is always worthwhile and couples who are anxious should never feel they are wasting our time. (*Mother and Baby,* August 1987).

There are approximately 3,500 'single-gene' disorders. These occur either because defective genes give the wrong chemical messages to the body, or because the body may have trouble interpreting these messages. This results in illness or a birth defect. There are other genes that do not seem to be defective, but they leave the body vulnerable to environmental agents such as viruses. There is, for example, a wayward gene that is suspected of allowing mumps to attack the pancreas, producing juvenile diabetes.

Before describing various genetic disorders it may be helpful to say something briefly about the way they are distributed in the fertilized egg. Every baby develops from a single cell, the fertilized egg. This cell contains all the information necessary for the development of mental and physical characteristics. The information is carried in twenty-three pairs of chromosomes, one half of each pair contributed by the mother, the other by the father, and each chromosome carries thousands of genes. It is the genes that determine particular features of the child, such as hair colour or blood group. But some of these genes occasionally do not work as we would like them to and they hang around and keep on being handed down from one generation to the next causing disease, or the disease may skip one generation and turn up in the next.

There are two basic types of genetic disorders.

1 *Those produced by a dominant gene.* This means that anyone who inherits the defective gene from either parent is bound to have the condition. A tragic example is Huntington's chorea – a very rare degenerative disease which does not produce symptoms until middle age. Consequently, some victims of the disease do not know they have it until after they have had children and possibly passed the faulty gene to them. On the other hand, there are people

who refrain from having children because they know that the disease runs in one branch of the family, only to discover, when it is too late, that they themselves have not inherited the disease and could therefore have had children.

2 *Those produced by a recessive gene.* These are the commonest forms of genetic disorders, in which a child will not inherit a disease unless both parents carry the faulty gene. An example is cystic fibrosis.

There are also multiple gene disorders. These are disorders that are said to 'run in families' (for example, coronary artery disease and asthma) which means that there is a genetic element present which is responsible for a susceptibility to the disorder, but it cannot be isolated or defined. Interaction between genes and environmental factors plays a part in the development of the disease.

Apart from single-gene disorders, there are also chromosome disorders, the most common of which is Down's syndrome. Unlike single-gene diseases, virtually all of these disorders can be detected through pre-natal testing and many through simple blood tests before conception.

The most common single gene and chromosomal disorders are described in the following pages.

HAEMOPHILIA

The term 'haemophilia' is applied to a group of blood disorders in which there is a life-long defect in the clotting factor which is known as Factor VIII. In the majority of cases there is a family history of the disease, but there are a few cases where the haemophiliac is the first in the line, due to some defect arising spontaneously in the mother's genes. The most common disorder is classic haemophilia, which is transmitted by both sexes but causes bleeding only in the male, except in rare circumstances.

Sufferers from haemophilia bleed much longer than normal after injury or operations. In those severely affected there can be spontaneous bleeding into joints and muscles and elsewhere in the body.

In the past ten to fifteen years effective treatment has been available for haemophiliacs and sufferers can now lead relatively normal lives, expect to marry and have children of their own.

When a man with haemophilia has children, none of his sons will be affected and they cannot pass on the condition. However, all his daughters will be carriers. With each pregnancy the daughter carrier will have a fifty-fifty chance of having a son with haemophilia and likewise a fifty-fifty chance of having a daughter who is a carrier.

If there is a history of haemophilia in the family of either partner, the couple should get the advice of a genetic counsellor about risks. We know that the risk of a woman carrier having a haemophiliac son is high. But the couple might also want to know what risk there is of having a severely affected child and what the prospects are for a son who is not too badly affected. These are questions which need to be discussed with your doctor and genetic counsellor.

In the past some women carriers decided against starting a family, others elected to abort all male fetuses. Prenatal diagnosis is now available. A blood sample can be taken from a male fetus, at eighteen to twenty weeks of pregnancy, by means of fetoscopy, to determine if the boy has haemophilia. If the test proves positive, the parents will then have to make the agonizing decision about whether or not to terminate the pregnancy. At such a late stage some parents see this as killing their unborn child, while others regard it as an act of mercy, a sort of prenatal euthanasia sparing the child all the possible miseries ahead of him. Both attitudes are understandable and the decision must be taken by parents with their doctor and genetic counsellor. Although interference in a problem of this kind is understandably resented by parents some doctors themselves have doubts about abortion.

For those who are not prepared to terminate a pregnancy, the decision must be made before conception as to whether or not they are willing to risk having a child with haemophilia. There are possible alternatives available: an adopted child or a child by a surrogate mother perhaps, but this latter solution is fraught with legal and emotional problems.

CYSTIC FIBROSIS

Cystic fibrosis (CF) is the commonest genetic condition in the Western world where it affects one in every 2,000 babies. One in twenty Caucasians (white Europeans as well as those from India and the Middle East) is a carrier of the CF gene, and when this occurs for both parents, there is a one-in-four chance that any child of theirs will inherit the condition. According to Professor Bob Williamson, of St Mary's Hospital Medical School, a leading CF researcher, it may be that carriers (who are completely unaffected) are more healthy than those who do not carry the CF gene.* The faulty gene that causes CF was identified in 1989 so that accurate carrier testing for most parents is now possible. This discovery also gives hope of better treatment through the development of a drug which will compensate for the protein defect (one vital component, an amino acid, is missing in cell linings) in the faulty gene. Researchers are also working on what will in effect amount to a cure: putting the normal gene into the lungs and other tissues, so that the cell itself makes the normal protein – but this is a long way in the future.

The condition mainly affects the lungs and digestive system. Its main characteristic is the thick and sticky mucus which accumulates in the lungs and must be cleared by regular physiotherapy (postural drainage). People with CF often have to take antibiotics to reduce the germs that tend to multiply in their lung secretions. Mucus may also block the ducts of various organs, in particular the pancreas, where it prevents the flow of the digestive enzymes. These enzymes are replaced with enzymes from the pancreas of a pig, in the form of tablets taken before meals. Without these tablets the CF patient would suffer malnutrition.

CF varies in severity. Some are very badly affected in childhood, some have such a mild form that it is not obvious until adulthood. The treatment of CF has greatly improved since it was first diagnosed in 1938, and now many people reach adulthood and can, with constant care, live full and productive lives. Doctors at CF clinics are often amazed at the resilience of patients and, according to Sir John Batten,

---

* Professor Bob Williamson writes:
Carriers of most autosomal recessive diseases are no healthier than the general population; this is only true in those rare cases where carriers have increased rapidly during a relatively small number of generations. In the case of cystic fibrosis, there are now something of the order of 30 million carriers worldwide even though the disease mutation probably occurred less than fifty thousand years ago. For a gene to spread at that rate, particularly in one population (Caucasians) and not among Asians and Blacks, certainly indicates the possibility that CF carriers may have a selective advantage. In particular, it has been suggested that carriers of cystic fibrosis might be resistant to cholera (because they secrete less water into their intestine and the damage in cholera is for the most part due to diarrhoea), or perhaps to tuberculosis (through the lung changes). It is not yet sure that CF carriers do have a selected advantage, but it is certainly a strong possibility.

President of the CF Research Trust (in a personal communication to us; we had a CF child) it is not unusual for them to possess a special quality of character which could be the result of adversity but could, he believes, be inherited with the defective gene, and goes some way to compensate for a CF patient's disability.

In the USA a group of young people with CF have formed a club. They are very positive and creative people, but at the same time generally have a realistic approach to their illness, and are known as 'Thursday's Children', because they have to 'work hard for a living'. In the UK there is an equally active and creative group of CF adults, who produce a regular newsletter and have their offices at the HQ of the CF Research Trust in Bromley, Kent.

Male CF sufferers are usually sterile, due to a blockage of the duct that carries the seminal fluid. Women with CF can become pregnant, but doctors often advise against their having children because of the damaging effect it can have on their health, particularly on their lung condition. But each patient is unique and responds in her own way to pregnancy, and there are those who do have children and who do not regret it. For example, a twenty-one-year-old mother of a one-year-old child said, in *A Survey of the Needs of CF Families in the Midlands* (Barnardo's Midlands, 1987): 'I was advised against pregnancy, but would advise other CF girls to go ahead as long as they have expert medical advice.' Another twenty-four-year-old mother of a four-year-old child said: 'Cystic fibrosis was not enough to stop me from having a child.' And another mother said: 'I thought it would be harder.'

All children born to patients with CF will be carriers of the disease, but their children will not be affected unless they marry another carrier of the disease. When a CF woman marries, she and her husband should seek expert advice about the risks of having a CF child.

SPINA BIFIDA AND HYDROCEPHALUS

Spina bifida and hydrocephalus are congenital disorders of the central nervous system, which is one of the first parts of the body to develop. When the embryo is twenty days old a groove appears in the centre of what will be the baby's back. This groove deepens and the edges above it join to form the neural tube. The front part expands to form the brain; the back part becomes the spinal cord.

Spina bifida and hydrocephalus are known as neural tube defects because they are caused by something that goes wrong at that early stage of development when the central nervous system begins to take shape. No one knows exactly what goes wrong (apart from the fact that the defect occurs in the neural tube) but it is believed that both genetic and environmental factors are involved. If a couple have had one affected child, the risk of recurrence is approximately one in twenty-five. It is believed that more than one gene may be implicated.

Spina bifida is a defect in part of the bony spine that helps protect the spinal cord. The nerves in that area – usually the lower spine – are exposed and unprotected and may also be defective. These nerves control the muscles of the legs, bladder and bowels and a child born with the defect may have some paralysis of the legs and incontinence. In others the defect may be so mild as to cause hardly any physical handicap.

Under normal circumstances, a fluid called cerebro-spinal fluid is secreted into a space around the brain, where it is absorbed into a membrane surrounding the space. But in hydrocephalus, due to a congenital abnormality, the fluid cannot be absorbed and therefore accumulates in the space. Increasing pressure causes the brain to swell and the head grows larger than normal. The defect can be detected in the uterus by means of X-ray or ultrasound. If the defect is well advanced before birth, it may be necessary, for the mother's own safety, to deliver the child by caesarean section. If the defect is not too advanced, it can be relieved after birth by an operation.

In a clinical trial in 1976 carried out by Professor R. W. Smithells of Liverpool, in which 387 women took part, it was found that the recurrence rate was dramatically reduced in those women who had previously had a child with a neural tube defect, by administering multi-vitamin tablets containing ten vitamins, folic acid, iron and minerals. The women were given the multi-vitamin tablets a month before they conceived because it is in the early stage of embryonic development that the damage occurs. Other studies in South Wales suggest that folic acid alone may help reduce the risk of recurrence.

Where couples have had a child with a neural tube defect or have a history of the defect in either of their families, the advice of a genetic counsellor should be sought before they conceive.

6

Difficulties of
Conceiving and Miscarriage

—

If you are unfortunate enough to have a fertility problem yourself, or you think you have, you will be glad to know that it is probably not so difficult to diagnose and to treat successfully. In fact, modern science has made it possible to make an accurate diagnosis of 90 per cent of all cases of infertility, compared with only 40 per cent ten or so years ago. There are, however, some fertility problems that are quite complex, and these include a number of problems that did not affect previous generations. These problems are related to the way we live today. You could say that in many of them nature is protesting at our lifestyle. A number of fertility problems and many of the problems of pregnancy are the result of inadequate preparation. Infertility can be caused by excessive smoking and alcohol consumption and, in general, a poor physical condition which may be brought about by a combination of causes, such as lack of exercise, a poor diet, or exposure to industrial chemicals, in addition to smoking and drinking. Overweight and marital strains can also be predisposing factors.

For most couples, however, infertility is not a problem though it may be a worry. And for many it is an unnecessary worry: 65 per cent of couples who try to conceive are successful within three months, 85 per cent within a year. There are some who take longer simply because the mathematical odds are temporarily running against them. There is only a 20 per cent chance of pregnancy in any given month and there are no symptoms of infertility, no aches and pains, which make it difficult for a couple to know when they should start worrying about their failure to conceive.

Usually a couple is considered eligible for professional counselling if they have failed to conceive after trying regularly for around six months or randomly for a year or more.

The problem may be a simple one like not understanding about fertile and infertile phases in the monthly cycle. Being in too much of a hurry to conceive after coming off the Pill can lead to a great deal of anxiety. There may be unfounded and inconsiderate accusations about who is to blame. Neither partner wants to believe he or she is infertile, so tensions build. It can, of course, be very disappointing for a couple to find that having a child is not as easy as they expected. But becoming pregnant sometimes requires a lot of patience and stamina, and anxiety over not being able to conceive does not help.

A couple who do not start thinking about having a family until they have been living together for a number of years may feel, if they have been actively trying to have a child, that they have left it too late. Age will not affect male fertility, but it is certainly an important factor in female fertility. After the age of thirty a woman's reproductive capacity begins to decline. An older woman might therefore be worried about her failure to conceive after actively trying to do so for several months. No matter what is worrying you, the fact that you *are* worried is a good enough reason to see a specialist, who will probably be able to reassure you and put you on the right track.

A couple may be apprehensive about going to hospital for a check-up. Talking to a stranger about the most intimate details of your life is never easy. The woman may resent being questioned about her bodily functions by a male gynaecologist or fertility specialist and both partners may find it difficult to talk about their sexual habits. In fact, it can be helpful to discuss these matters in a clinical setting and there should be no question of apportioning blame: no one should feel guilty.

There will be an initial discussion about the nature of the problem as you see it. The specialist will want to know your medical history. Then both partners will be physically examined – this will include a genital examination. If there is not a simple explanation, the specialist will then carry out a fertility investigation to provide a precise answer to the problem.

Male Infertility

The first step is to determine the man's role in the couple's fertility problem. Men who have had little or no education in childbirth may regard infertility as a woman's problem, but in fact they are implicated in 30 to 40 per cent of all cases of infertility. The specialist will ask the man to provide a sample of semen, recommending that this should be taken following the usual interval of intercourse. If the couple have sex twice a week the man may be asked to take the sample after an interval of three days, or if they have more frequent sex, which may affect the sperm count, they may be advised to abstain for two or three days before the sample is taken.

Many specialists insist that the specimen should be taken in the hospital so that it is not exposed to any change of temperature or other damage in transit. This poses a problem for some men who may feel, as some still do, that there is something shameful about masturbation, and there are those who simply cannot masturbate no matter what privacy they are given and need to be in their own house to take the specimen – this is usually allowed so long as great care is taken in protecting the semen from heat (not above 64° F) and it is delivered to the hospital laboratory within two or three hours.

Sperm are examined for three main characteristics: their shape (morphology), their movement (motility) and their number.

● *Morphology.* The normal oval-shaped forms represent about 85 per cent of an ejaculate. There are others with large heads, small heads, duplicate heads, tail defects and tapering forms. There are always a small number of abnormal forms in every ejaculate. An infertile male may have more than the normal number.

● *Motility.* In a test tube motility lasts for about two hours; in the womb it goes on for forty-eight hours or more. The laboratory technician will note the percentage of sperm that are moving and evaluate their swimming ability. Good motility means the sperm are moving in a straight line with good power. Sometimes only the tails may be wagging or there may be no movement at all.

● *Number*. The number varies, but 60 million sperm per ejaculate is regarded as desirable. However, any sperm count of 40 million per ejaculate, with good motility, should be sufficient to produce a pregnancy. Counts of 20 to 30 million are considered low, but most specialists believe that as long as some sperm are present there is always a possibility of pregnancy. There is a small number of men who produce too many sperm which prevents movement: they clump together head to head (agglutination). Artificial insemination, in which the ejaculate is split, can solve the problem.

A semen analysis may reveal other problems. The sluggish movement of sperm may indicate varicoceles, which are varicose veins in the scrotal sac. This condition accounts for 40 per cent of male cases of infertility. It can be corrected by surgery.

Absent sperm in the semen may indicate the failure of sperm production in the testes or a blockage in the transport system.

If the sugar, fructose, which is manufactured in the seminal vesicles (two small bladders at the back of the urinary bladder), is missing from sperm it indicates a blockage in the ejaculatory duct or a very rare birth defect, the absence of the vas deferens, the tube which connects the epididymus (a duct on the back surface of the testicles where sperm is stored) with the prostate gland, which contributes fluid to the semen. Without the vas deferens a man can have a normal sex life, but his ejaculate has no semen and consists chiefly of prostate fluid.

It is a clear indication of infection if the semen contains white blood cells (pus cells) and the sperm are dead.

If the sperm count is low with poor motility, a specialist will ask more searching questions about your medical history and lifestyle – for instance, if you had mumps as a child and, if so, whether it spread to the testes, where it can destroy reproductive cells; whether you are working in a job in which you are exposed to radiation; if you have had a venereal disease; if you smoke or drink excessively; if your diet is poor; and questions about whether you are disturbed about anything in your life besides your infertility problem, and so on. The answers to some of these questions may suggest a solution to your problem.

If this is the first time you have considered the possibility that your lifestyle and medical history may affect your fertility, then, whether the problem is easily solved or not, it is obvious that you are unprepared for pregnancy. These are the sort of questions a couple should ask themselves before they attempt to conceive.

HORMONAL DEFECTS

About 8.5 per cent of fertility problems in men are associated with a malfunction of the endocrine system (the glands of internal secretion, such as the pituitary gland just below the brain which produces hormones that are essential for the maintenance of sexual function). Hormonal defects involve not only the glands concerned with sex, but others such as the thyroid gland, which controls the rate at which body fuel is used, and parts of the pancreas that produce insulin to regulate the body's use of sugar. Both these glands can interfere with reproductive processes. Sometimes when a shortage or excess of hormones is found to be the cause of infertility, this can be treated through providing additional amounts of hormone (replacement therapy) or by decreasing the excess amount of hormone present. But it is usually more complicated than that because there are glands that work in pairs according to an intricate feedback mechanism. The hypothalamus, for instance, which is just above the pituitary, regulates the hormones released by the pituitary. One of the amazing functions of the hypothalamus, which is not properly understood, is that it can convert thoughts into physiology; so that thinking about sex, for instance, can activate the mechanism that can lead to an erection. When there is a breakdown in the system that regulates sperm production it is not always easy to determine which glandular partner is at fault. If, however, either one is not functioning properly and the pituitary is not releasing the hormones that regulate sperm production, the missing hormones are administered directly to the testicles. Hormone levels in men are tested with one blood sample. This will provide all the data a specialist needs to determine any failure in the endocrine system that may be the cause of infertility. The connection between the production of hormones in both sexes and emotional disturbance is a fascinating inter-disciplinary area of research.

ENDANGERED SPERM

Low sperm counts are becoming a problem in some parts of the world, including the USA, where there is talk of 'the endangered sperm'. There is a downward trend in sperm densities and some scientists believe that this might be due to increased exposure to a number of industrial chemicals.

To improve the quality of their sperm (before conception) men should cut down on alcohol, give up smoking and certainly avoid street drugs such as marijuana, which are known to interfere with sperm production. Stress can also have an effect on glandular functioning.

Sexually transmitted diseases, a number of infections (even flu), and certain chronic illnesses such as diabetes may reduce the sperm count, as may the drugs used to treat them. Among the drugs implicated in male infertility are: opiates (used as painkillers), cimetidine (used for ulcers), propranolol (used for heart conditions) and drugs used for high blood pressure.

IMPOTENCE

One of the commonest male problems is impotence, which means that a man is not able to have an erection long enough to have successful sexual intercourse. Men may experience temporary impotence after drinking too much alcohol. There are, however, an estimated two million men in the United Kingdom who are permanently impotent. Sometimes impotence is a side-effect of medication, particularly medicines prescribed for high blood pressure. There are also psychological causes, including the kind of impotence which is caused by 'performance anxiety' – the fear of not performing well during sexual intercourse.

Men with diabetes are often impotent, though it is not, as some think, inevitable and it may be only temporary. The cause is not known, but it is believed that nerves or blood vessels controlling blood flow to the penis may be damaged as a result of the disease. To avoid impotence, the diabetic man should keep his diabetes in tight control.

Usually, physical impotence develops over a period of months or years. There is a gradual loss of penile firmness – it takes progressively longer to achieve an erection and becomes increasingly difficult to maintain one. To determine if there is any physical problem there are hormone tests and tests for blood flow to the penis. One unmistakable symptom of impotence is the absence of night-time or morning erections that occur regularly in a healthy man.

There are many treatments available for impotence. Where there is a psychological cause, counselling very often gets to the root of the problem, particularly if both partners attend counselling sessions together. For diabetic men impotence will often be cured when they learn that their problem need not be permanent. Impotence caused by hormonal problems can sometimes be treated with medication. And if a medicine is causing the impotence, the doctor should be asked to prescribe alternative treatment. Impotence that results from permanent damage to the blood vessels or nerves can also be treated by penile implants.

CRYPTORCHISM

This is the retention of one or both of the testes in the abdominal cavity. It is a condition which should be corrected in childhood by the administration of chorionic gonadotropic hormones (which are the same as those formed in the pituitary and are concerned with reproduction) that affect the activity of the testes, or surgery. Testicular descent which is delayed beyond puberty usually results in sterility.

THYROID GLAND

The way this gland functions can be tested by measuring how it takes up a measured amount of iodine. Excess thyroid hormone (hyperthyroidism) or a deficiency (hypothyroidism) affect the gonadotropic hormones released by the pituitary. If thyroid malfunction is established, treatment is given to improve the quality of sperm. Three months usually elapse before the treatment is effective.

RETROGRADE EJACULATION

This is a condition in which the semen flows up into the bladder instead of being ejaculated through the urethra. The semen is then discharged in the urine which will be milky white. The reason for the condition is that the muscle at the base of the bladder has been weakened and does not close to allow the free passage of the semen through the urethra. Often the muscle can be repaired with medication. The condition can be a complication of diabetes or a result of medication for some other condition such as high blood pressure. If the condition does not respond to medication, a man can still father children by artificial insemination, in which semen retrieved from the bladder is used.

Female Infertility

Women's infertility is much more complicated than men's. To be fit for pregnancy a woman must enjoy good health and her reproductive system must be functioning efficiently. If something goes wrong in any part of the reproductive system – the vagina, cervix, fallopian tubes, ovaries and womb – or the glands which control fertility, it will affect a woman's ability to conceive.

Many fertility problems in women are related to egg production and release. Because of a disturbance in the hormonal system – it may be a fault in the connection between the hypothalamus and pituitary glands or between the pituitary and the ovaries, or the ovaries themselves may not be responding to signals from the pituitary – the egg may not mature properly; or if it does grow, it may not be released from the ovary at the appropriate time.

There are four reproductive hormones: the luteinizing hormone (LH) and the follicle-stimulating hormone (FSH), which are released from the pituitary and together are called the gonadotropins ('tropin' means 'directed towards') because their targets are the sex glands or gonads (ovaries or testes). LH and FSH stimulate the female hormones, oestrogen and progesterone, to do their work which is concerned with the ripening and release of the egg and the preparation of the lining of the womb (endometrium) to receive the blastocyst (a cluster of cells that develop after fertilization of the egg). Blood tests can detect any dysfunctioning in the production and operation of these hormones. The four main dysfunctions are known as PRRP: Prime, Respond, Release, Progesterone.

1 *Failure to prime the ovaries:* low FSH, which stimulates the cells in the ovaries to pump out oestrogen, encouraging the lining of the uterus to build up to receive and nourish the implanted early embryo (blastocyst); no LH surge which stimulates the release of an egg.

2 *Failure of ovaries to respond:* low oestrogen production.

3 *Failure of egg to release:* no LH surge or faulty LH receptor sites on the follicle.

4 *Failure in progesterone production:* poor development of the follicle, weak LH surge, or faulty LH receptors.[1]

Stress and illness can interfere with the functioning of the reproductive process and cause infertility. Your medical history may provide clues about possible causes, especially if there is a record of a serious illness such as a sexually transmitted disease or if there is a family history of diabetes or other illnesses that could be inherited. You may be suffering from some undiagnosed illness such as an overactive or underactive thyroid gland or infections such as Pelvic Inflammatory Disease (PID) or chlamydia (see also Chapter 5).

CONTRACEPTIVES

You can see the way the various segments of the hormonal axis function in the way the Pill works by kidding the controlling centre that a woman is pregnant, and thus preventing the production of the hormones which are secreted cyclically and are responsible for the ripening and release of an egg. When the concentration of the ovarian hormones oestrogen and progesterone is high the production of FSH and LH in the pituitary is suppressed by a feedback mechanism. Contrary to popular belief, the length of time a woman stays on the Pill does not in itself seem to affect fertility, but an erratic use of the Pill does; stopping and starting jolts the ovulatory system on and off, which results in loss of buoyancy. Problems may arise in a woman who has used the Pill erratically over a number of years and has delayed child-bearing until her thirties; after a series of shocks the controlling centre may take a long time to recover or may simply refuse to become active again even after a year. When this happens, fertility drugs can help the ovulatory system to start up again. Fertility drugs work in the opposite way to the Pill by kidding the brain control centre that it is not producing the hormones necessary to ripen and release the egg and prepare the lining of the uterus to receive the blastocyst. The result is a flood of hormones into the ovaries; and there is a risk of multiple pregnancy.

Another contraceptive which may affect fertility is the IUD (see page 161), which some doctors say should not be used by women who wish to have children because of the risk of infection and damage to the tubes.

PELVIC INFLAMMATORY DISEASE

This is the single most important cause of the rising incidence of infertility in Western Europe and the USA. It is a sexually transmitted disease caused by bacteria entering the pelvic cavity through the cervix. It is difficult to diagnose because symptoms are the same as various other diseases: fever, abdominal pain, possibly some bleeding through the vagina (PID and other sexually transmitted diseases which cause infertility are described in Chapter 5). A woman who has had one attack of PID has a 15 per cent risk of becoming infertile. After two infections the risk rises to 50 per cent and after three it is 75 per cent.

POLYCYSTIC OVARIES

A common and extremely complex cause of ovulatory failure is polycystic ovarian disease. Something goes wrong in the hormonal axis between the brain control centre and the ovaries: it seems that either the pituitary gland is sending the wrong signals to the ovaries or the ovaries are sending the wrong signals back along the feedback loop. The result is the follicles (small sacs in the ovaries in which eggs develop) do not release an egg and swell to turn into cysts inside the ovaries. The symptoms are infrequent periods, excessive hair on the face and breasts (hirsutism), obesity, and the characteristic large ovaries with multiple cysts. Polycystic ovaries can be treated successfully with fertility drugs. If they fail, an operation called a 'wedge' resection usually results in a return to ovulation and regular menstruation and actually improves fertility. In the operation the surgeon removes a wedge-shaped segment of the ovary, permitting the eggs to be released.

ADRENAL HYPERPLASIA

This is a condition which has some of the symptoms of polycystic ovaries, including hirsutism and the irregularity or absence of menstruation. As the name implies, its main characteristic is an enlarged adrenal gland which produces an excess of hormones. It is usually treated with small doses of the hormone cortisone, which depress the action of the adrenal glands and thus reduce the amount of hormones produced. After a few months' treatment there is an improvement in fertility following the restoration of regular menstruation.

ENDOMETRIOSIS

Endometriosis is frequently overlooked as a cause of infertility. The condition is characterized by cells from the lining of the womb (endometrium) breaking loose and emigrating to other parts of the pelvic cavity. These break-away cells respond to hormones in the same way as the cells in the womb in preparation for a fertilized egg, but are unable to separate and be cast off during the following menstrual period. The cells may invade the covering of the ovary to form cysts. If the condition interferes with conception, surgery is recommended to remove the growths. The condition can be treated with hormonal therapy, but surgery has been found to be more successful in treating the resultant infertility.

DRUGS

Drugs can cause a rise in the levels of the hormone prolactin, which is produced by the pituitary gland to stimulate milk production. Antidepressants, anti-hypertensives (for high blood pressure), hallucinogens, painkillers and alcohol can cause ovulation failure due to prolactin levels rising. When the drug is withdrawn levels are reduced and fertility is improved.

DAMAGE TO THE FALLOPIAN TUBES

The fallopian tubes may be damaged by infections, including PID and endometriosis, or by the consequences of abdominal surgery. There may be damage to the transport mechanism in the tubes: the fimbria and cilia. The fimbria, which are like minute fingers, catch the ovum as it starts its journey to the uterus, and the fine hairs called the cilia waft the ovum down the tube; these are easily damaged by infection. The fimbria may get stuck together in an amorphous mass and form a blockage; the cilia may be destroyed and unfortunately do not grow again. Absence of cilia is a major cause of infertility. To establish the nature and extent of the damage several tests are carried out, which will include a laparoscopy, in which a small incision is made in the belly-button in order to look inside the womb, or special X-ray studies. Tube repair is a difficult operation and there is no guarantee of success in the sense of curing the infertility. It is therefore extremely important to do everything possible to avoid infection.

FAULTY IMMUNE SYSTEM

A healthy body with an unimpaired immune system is protected from the invasion of foreign bodies, such as viruses or foreign proteins, by 'antibodies' that repel an invader. Sometimes the body is overwhelmed by an invader, but usually it is able to manufacture or can be helped to manufacture (by the use of a vaccine) an antibody to a variety of diseases, and in many illnesses the immune system works efficiently even without medical intervention. In fact many of the illnesses that a doctor sees are self-limiting. There are, however, occasions when the immune system misfires and there are many major and minor illnesses – from hayfever, to multiple sclerosis, perhaps even cancer – that are at least partly caused by some malfunction of the immune system. This happens in some cases of infertility where antibodies develop which reject sperm. The treatment recommended for this condition is the use of condoms which result in a reduction of the antibody concentration, medically known as 'titre'. When the titre is as low as it will go, the fertile period of the woman is determined, and a couple is advised to drop the use of the condom. Many couples who have followed this procedure have conceived and had children.

EMOTIONAL DISTURBANCES

Doctors in the past have tended to treat some women's complaints rather cavalierly, especially complaints which are difficult to treat such as painful periods or endometriosis. Women were told their problems were mainly psychological: 'Stop worrying, and you'll find you'll get better.' But they didn't get better; and they felt guilty and were worried about being worried. Few things are more depressing than being told that the illness which is making your life a misery is not 'real' or that 'it is all in the mind'. This attitude to illness has resulted in recent years in a backlash, so that now the cause of most illnesses, including psychiatric illness, is said to be chemical or physical.

Both attitudes – 'Stop worrying, it's all in the mind', and 'Stop worrying, there's a perfectly simple physical explanation' – are wrong. To the sensitive physician diagnosis is mainly a matter of going round in circles. That is to say, it is a matter of looking at every aspect of an illness and seeing how each part interrelates and then deciding which should be given priority, without ignoring the rest. That is the modern holistic approach to illness, practised by orthodox physicians as well as those involved in the popular complementary therapies. It is almost a cliché now to say that in all illnesses the mind, the body and the environment are involved, but it is true nevertheless and particularly true in regard to fertility problems.

An important advance in recent years is the recognition of the 'infertility stress syndrome'. People involved in counselling couples who have fertility problems say that both partners are under enormous psychological stress, and the stress increases as the couples go through investigations and subsequent treatment. Stress often upsets marital relations and makes existing problems worse. Couples who are in this situation and feel that their marriage is under threat should make sure that they see a fertility specialist who is fully aware of these emotional problems. Fortunately most fertility specialists now consider professional psychological evaluation an important part of their investigations.

SEXUAL PROBLEMS

One of the problems standing in the way of successful conception is the problem of sex. Sexual problems may be a symptom of stress of one kind or another, caused by problems at work, financial difficulties or emotional entanglements outside the home. A loving relationship may, of course, exist in spite of sexual problems. Indeed, it is rare to find a perfectly compatible couple whose sex life is ideal. Even if it is blissful at first, it will not necessarily go on being so; there will be emotional troughs and peaks, particularly during pregnancy when sex may become a problem.

Impaired sexual arousal and orgasmic dysfunction may possibly be due to some undiagnosed hormonal problem. It is customary nowadays to separate sexual problems from marital problems. Sexual problems in the male include premature ejaculation, which is particularly common in young men and is usually caused by psychological fears; and the opposite condition, retarded ejaculation, which is rare.

Contacting the Association of Sex and Marital Therapists (ASMT) could be useful, as could sexuality workshops, run by individual counsellors, therapy groups or institutions.

In Vitro Fertilization (IVF)

There is always the possibility that a couple's fertility problem may never be solved and they may wonder if their relationship is stable enough to survive such a crisis. How will they feel about having to abandon their dream of having a child? Does the success of their relationship depend on having children?

Infertility has sometimes led to marriage breakdowns. Couples become hostile and keep blaming one another for their failure to conceive. Having a baby comes to dominate their lives and making love may become mechanical. Sexual intercourse has to take place at a particular time and in a particular way. Tensions build. For some, after months of trying, nothing works and they are told there is no cure.

In spite of medical advances in the treatment of infertility, there are still many couples who are unable to have a child in the normal way; and some of them may want to try in vitro fertilization (IVF). This is a technique pioneered by Dr Robert Edwards and Mr Patrick Steptoe in the late 1970s, in which eggs are taken from a woman's ovary, fertilized with male sperm in a laboratory petri-dish (in vitro) and returned to the womb. Since 1978 when the first test-tube baby was born, IVF clinics have been set up in various parts of the world. But the technique is anything but simple and there is a high failure rate.

Not everyone can accept the idea of having a child conceived in a test tube or having an egg fertilized by the donor sperm of a complete stranger (AID–artificial insemination by donor). Many questions will be asked by an anxious couple who are considering such a procedure. For instance, there is the fundamental question of why a couple want a child so much that they are willing to accept a procedure which some say is 'against nature' and which can be very stressful because of the uncertainty of success or, if there is initial success, the possibility of a miscarriage at some stage of the pregnancy. If they do agree to IVF and the procedure works for them, they may wonder how the child will feel about it when he/she hears that he/she was a test-tube baby. Will the child suffer if he/she does not know the identity of one of his/her parents?

Christine Walby, Director of Social Services for Solihull, believes (*Guardian*, 13 July 1989) the 'identity factor' is crucial. 'The future happiness and emotional security of those conceived in this clinical way is being ignored,' she says. 'It's important for a person to feel part of some chain of physiological continuity ... People without the necessary information about their natural parents have a big bit missing.' She believes test-tube children will suffer mostly because they were not conceived in a loving relationship.

On the other hand, E. Wood, a correspondent to the *Guardian* (22 July 1989), incensed at the views of Christine Walby, wrote: 'IVF is a deeply stressful procedure which makes demands upon relationships that can only be met where two people are able to love and support each other. Children conceived in a test tube stand just as good a chance, if not better, of being the fruit of a loving union.'

There are some infertile couples who are quite happy at first to accept childlessness, but later the woman may suddenly discover in herself a strong desire to have a baby and is unhappy at being denied this fundamental biological need. If the couple then decide to try IVF and the procedure does not work for them, what will be the psychological consequences? Sadly, the chances are the procedure will not work. 'IVF is like playing pinball,' says Professor Robert Winston of Hammersmith Hospital (*Bella*, 21 May 1988). 'Though everyone can have a go, only a few will hit the high scores.' The possibility of being childless, and what it will do to a marriage, and whether having children is terribly important to one or both partners should be discussed by couples before conception, remote though the problem may seem at the time. Living without children – the failure of your plan for parenthood – is something you should consider; it is as important as how your life will change when you have children.

Dorothea Garrett Boswell is one of the many who have tried in vitro fertilization so far (at time of going to press) without success. 'You tell yourself you didn't expect it to work,' she says (*Guardian*, 19 July 1989), 'but it is still devastating. We have decided we will have two more attempts, after which the success rate drops dramatically. Then it is time to face the inevitable. That kindly meant advice not to give up hope is mistaken. Perhaps only by giving up hope is it possible to grieve the loss of the child you never had and make a future alone. Together.'

Most people have no qualms about the fundamental principle of the IVF technique. Everyone is happy about the joy and benefit it can give to an otherwise childless couple. Problems arise from secondary considerations, and these include the fear that many people have concerning man's new-found ability to create human life; and there are those who object to research being carried out on 'spare embryos', even though it may have the laudable aim of trying to unravel some of the mysteries of genetic disorders. 'Where is all this leading?' they sometimes ask. IVF, more than any other medical advance, has opened a Pandora's box of ethical dilemmas concerned with the problem of when life begins and the value we place on it. Some argue that an IVF embryo is an early form of human life and should be protected against any kind of experimentation.

Recognizing the moral dilemmas thrown up by IVF techniques, a committee of inquiry, chaired by the philosopher Dame Mary Warnock, was set up in 1984 by the government. In their report the committee recognized people's need and desire to set moral boundaries and, following the inquiry, the Voluntary Licensing Authority for Human In Vitro Fertilization was established. In their first report in 1986 the committee agreed that the development of IVF was being handled in a responsible and sensitive way.

The problems for which IVF are considered appropriate are:

● where there is irreparable disease or surgical loss of the fallopian tubes

● where the cause of infertility cannot be explained

● where cervical hostility blocks the passage of sperm

● where the tissue lining the womb breaks away to form blockages and scarring inside the pelvic cavity (endometriosis)

● where the quality of a man's sperm is so poor that it can never achieve fertilization or where sperm is diverted to the bladder and no treatment can prevent this.

IVF PROCEDURE

The eggs are 'harvested' through an instrument called a laparoscope inserted in the navel. To make sure the woman produces more than one egg the process of ovulation is helped along with a fertility drug – if more than one egg is implanted, there is a better chance of success. The eggs are placed in a culture medium and allowed to mature for several hours before the sperm are introduced. When fertilization takes place and the fused cell divides several times, an indication that the embryo is developing normally, it is transferred to the womb. This is the most difficult and least successful part of the process: it succeeds only 20 per cent of the time in any given cycle, and for this reason more than one egg is implanted at a time, which doubles or triples the chance of a successful pregnancy.

When the eggs are being incubated the woman usually receives injections of progesterone to help prepare the uterus to receive the fertilized ova. The timing of the transfer must be precise; if at the moment when the transfer is carried out the endometrium lacks progesterone, the embryo will fail to implant. About a third of the embryos are spontaneously aborted in the first twelve weeks and another 10 to 15 per cent later in the pregnancy. So waiting for the outcome of the procedure, with the possibility of a miscarriage, can be a very difficult and stressful time for a couple. Bearing in mind the low success rate of IVF and, if private facilities are used, the high financial cost, it would seem prudent for a couple to make absolutely sure that their infertility has been thoroughly investigated before taking their chance with IVF.

There are a number of IVF centres in London and a few in the provinces. Nearly all of them have long waiting lists. For NHS services you may have to wait four or five years. At present only one – St Mary's in Manchester – is supported by the NHS alone in providing the facility for its patients. There are some NHS centres that ask patients for a donation, but others do not charge a set fee and do not press patients to contribute. A list of approved centres can be provided by the Voluntary Licensing Authority for Human In Vitro Fertilization and Embryology.

GAMETE INTRA-FALLOPIAN TRANSFER (GIFT)
A treatment similar to IVF, but with an important difference is known as GIFT – Gamete Intra-Fallopian Transfer. In this case the whole process of fertilization does not take place outside the

body in a petri-dish, but the eggs and sperm are simply mixed and placed straight away into one of the fallopian tubes for fertilization to take place within the body. Like IVF, it has a high failure rate. It may appeal to those who have moral qualms about fertilization taking place in a laboratory petri-dish.

Miscarriage

It is one thing to be disappointed or depressed because you are unable to have a baby because of a fertility problem, but often there is an answer to the problem. However, it is another thing to be able to conceive, to have a baby growing inside you and then suddenly to lose it. Nothing can be more distressing.

Margaret Leroy, in her book *Miscarriage*, describes one woman's agony at losing a child before birth.[2] Sally lost her baby at eleven weeks: 'I cried constantly, broke down in public on two separate occasions, could think and talk of nothing else. Paul came home from work every day to find me lying on the bed asking again and again why my baby had died.' Emma, who lost her baby at twenty weeks, said: 'This grief seems unbearable and unending, it seems to give rise to an almost physical internal pain.'

Can such distressing experiences be avoided? Is there anything one can do before conception to prevent a miscarriage? While asking these questions, we are aware that they are the sort of questions a woman usually asks herself after she has had a miscarriage and outsiders should try to avoid saying anything that could add to this distress. Most couples are eager to do everything possible to maintain a pregnancy, yet most miscarriages occur because of an unavoidable spontaneous, natural process. A couple who lose a child before birth usually have nothing for which they can blame themselves. A feeling of guilt, though understandable, is the most destructive of all emotions, and should not be indulged in: life is full of hazards and we all make mistakes. The 'if only' feeling – 'If only I had done something different, he/she might have been alive today' – is a feeling common to many people who experience a bereavement, and miscarriage is a bereavement. But such self-recrimination is like trying to play a record backwards: it cannot be done, you cannot change the past. You must go on living, and while accepting the grief and not pushing it away (what Freud called 'the grief work' is necessary and healthy, though difficult in the case of an unborn child whose life has hardly begun and whose passing is marked only in the mind), the important thing is to learn something from the experience, no matter how distressing it is. The Miscarriage Association is an organization which can help women through their grief and advise on other problems related to miscarriage (see Further Information section at the end of book).

The woman who has suffered in this way should remember that miscarriages are very common and can happen to anyone. They may occur so early that they are not noticed and feel just like a heavy period: these are often referred to as 'silent abortions'. In fact, a great many fertilized eggs are rejected by the woman's immune system before implantation. Very often miscarriages can be viewed as a kindness performed by the body because it recognizes a defect in the developing embryo and rejects it.

Generally speaking, there are three main causes of miscarriage: (1) a defective embryo or fetus; (2) faulty implantation of the fertilized ovum in the uterus, or other physical problems associated with the uterus or cervix; (3) hormonal deficiencies.

A defective embryo or fetus may be caused by genetic abnormalities, the result of inherited disease, or exposure to a toxic substance (called a teratogen) such as radiation and certain chemicals before, during or after conception, or an illness suffered by the mother during the first three months of pregnancy. A number of birth defects, such as Down's syndrome, Tay-Sachs and Huntington's chorea (see Chapter 5) are caused by chromosomal defects. Fortunately, very few defective embryos develop to full maturity: 98 per cent are aborted before the end of the fourth month.

The risk of a second miscarriage depends on the reasons for your first one, so it is important to try to establish a cause. Besides the reasons given above, some are the result of a severe shock, like falling downstairs or a serious operation carried out during pregnancy.

Although many miscarriages are unavoidable, there are some that can be traced back to lack of care before conception. The woman's ovum and the man's sperm are, as we have seen, sometimes damaged before they meet up. The main preventable causes of miscarriage are described in other chapters, but, by way of a summary, they include the following.

1 *Alcohol*. Alcohol is recognized as a potential hazard and even social drinking can lead to miscarriage. Before conception both men and women need to cut down on alcohol to prevent embryonic damage and miscarriage (see Chapter 2).

2 *Smoking*. Smoking before and after conception, in both men and women, can harm the embryo and increase the risk of miscarriage. Smoking should be given up before conception (see Chapter 2).

3 *Industrial chemicals*. Chemicals used in certain industries, such as polyvinyl chloride and other chemicals used in the plastics industry, are linked to an increased incidence of miscarriages. (See Chapter 8 for a list of hazards in industry.)

4 *Drugs*. Alarm bells rang following the thalidomide tragedy, when what was considered a harmless drug, promoted as a sleeping tablet in West Germany and sold over the counter without prescription, turned out to be one of the most damaging of teratogenic poisons. We do not know enough about some powerful drugs so their use or over-use should be avoided before and during pregnancy. The medical profession is aware of the possible dangers, so if you are preparing for pregnancy you should let your doctor know. This applies to the man as well as the woman because of possible damage to sperm. One study found an increased miscarriage rate among women sufferers from migraine, and among the wives of male migraine sufferers, which was attributed to the use of ergotamine preparations.[3]

5 *Environmental hazards*. There is very little research concerning the connection between environmental hazards and miscarriage, but common-sense tells you that any poison in the environment could harm the fetus and lead to miscarriage. Living near a toxic waste dump or walking through fields that have been sprayed with pesticides could cause ill health and endanger the health of an unborn baby. One Finnish study has shown that women gardeners often bear children with muscular and skeletal deformities.[4]

6 *Diet*. A good diet will minimize the risk of miscarriage due to environmental hazards. Women in low-income groups, whose diet

is usually lacking in some of the essential nutrients, suffer more miscarriages than those in higher income groups who have an adequate diet. There is plenty of evidence linking vitamin deficiencies with reproductive problems. Certain foods should be avoided because of the possible presence of bacteria, such as listeria, which are known to cause miscarriage (see Chapter 3).

7 *Radiation.* The damage that ionizing radiation, which is a high-frequency form of energy, can cause to the unborn baby is well recognized. This form of radiation is emitted from X-rays. If you are planning a pregnancy and you need an X-ray for some undiagnosed problem, you should tell your doctor or dentist who will arrange for an X-ray to be postponed or cancelled, if it is not absolutely necessary, or carried out when it can cause the least possible damage, before ovulation. There is some evidence that electro-magnetic radiation from power lines may cause miscarriage, so try, if possible, to avoid living too close to them (see Chapter 2). VDUs emit various forms of radiation apart from ionizing radiation: they are radio frequency (RF), very low frequency (VLF) and extremely low frequency (ELF) which combined may present a hazard. If you work with VDUs it would be prudent to avoid too prolonged or unnecessary exposure (see Chapter 8).

8 *Stress.* The relationship between emotional disturbance and miscarriage is difficult to prove. However, sometimes the mind does seem to play cruel tricks. There are fantasies that are 'real' in the sense that they produce real effects: an unreasonable fear may produce a rapid pulse and other physical symptoms. Worrying about another miscarriage in women who have already suffered one or more is difficult to avoid; but many doctors will tell you that, if there is no other obvious cause of miscarriage, one of the best ways of avoiding a recurrence is to stop worrying. Studies have demonstrated that if a woman is given new hope by the offer of a different kind of treatment from anything she has had before, even if it is a placebo – a dummy treatment – it has a high success rate. The positive attitude of the doctor, optimal psychological support of friends and relatives, especially your partner, will help to overcome a nagging fear. Meditation, yoga, relaxation exercises will also help. It is important to get into the right state of mind, and establish a healthy lifestyle before conception; this will help to

create the right conditions for a successful pregnancy and minimize the risk of miscarriage.

9 *Exercise*. Exercise is important for your health before and during pregnancy, but strenuous exercise, such as squash, can be risky: it raises body heat and impairs blood flow to the uterus. There is evidence that some athletes have difficulty in conceiving (see Chapter 4).

10 *Spacing and recurrent miscarriages*. If you have had a miscarriage, you should not be in too much of a hurry to try again. You should allow yourself time to recover from the shock and make sure you are fully restored to health before planning another pregnancy. If miscarriages occur again and again, it may be due to a fertility problem, in which case you should seek specialist advice. After one miscarriage the statistical chance of another is only 20 per cent. After two miscarriages there is an even better chance that your next attempt will be successful.

11 *Disease*. There are some diseases that make pregnancy difficult. These include diabetes, chronic high blood pressure, heart disease, kidney disease, and thyroid problems (see Chapter 5).

One of the problems of couples who suffer recurrent miscarriages is that there is a slow flowering of love for their baby when at last a pregnancy goes to full-term. Teresa Kewley, who wrote an account of her miscarriage in *Spare Rib* said: 'Pregnancy became an obsession. I had to get pregnant. I didn't even see the end product, the baby, in my mind. I just needed to be able to say "I am pregnant." In fact when I finally did get pregnant with my daughter I was very upset when she was born because I was no longer pregnant! I rejected her and didn't want to know her at all for a few days while I got over my resentment with the pregnancy being over.' But it does come right in the end. The baby sees to that. It has a survival mechanism called lovableness.

7

Contraception

Human beings are a remarkably fertile species. It is calculated that if each sperm in a single average ejaculation were able to find an egg, the resulting pregnancies would be enough to populate the whole of North and South America.

Contraceptives are designed to prevent those energetic sperm from getting to the egg (as in the case of the condom and diaphragm) or to stop the fertilized egg implanting (IUD) – though the latest research from the World Health Organization (1987) shows that IUDs not only have the capacity to interfere with implantation, but actually prevent the egg and sperm from meeting – or to interfere with hormonal 'triggers' in order to prevent the release of an egg (the Pill).

Whatever the advantages or disadvantages of a particular contraceptive, the choice should be a joint decision and it is a good idea for couples to explore together the pros and cons of the different types, taking into consideration safety, ease of use and health. No method is 100 per cent effective. All methods – apart from IUD and sterilization – are *only* as good and efficient as the user. This is emphasized in the literature of the Family Planning Association which quotes 'user-failure' rates as an indication of how good or less good a method can be in practice.

The Pill

When the contraceptive pill was introduced nearly thirty years ago, for most women it meant freedom at last from the constant fear of an unwanted pregnancy. It was by far the most reliable of all forms of contraception. Every day over 50 million women around the world still take it even though we are now being told about possible side-effects, some of which are very serious. However, although the Pill has not lived up to expectations, medical authorities insist that its advantages far outweigh its risks. Even so, this may worry some women who feel that any serious risk, however slight, is unacceptable. At any rate, on such an important matter, you have a right to know the facts and must make up your own mind.

For most women the Pill has undoubtedly had some good social effects. It has helped to bring about a big change in their role, giving them the same freedom as men to pursue a career if they wish, without any unwelcome interruption for child-bearing. And it has allowed them to decide (without fear of accident) how many children they are going to have, when they are going to have them, or whether to have them at all and to enjoy sexual intercourse and love-making.

HOW THE PILL WORKS

When a woman is physically mature an egg, or ovum, usually ripens and leaves the ovary once a month to travel down the fallopian tube. This is called ovulation. Fertilization takes place when the male sperm merges with the ovum. There are two types of contraceptive pill that prevent this from happening.

1 *The combined pill.* This contains a combination of oestrogen and progestogen and is the most widely used and most effective when taken correctly and according to instructions. It works by suppressing ovulation; by thickening the mucus at the entrance to the womb and thus discouraging the passage of sperm into the womb; by altering the mobility of the fallopian tubes; and by acting on the endometrium (the lining of the womb) to prevent implantation of a fertilized egg. If you have a twenty-one or twenty-two day pack you will have a break of six or seven days before starting the next pack, during which time you will have some bleeding. Some women take the twenty-eight day pill – called

the everyday or ED pill. Each pack of twenty-eight day ED pills includes twenty-one active pills and seven dummy (inactive) pills which contain no hormones. They are designed for women who prefer to take a pill every day. You will usually have some bleeding while taking the dummy pills.

Combined pills come in three forms: *monophasic*, where each pill is identical; *triphasic*, where the relation of oestrogen to progestogen varies three times in the cycle; and *biphasic*, where the ratio varies twice in the cycle. It is important that phasic pills are taken in the correct sequence.

2 *The progestogen-only pill.* The mini-pill is taken every day without a break, even through menstruation. It does not prevent ovulation in 60 per cent of cycles, so there is a slight risk of becoming pregnant while taking it. It has the effect of thickening the mucus at the entrance of the cervix and altering the movement of the fallopian tubes to prevent fertilization, and altering the lining of the womb to prevent implantation. It can be taken during breast-feeding. Common effects are irregular bleeding, which is usually sorted out by changing to another progestogen-only pill, and amenorrhoea (absence of menstruation), usually because the pill has prevented ovulation.

THE PILL AND PRE-CONCEPTUAL HEALTH

The Pill is disapproved of by some people who believe that you cannot tamper with nature without suffering ill effects. 'Do we really think that a drug which effects so many different changes in the body is not going to affect our health?' says Dr Peggy Norris, Hon. Secretary of the Medical Education Trust. 'Or has nature got things wrong?' For others, such as the Catholic Church, the Pill, like all forms of contraception apart from natural family planning (NFP), defies God's will or purpose.

The Pill is unacceptable to the Foresight Association for the Promotion of Pre-conceptual Care, who campaign for a healthier lifestyle, free from over-dependence on chemicals (in food or medicine), as the best way of ensuring a trouble-free pregnancy; and they also advocate NFP.

With many people who are troubled about the Pill there is a painful tug of war going on between the heart and the head. The result very often is confusion. If you are confused, see either your GP if he/she offers a family planning service or go to a NHS family planning clinic (see Further Information, page 253). If you lean towards a more natural method of contraception, go to a Natural Family Planning clinic or a Foresight doctor.

The Pill sometimes arouses strong emotions and conflict between those who are for it and those who are against it. The careful, unemotional scientist pursues her/his researches in the clinical setting of the laboratory, looking for hard evidence and discounting the views of those who have fears but very little evidence to offer. But it must be said that it is very often a fear, an intuition, a hunch, a 'gut' feeling that is the starting point of research. Is the Pill one of medicine's mistakes? Some people seem to think so. But this is not confirmed by the painstaking scientific research going on all around the world which has not at present come up with anything to undermine a *healthy* woman's confidence in the Pill. It is believed, however, that there may be risks in certain groups of women and these are being investigated very thoroughly.

Serious risks associated with the Pill may include breast cancer, particularly in young women who go on using the Pill for a long time before they have a full-term pregnancy. However, research in this area is still inconclusive and contradictory. Scientists also suspected a link between breast cancer in some women and the older high-dose contraceptive pills; but it has been standard practice for many years to prescribe the lowest effective dose of pill for women.

Alarmist reports in the press linking the Pill with breast cancer have tended to misquote researchers to give the impression that the connection has been established beyond any doubt. But although the possibility is not denied, scientists around the world are still working towards formulating some kind of conclusion and recommendations concerning the use of the Pill. Certainly, studies have suggested that various groups of women may be more at risk and these may include young women under twenty-five who use the Pill for long periods of time. But there is a need for further confirmatory research before advice can be given with any certainty.

For most women, however, the low-dose Pill is generally regarded as a safe method. It should be avoided if you are among what is regarded as the higher than average risk groups: that is, if you have high blood pressure, diabetes, a history of thrombosis in the family, if you are overweight, smoke excessively, or if you are over forty-five. Smokers are advised by the Family Planning Association to change methods at thirty-five. But it is emphasized that you should have regular check-ups, particularly of blood pressure, to make sure you are really fit. The Pill may increase blood pressure.

A few women may develop a blood clot which can block a vein or artery; this can be a very serious condition. The risk is greater in those mentioned above – smokers, diabetics, etc. It may not be wise for them to take the Pill if a close blood relative has developed heart disease and/or thrombosis at an early age.

The Pill is also blamed for the fact that cervical cancer is now increasing in women below the age of thirty-five. It is believed that there may be a link between this form of cancer and the Pill, though this is still a contentious issue.

On the plus side, there are quite a number of things to be said, apart from the proven reliability of the Pill and its great advantage of not interfering with intercourse. The Pill does prevent unwanted pregnancy, which is probably the biggest tragedy of all for a young girl or, for that matter, any woman. The Pill reduces the risk of some non-cancerous breast disease, fibroids and a type of cyst on the ovary. It also protects against cancer of the ovary, cancer of the uterus and some pelvic infections, and maintains this protection for many years after its use is discontinued.

The efficiency of the Pill is reduced by a wide variety of medicines, including some antibiotics, anticoagulant and anti-arthritic drugs. If you are prescribed medicine of any kind you should ask your doctor if it can reduce the effect of the Pill. Severe vomiting and diarrhoea and other gastric and intestinal disorders, such as colitis, may also lessen the effect of the Pill.

Other problems associated with the Pill are:

● cramps and pains in the legs – if this occurs, you should see a doctor

● migraines and headaches if they are worse or occur for the first time while you are on the Pill

● weight gain, which may be a problem when you first start taking the Pill, but not after the second or third packs – if there is still an increase of weight, it can easily be remedied by changing to another brand of Pill

• bleeding at odd times in the first months sometimes occurs (breakthrough bleeding); it usually settles, but if not, the problem should be discussed with your doctor or clinic

• breast tenderness and enlargement, partly due to water retention

• discomfort or soreness if wearing contact lenses, but this is less likely today with low-dose pills

• skin conditions, including eczema and pigmentation of the face (chloasma), which sometimes happens in pregnancy too – in bright sunlight a protective cream is advised but the condition may remain permanently.

Despite the problems, the Pill has given a new lease of life to those women whose hormone balance is not functioning well, or who have irregular or heavy periods.

COMING OFF THE PILL

If you are planning to have a baby, you should stop the Pill and then have two natural periods before you try to get pregnant. A condom can be used for that time. After two natural periods it is easier to work out when the baby is due. The first post-Pill menstruation may not occur for up to ninety days after the Pill has been discontinued; this happens particularly in women who come off the Pill in their thirties. It is important that the woman should be aware of the possibility of a delay in the return of fertility, otherwise worry about it could further slow down conception (see Chapter 6).

Injectable Contraception

The injectable method is useful to some women who find daily pill-taking hard to remember and are unable to use other methods for medical reasons or simply because they don't want to. In the UK the most common injectable contraceptive is Depo-Provera, which contains a hormone similar to that in the mini-pill. It should be offered only to women who cannot use other methods and should be regarded as a last resort. The injection lasts two or more months.

The most common side-effect, like the mini-pill, is that it alters menstruation. Some women have fewer or no periods after one or more injections. A few women may have light bleeding. The absence of periods, or light periods, in relation to this method is not considered harmful to your health. However, women whose diet is deficient in iron, who have frequent and/or heavy bleeds will in all probability suffer from anaemia.

Some women gain weight using this method, and some may suffer from depression which may or may not be related to Depo-Provera. Some women find that when they stop injections there is a delay of up to a year before the return to regular periods and fertility. As with the contraceptive pill, there is the possible risk of cancer in some groups of women, but this remains unresolved. You should not choose this method, or for that matter any other method, without the consent of your partner and you should discuss with your doctor any possible side-effects and the suitability of the injection in your case. Ask your doctor for the manufacturer's leaflet on Depo-Provera which is available to help you decide.

The Condom

The condom is a sheath of latex rubber that fits over the erect penis and prevents sperm from entering the vagina. It stretches to fit closely to most sizes and shapes of penis. It generally has a teat at the end to collect the sperm.

After the introduction of the Pill, sales of condoms declined, but they are now coming back into use because of the HIV and AIDS scare. They are regarded as an effective way of reducing the risk of sexually transmitted infections. The campaign to prevent the spread of HIV recommends the use of the condom: but this is aimed mainly at men and women who have a number of sexual partners or a new partner whose sexual history is unknown. The condom should always be used for casual sexual encounters.

Good condoms are very effective, having a failure rate which is said to be as low as two per hundred user-years. Generally speaking, however, the failure rate is higher, mainly, it is believed, because of poor use but also because there are condoms of poor quality on sale that do not conform to the British standard BS 3704. Good quality condoms that conform to the British standard carry the kite-mark, so it would be advisable to use these brands. There is no internationally recognized standard, so it would be as well to carry a supply of kite-marked condoms when going abroad.

Condoms can deteriorate over time, especially if they are stored in a warm damp atmosphere or are kept too long in a wallet or similar container.

One of the disadvantages of the condom can be that it interrupts intercourse. Last-minute fumbling for the condom can be embarrassing and the attempt to fit it can result in an erection subsiding or the woman losing interest. However, it can be put on as part of love play, thus enhancing excitement. It is also said that the condom dulls genital sensation, thus reducing the enjoyment of sex for women as well as men. However, loss of sensitivity is reduced by some of the latest, finer varieties which are lubricated with spermicides. But much of this may be related to emotional concern rather than physical reality. Couples must be careful not to fall asleep, still entwined, before removing the condom.

Diaphragm, Caps and the Sponge

The diaphragm (vaginal cap) is a circular dome made of thin rubber with a pliable metal rim that fits over the cervix. There are three kinds: flat spring, coil spring and arcing spring. Cervical caps are smaller devices designed to fit over the cervix, and again there are three kinds: the cervical cap itself, the vault cap and the vimule cap. All are usually referred to as 'caps' because they are used in a similar way, and work in the same way. The sponge is made of polyurethane foam and already has a spermicide in it. A doctor or nurse should advise you on what kind of cap is suitable for you and how to use it.

A cap acts both as a barrier to prevent sperm from reaching the womb and as a receptacle for holding spermicide near the cervix. When used properly it is very effective and has no serious side-effects. Some women, however, find its use results in a greater susceptibility to cystitis and other urinary tract infections; but this can be improved by changing to a different cap or, obviously, changing to a different method of contraception.

After the introduction of the Pill and IUD the diaphragm lost its popularity. It is, however, coming back into favour among some women who are worried about the long-term effects of the Pill and IUD use.

The diaphragm/cap has a life of at least a year, but should be carefully checked before use. It should not, of course, be used if the ring is bent out of shape, or if the rubber deteriorates because it is badly stored, or if it is damaged by fingernails or rings. Oil-based spermicides or lubricants should not be used with the diaphragm because they may damage the rubber.

Tests show that for every hundred women who use the cap very carefully and consistently, two will become pregnant in a year. But with less careful and consistent use, two to fifteen will become pregnant. The sponge is believed to be a lot less reliable, and the Family Planning Association advise you not to use it if avoiding pregnancy is very important to you.

The IUD (intra-uterine device)

The IUD is a plastic and copper device which is inserted in the womb and left there for some considerable time – three to five years depending on the type fitted. They come in various shapes and sizes but are mostly about an inch and a half long and rather less than that in width. They are a very reliable form of contraception and their reliability increases with use. They work, as recent research shows, not only by interfering with implantation, but by preventing the egg and sperm from meeting.

One of their main advantages is that once fitted there is nothing to remember and nothing to take or use daily. But it is important that they are fitted correctly.

The IUD is not recommended for young women or those who are not in a mutually faithful relationship because of the risk of infection which, if it occurs, can damage one or both fallopian tubes, thus causing infertility. If pregnancy does occur while the IUD is still in the womb it is more than likely to be ectopic: that is, one which develops in one of the fallopian tubes and cannot be sustained.

The Female Condom

A new contraceptive, known as the female condom, has recently been developed by an international group of gynaecologists. A combination of a diaphragm and a condom, it is made of strong polyurethane or latex material and is inserted into the vagina before intercourse, giving it an advantage over the male condom, which may interfere with love-making. It is claimed to be just as effective as its male counterpart against sexually transmitted diseases, including HIV. However, research is still being carried out and at present there are no results yet as to its efficacy either against pregnancy or HIV.

Although the female condom covers the whole surface of the vagina, it is not skin-tight like the male condom, allowing the penis to move freely within the device. The promoters say there is no problem about fitting – 'it is as simple to insert as a tampon' – but, again, researchers who are testing the condom are not absolutely sure about this. A thin flexible plastic ring on its outer edge holds it in position over the woman's genitalia and prevents it from being accidentally pushed into the vagina during intercourse. It is pre-lubricated, so no additional creams or jellies are needed. Like the male condom, it is used only once and then discarded.

Morning-after Emergency Birth Control

Accidents do happen sometimes – condoms rupturing or slipping off, for example. If something like this happens to you, there are two emergency methods that are available. It is important to take prompt action the following morning. The two methods are a pill and an IUD, which will usually prevent an unwanted pregnancy. Two special doses of a pill, which must be prescribed by a doctor, are taken twelve hours apart. The sooner the treatment starts the better – certainly not later than three days (seventy-two hours) after sex. The treatment may cause sickness, which may mean taking more pills. It is important to check with your doctor after treatment.

The other method involves fitting an IUD in your womb and this will be done by your doctor. Again, the sooner this is done the better – not later than five days after sex. It is almost 100 per cent effective, but it is not suitable for all women, so you should discuss this with your doctor.

Natural Family Planning

In the last decade we have seen a longing, especially among young people, to return to a way of life that is in harmony with nature and not at war with it. This longing is expressed in a support for the ecological movement, the current emphasis on 'healthy' living, the refusal to kowtow to the authoritarianism of orthodox medicine and the demand by growing numbers of men and women to control their own lives and free their bodies from the tyranny of drugs.

Disillusion with the Pill is part of this general movement away from unnatural methods of regulating our lives. Women in particular, who have to suffer the side-effects of some of the artificial methods of contraception described in this chapter, are not convinced that their advantages outweigh their risks.

Those who advocate natural family planning (NFP) believe that theirs is the only really sensible and enjoyable way of planning or avoiding pregnancy. They do emphasize, however, that NFP needs to be taught personally and cannot be learned successfully by reading alone.

NFP depends on the woman becoming so familiar with her menstrual cycle that she can accurately identify her infertile and fertile days. There is still a feeling among many people that NFP is not reliable and, sadly, professionals perpetuate this myth. The reason for this is that the old-fashioned rhythm method which was based on calendar calculations, was, as is generally recognized now, both unreliable and unacceptably restrictive. The method was associated with religious scruples and was described unkindly as 'Vatican roulette'.

Calendar calculations, though still used in combination with other methods, are no longer recommended as a single reliable form of NFP. In recent years there has been a great deal of research carried out into the effectiveness of NFP and there is no doubt that it is now possible to work out reliable methods tailor-made to suit individual requirements. In Britain NFP teachers are trained by the National Association for Natural Family Planning, which is currently based at the Queen Elizabeth Hospital, Birmingham, or the Natural Family Planning Service of the Catholic Marriage Advisory Council.

There are three methods of natural family planning, all of which aim at determining, as accurately as possible, the beginning and end of the fertile phase in the menstrual cycle.

1 *The temperature method.* In most women the basal body temperature (which is the temperature of the body at rest) rises by several points of a degree just after ovulation and does not fall again until a day or two before the next period starts. A pattern of a low temperature for the first part of a cycle and a higher temperature for the second part can be seen easily if an accurate record of daily temperatures is taken throughout the cycle. This method, however, does not detect the potential fertility of the days before ovulation when intercourse could leave sperm in the womb which could fertilize the egg when it is released. If, however, sexual intercourse is restricted to the latter part of the cycle, the temperature method can be up to 99 per cent effective in avoiding an unwanted pregnancy. This compares favourably with

other methods of contraception which are regarded as reliable.

One of the advantages of this method is that the male partner can play a part by taking responsibility for temperature charting and interpretation. A disadvantage for those wanting to achieve a pregnancy is that it does not detect the beginning of the fertile phase. It can be of most help to those who do not want to conceive, but restricts intercourse to about a third of the cycle.

2 *The cervical mucus method.* This is also known as the Ovulation Method or Billings Method after the doctors Evelyn and John Billings who first described the way fertile and infertile days could be recognized by the changes that take place in the cervical mucus.

At the time of ovulation the mucus changes from being thick, tacky and opaque to being thin, clear and profuse. You can learn to recognize these changes by examining your own mucus. In the infertile phase the mucus breaks easily when held between thumb and forefinger. In the fertile phase the mucus has an elastic quality and can be stretched for several centimetres when held between thumb and forefinger. It is compared by some women to raw egg-white.

These changes can be recognized by distinct sensations in the vulva, which feels dry in the infertile phase and wet in the fertile phase. A chart is used in which different kinds of symbols or coloured pencil or stamps indicate the changes that take place (see box).

THE MUCUS ONLY APPROACH – THE BILLINGS METHOD

Regular cycle

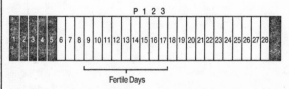

Fertile Days

This is a chart of the so-called 'text-book' cycle, where periods occur every four weeks. The woman starts her chart on the first day of her period. Studies have shown that pregnancy rate on the first four days of a genuine period is virtually zero. Thereafter, the key to fertility is the presence or absence of cervical mucus. Days 6, 7 and 8 were recorded

---

as DRY with no mucus, and were therefore infertile. On day 9 mucus appeared and so fertility began. Mucus continued until day 14 and therefore all these days were fertile days. The last day of fertile mucus is marked peak (P) day, and classically the egg is released the day after – i.e. day 15 on this chart. Since the egg lives forty-eight hours, days 16 and 17, although DRY, are still potentially fertile. From day 18 the rest of the cycle is infertile.

Short cycle

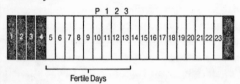

Fertile Days

This is a chart of a short cycle, where a period came only twenty-four days after the start of the previous one. This is caused by an early ovulation. As the period stopped, the egg ripened immediately, producing cervical mucus from days 5 to 10. The mucus disappeared on day 11, when ovulation most likely occurred, allowing two more drying up days for the lifespan of the egg. From day 14 the remaining days of the cycle are infertile. In short cycles like this one, there is no infertile phase before ovulation.

Long cycle

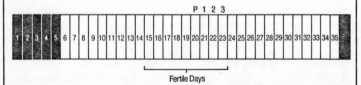

Fertile Days

This chart represents a long cycle: some women have cycles even longer than this one. This is caused by a very long ovulation, which for some women is their normal pattern, but for others occurs only at times of illness, stress, breast-feeding and menopause. After the period, because the egg did not ripen, there was no mucus production and infertility continued for several days, until day 14. On day 15, mucus appeared and continued until day 20, allowing the statutory three drying up days after P day. Infertility returned on day 24 until the end of the cycle.

It takes time for a woman to become familiar with her own mucus pattern and this should at first be learned with the guidance of a NFP counsellor (see details at end of the book). It also calls for a degree of commitment by both partners to make the method work. Couples have said that co-operating to make the method work gives them a sense of mutual understanding and closeness. For couples wishing to achieve a pregnancy the mucus method is undoubtedly the best because it can predict the peak of fertility in the cycle.

3 *Multiple-index methods.* These are methods which combine two or more indicators of fertility, including breast tenderness, texture and width of the cervix, as well as calendar calculations, the temperature and mucus methods. The various combinations of indicators of fertility include the following:

● *Symptothermal methods.* This combines the temperature method with other indicators of impending ovulation such as changes in mucus and cervix.

● *Calculothermal method.* This involves the calendar method to predict the beginning of the fertile phase with the temperature method to determine its end.

● *Mucothermal method.* This uses the mucus method to identify the beginning of the fertile phase with the temperature method to detect its end.

● *Mucus method plus calendar calculations.* Calendar calculations are used to predict the beginning of the fertile phase while the mucus method is used to determine its end.

● *Mucus method plus cervical changes.* Women on night shift or doing other work which makes it difficult to carry out the temperature method can combine the mucus method with noting cervical changes to determine the beginning and end of the fertile phase.

8

Health and Safety
in the Home and at Work

Most of us live in a high-tech environment surrounded by potentially dangerous appliances – television sets, videos, microwave cookers, electric kettles, toasters, razors, electric blankets; any one of these could give you an electric shock and some of them could kill in certain circumstances. They can also cause fires. It is well known that there are more accidents in the home than on the roads; and most of the accidents, some fatal, are caused because we think of the home as a safe refuge from the stresses and dangers outside. Accidents happen quickly: a simple, thoughtless act, such as allowing the handle of a saucepan to stick out from the stove could lead to someone knocking it and spilling the contents of the pan, perhaps scalding themselves or setting oil from a chip pan alight. (There are 15,000 chip pan fires reported every year.)

Not nearly enough trouble is taken to make the home a safe place to live in. We have enforceable safety standards for offices and factories, but not for the home. It is therefore very important that a couple who are planning a family should take extra care about such things as wiring and all electrical appliances. Safety in the home is of paramount importance if you are expecting one day to see a child crawling or toddling around. For example wires to ironing boards, television sets and so on could be hazardous if they are left trailing across a room. Loose carpets are also a cause of accidents, especially stair carpets. A pregnant woman could easily trip over such obstacles and sustain injuries which could put her child at risk.

A couple planning to start a family must be their own health and safety officers and look at everything in the home with a critical eye. They should ask, 'Do I really need a loose rug in the hall?' or 'Can the medicine cupboard be reached by small hands?' or 'Is there enough air circulating in the room?' or 'Shouldn't we do something about that damp corner in the bedroom?' There are hundreds more such questions that should be asked about safety and health in the home.

Health and Safety in the Home

ELECTRICITY

Getting fit for pregnancy means looking at everything in your lives that could affect your health and safety, and this must include your home environment. You don't have to be obsessional about this, worrying about every small thing that could go wrong. You do, however, have to do some basic, common-sense planning; for instance, take a close look at the electricity when you move into a new home, and make absolutely sure your wiring is safe. Call in a good electrical contractor, preferably one who is approved by the National Inspection Council for Electrical Installation Contracting (NICEIC) in the UK.

You may have to have your home completely re-wired and this could be expensive. Faulty wiring, however, could result in even more expensive – and dangerous – problems. Most electricity boards and some electrical contractors have credit schemes that allow you to spread the cost over a reasonable period. On the other hand, you may find your local authority will offer you an improvement grant to cover the cost.

You should also take a look at your plugs and electrical appliances. The following are some points to bear in mind.

Plugs. Do not use plug adaptors. They may be convenient as temporary measures but they will encourage you to overload a socket. It is safer to have one plug for each socket; or you could, with safety, use a double socket fitted in place of a single.

Electric blankets. Never plug an electric blanket into an adaptor in which another appliance is already plugged, or in a light fitting. Do not use an overblanket under you or an underblanket over you.

Electric blankets should be stored flat, and an underblanket can be kept on the bed all the year round. Check your blanket regularly for signs of wear such as scorch marks, frayed edges, damaged flexible cord. You should get an expert to service electric blankets at least every two years.

Microwave cookers. The early microwave cookers did not have adequate sealing mechanisms and could be dangerous, but the latest are subjected to stringent safety tests by the British Electrotechnical Approvals Board. There are a number of basic precautions which are always covered in the instruction leaflet. As with all instruction leaflets issued with electrical appliances, this should be read carefully. There are fears that the microwave cooker could be damaging because of ionizing radiation. But it is unlikely that this could be a hazard as they are generally used for only a short time and are fairly well screened. The main danger of microwave cookers is that they vary greatly in their ability to heat food evenly and may leave cold spots where food poisoning organisms survive (see pages 178–9).

Light fittings. Do not fit an electrical appliance to a light fitting. Do not use shades that are not suitable for the wattage of the bulb. The recommended wattage should be stated on the label of the shade. Always switch off the light before changing a bulb.

Kettles. Always switch off and unplug from the wall socket before pouring from kettles. A coiled kettle flex might be a good investment for the future if you are planning a family and cordless jugs are now on the market which are heated on a power base. These will prevent a child from pulling a dangling cord and toppling a kettle off the worktop – a frequent cause of serious burns and scalds. Every year there are 300 or so kettle accidents involving young children.

Toasters. These must always be switched off, unplugged and allowed to cool if something such as a piece of burnt toast gets stuck inside them. Never poke them with a knife or fork. Simply turning the toaster over, then shaking it gently may remove the toast. Otherwise remove it with your fingers or a pair of tweezers when the elements have cooled.

Washing machines. A washing machine uses a lot of water, so make sure the flex and plug are dry at all times.

Irons. Always allow the iron to cool completely before wrapping the flex round it and storing it away. A cordless iron is now being marketed; like the jug kettle, it is heated on a power base.

Vacuum cleaners. These should be serviced regularly. Flexes should be checked frequently and replaced at the first sign of wear.

IS YOUR WATER SAFE?

It would be wise to check your water for pollutants, particularly if you live in an old house which may still have lead piping or you are worried about the possibility of your water supply coming from an area such as East Anglia where there is a problem of pollution from agricultural nitrates. Do not be taken in by the tactics of some water filter advertisers who, while scaring you to death about the poisons in your water, will offer to check it for chemical levels free of charge. Maybe it should be checked but not by a manufacturer who is pushing a particular brand of water filter. The filter could be unnecessary in your particular area, it might be ineffective against some pollutants or it may even increase the pollution in your tap water. The Thames Water Authority has found bacteria levels as much as 1,000 times higher in some filtered water than in the tap water.

There is, however, some truth in the allegation that not all of Britain's water is of very good quality. A report published in 1986 by the Consumers' Association said that nearly a quarter of Britain's population may be drinking sub-standard water. In 1987 the EEC regarded the problem as so serious that they threatened to sue Britain unless action was taken to meet EEC standards.

The main pollutants in water, which vary from place to place, are lead, nitrate, aluminium, iron and manganese. The most serious problems are pollution by lead and nitrates. Britain was granted a four-year delay in implementation of EEC standards on lead, but it is unlikely that the deadline will be met in the case of thousands of homes where lead plumbing is still in use. So check the plumbing if you live in an old house.

As regards the other main area of concern – agricultural nitrates – serious ground water pollution has been recorded in some regions. Nitrates can and do get into water supplies via underground aquifers. Small quantities of nitrate can do no harm, but high levels are dangerous and can reduce oxygen levels in the blood causing an illness known as blue baby syndrome. A 1980 EEC directive set a maximum admissible concentration of 50 mg per litre of nitrates in water. The British government, however, insisted that this standard was set too low and the level was subsequently relaxed to 80 mg per litre. At the same time the government allowed water suppliers to average their results over a three-month period, instead of basing results on spot checks as the directive had indicated.

The government's attempt to get round the directive concerning nitrates was reported to the European Commission by Friends of the Earth in 1987. As a result, the new privatized water industry must now spend an estimated £6 billion on improving standards in order to conform to the EC directive.

In the meantime you, the consumer, must take action if you are at all worried about the presence of nitrates in your water supply. What can you do about it? If you are worried about pollutants of any kind in your water, you should first of all approach your water authority direct or call your environmental health officer at your local town hall or civic centre. If the problem seems to be bacterial, they will call and take a sample of your water for testing by the public health laboratory service. If the problem is chemical, the sample will be taken to the public analyst. Both these services are free so long as they are obtained through the environmental health officers.

On the other hand, you can search round for a suitable water filter, but take great care in the choice you make. There are filters that claim to remove nitrates, lead and other pollutants. Study the claims made for each water filter and, if you are at all doubtful, ask for independent laboratory reports. Remember, if your water is contaminated, not only could you be damaging your own health, but you may be putting an unborn child at risk if you do become pregnant.

GLASS

Every year more than 40,000 people – about a quarter of them children – need hospital treatment for accidents involving glass. Many of these accidents happen in the home while people are simply pottering about doing odd jobs or children are playing. Wine or beer glasses left on the floor beside a chair can be accidentally trodden on and glasses left on low tables or chairs are hazardous. For casual or late-night drinking it might be a good idea to use only plastic cups and glasses. Your best cut glass should be reserved for the dinner table. Do not serve children with soft drinks in wine glasses. Plastic cups, glasses and jugs should be on your list of things to buy for the home before you start your family.

Serious accidents can happen when people fall against windows or glass doors. Ordinary window glass is brittle and shatters into pieces with razor-sharp edges. Replacing this with safety glazing in vulnerable areas, such as patio doors or ordinary doors with glass panels, or bath and shower screens, would prevent many serious injuries. Safety glass is thick and less likely to break – but if it does the pieces are less dangerous without the sharp edges. A safety film for glass, which prevents shattering, is obtainable from Mothercare shops.

PAINTWORK

Most pre-war houses are likely to contain a lot of lead in their paintwork. You should therefore be careful when stripping off old layers of paint not to spread around dust which may be full of lead. The easiest solution is to paint over with new, low-lead paint. If you do strip off, keep doors closed but windows wide open to keep the room ventilated. Do not rub down with dry sandpaper and do not burn off the paint with a blow lamp which causes fumes.

The best way to remove the paint is to soak it thoroughly with warm water and then rub down with a waterproof abrasive paper. When you clean up afterwards dispose of bits and pieces of old paintwork and dust sweepings in a plastic bag in a dustbin. Do not burn it. Then have a shower and change into clean clothes.

If you buy a second-hand cot for your baby, you will probably want to give it a fresh coat of paint. Be sure to use a low-lead paint. Better still, use only emulsion paint which contains no lead.

AIR FILTERS

The air in the average house is full of dust, smoke, kitchen smells and other pollutants. It would therefore seem quite a good idea to install an air-filter machine. To do this effectively, however, rather larger banks of filters are required than are found in domestic machines. A *Which?* report in June 1983 showed that although domestic filters do remove smoke and smells, they do so in such a minor way that it seems unlikely that you would notice the difference apart from a masking smell produced by the scented filters. Instead open a window for a few minutes regularly during the day to keep the air circulating. This would not be a good idea if you live on a busy road, however, because you could let in more pollutants than you let out.

HYGIENE

Hygiene in the home is, like safety, often neglected. In restaurants or hotels the utmost importance is attached to hygiene; any lapse in standards can result in prosecution. If the same applied to many homes, there would probably be quite a few people who would find themselves in trouble.

The main problem in the home, as in restaurants, is bacteria. Bacteria thrive in a warm, moist atmosphere where, once established, they can double their numbers every twenty minutes. Bacteria live in food, even when it is kept in a fridge. They breed rapidly in any food that is left standing for long on a table or stove. A lot of the food we eat is, in its raw state, full of bacteria, so be careful not to store your food in a warm atmosphere where the bacteria will flourish. Any suspect food, especially meat and leftover food, should be cooked long enough to kill any bacteria – but, in the case of food rich in vitamins and minerals, not so long that all the goodness is cooked out of it. Poultry that is not cooked properly can be especially dangerous. Be careful to defrost poultry thoroughly before cooking because bacteria can remain alive in the centre of frozen food, even after cooking.

Most of the food poisoning outbreaks notified to doctors are caused either by salmonella or staphylococcus bacteria. Staphylococcus bacteria are fairly common. They appear under the microscope to look like little clumps of grapes and are found wherever there is dirt or particles of rotting food. They cause boils and may remain on the skin after a boil is cured; and from there they can find their way into food. Our skin plays host to a remarkable number of bacteria. At any one time there can be as many as three million on one square centimetre of your skin. These do us no harm so long as they remain on the skin, but if there is a cut, the bacteria can cause infection. You should always wash your hands thoroughly (but not in the kitchen sink) before preparing food. Cuts and sores should be covered with a waterproof dressing. Always keep lids on waste bins, and clean them regularly. Clean working surfaces with hot soapy water before placing food on them.

You should be careful about where you buy food. Do not buy it from shops where you suspect those handling the food are careless about hygiene. Ensure that food is well wrapped and cannot be contaminated on the way home, for example in the boots of cars or taxis which may not be particularly clean and may contain residues of other food parcels or items of soiled clothing.

Lavatories, of course, are a high risk area in terms of bacteria. The lavatory seat and lid, cistern, handle, and door knob or handle should be regularly wiped with a clean, damp cloth and disinfectant. The lavatory bowl should be frequently treated with disinfectant left overnight in the water before flushing away.

FOOD POISONING

Causes

- Food prepared long before consumption and not refrigerated
- Cooling cooked food too slowly before refrigeration
- Use of cooked food already contaminated
- Not reheating cooked food at high enough temperatures
- Undercooking
- Not completely thawing poultry

- Storing cooked food close to raw food, resulting in cross-contamination
- Preparing food on contaminated surfaces
- Contaminated dishes
- Cleaning dishes with dirty dish cloths
- Dishes washed in same water as pet bowls
- Infected food handlers
- Use of left-overs

Salmonella enteridis infection

Cases of food poisoning are on the increase, especially the much-publicized salmonella enteridis infection and listeriosis. Pregnant women are among those most at risk from these food-borne infections and, although symptoms may be hardly noticeable, they could lead to miscarriage or meningitis in the newborn child. The facts concerning the way these infections are transmitted are difficult to ascertain, but there is little doubt that an epidemic of salmonella enteridis infection is affecting poultry flocks in Britain and, even though a campaign is promised to clean up the poultry industry, it will be some time before the infection is stamped out. A great deal of the blame for this must be placed at the door of modern farming, food production and distribution practices. Add to this poor hygiene in the home, and we have a situation that is very serious, if not alarming.

It is believed that about 60 per cent of all poultry are infected with salmonella enteridis infection. The best suppliers say that they are able to reduce this incidence to 20 per cent but this is still 20 per cent too much. Salmonella bacteria can survive in the fridge, and even after cooking, if the poultry is not thawed out properly.

It is not certain, however, whether salmonella is actually in the eggs of infected poultry or has been introduced into them during handling or preparation. Given the uncertainty and the lack of information on egg safety and hygiene (at the time of going to press), it is wise to follow government advice.

- For healthy people there is very little risk from eating cooked eggs.

- Vulnerable people – the elderly, the sick, toddlers and pregnant women – should only eat eggs cooked until both yoke and white are solid.

- Avoid eating raw eggs or foods made with them such as mayonnaise.

- Cooked egg dishes should always be eaten as soon as possible.

Some free-range poultry farmers claim that their eggs are completely free of infection. The reasons for this, they say, are that (1) they don't overstock; (2) they don't feed their poultry with imported meal, some of which is made up of fish, bones and feathers, dried blood and offal, and may contain carcasses of infected poultry; and (3) free-range poultry do not suffer from the stresses of overcrowding suffered by livestock in intensive farming.

If you buy free-range eggs, make sure that the poultry are kept in the following conditions:

- where there is no overstocking, which results in the ground being ripped to pieces, giving the appearance of a paddy field;

- where the ground has about 80 per cent vegetation;

- where poultry feed is free of imported carcasses and bone-meal.

Listeriosis

Listeriosis, like salmonella infection, first came into prominence in 1988. The spread of the disease has been attributed to intensive farming and the complacency in the livestock industry where not much concern is shown for infective agents if they do not cause significant economic losses through illness in flocks and herds.[1] The bacteria *listeria monocytogenes*, which cause the disease, have been found in pre-cooked, chilled food (especially poultry) and soft cheeses. The incubation period can be several weeks. The World Health Organization believes that listeriosis is mainly a food-borne infection, but there have been rare instances of veterinary surgeons and poultry workers becoming infected through contact with diseased livestock.

There are two principal types of illness. In the elderly and patients with impaired immunity it could take the form of a severe type of blood poisoning with a one-in-three risk of death. The other vulnerable group is pregnant women who develop a flu-like illness which may be very slight. However, if the listeria spreads to the unborn baby it could cause either miscarriage or the birth of an infected or even dead baby. Rarer forms of the disease affect babies after birth and occasionally otherwise healthy adults can get meningitis.

The following foodstuffs contain listeria. They are a particular risk to the groups mentioned above and should be avoided by them as well as by couples who are planning a pregnancy: cook/chill food – listeria has been found in cook/chill food, even when this is supplied by reputable supermarkets and checked within the expiry date; soft cheeses, particularly those made from goats' and ewes' milk; prepared salads; salamis and meat pâtés. In addition to practising good hygiene in the kitchen, it would be advisable to avoid these foods.

An investigation carried out by the Association for Consumer Research found listeria in some ice-creams. Ice-creams were bought by two hygiene inspectors in Yorkshire and London in April and May 1989, and tested for bacteria. Of the forty-seven ice-creams bought, twenty-one showed up badly in tests. Soft ice-creams scored worst in the total bacterial count: twelve out of twenty-eight had unacceptably high counts. Four out of the twenty-eight contained the food-poisoning bacteria E-coli or listeria.[2]

If you buy ice-cream, make sure that scoop ice-cream is kept cold enough; check that the scoop is being rinsed in clean water; and buy from an outlet with a rapid turnover of stock.

Manufacturers, food handlers and retail outlets are usually blamed for contaminated food, but your own fridge could be a source of contamination. It should be kept spotlessly clean; temperatures should be maintained that will keep the food fresh. Do not keep raw meat close to other food; remove any food that has 'gone off' or has been kept beyond the expiry date. In short, keep the fridge well-organized and clean.

Another health hazard may be the microwave oven. Some cook/chill foods may not be suitable for the microwave. The ovens vary greatly in their ability to heat evenly – cook/chill foods should be fully heated to the 70°C recommended by the Department of Health – leaving cold spots in the middle of the food, thus allowing food-poisoning organisms to survive.

PETS

Pets are often a source of infection; so although a dog or cat can be a wonderful companion, it may not be a good idea to have one around until after you have established your family (see Toxoplasmosis and Toxocariasis, Chapter 5).

PESTS

Flies, cockroaches and other 'creepy-crawlies' are attracted to the kitchen area, although in the modern urban home they are not the problem they used to be. But flies can still be a terrible nuisance in the summer months. They carry a wide variety of bacteria and can contaminate everything they touch. The best way to keep them at bay is to make sure all surfaces are scrupulously clean and that food is always covered. Cockroaches too can spread disease. At the first sign of cockroaches, which are nocturnal creatures, dust and spray all surfaces with insecticide overnight, but wash down in the morning with hot soapy water. Cockroach eggs, which are small capsules, or flakes of their black or brown skins, are the visible signs of infestation.

Rats and mice are extremely dangerous creatures, carrying bacteria and viruses, and must be destroyed immediately. Like other pests, they are not so common in urban homes, but at the first sign of their presence, you should contact your local council who may send an expert to dispose of them or advise you on how to do this yourself. Be careful to keep children and pets away from any poisoned bait.

In conclusion, it cannot be emphasized too strongly that hygiene is of paramount importance in the family home. Little fingers can get into all kinds of dirty places where bacteria flourish, and infections can easily be picked up by children. Make sure that you are going to introduce your baby into a home which has the minimum of health and safety hazards.

First Aid and Home Nursing

Courses in first aid and home nursing are well worthwhile for a couple who are about to start a family. Your doctor or local council will advise you on where such courses are held. In the years ahead there are bound to be occasions when accidents happen and illness strikes; you will need a cool head to cope and your knowledge will prevent unnecessary complications as well as reassuring the sick or injured person. Your knowledge of some simple procedure, like mouth-to-mouth resuscitation, may even save a life.

Always keep a first-aid kit in the home as well as in the car. The kit should contain:

- TCP, Dettol or iodine
- clinical thermometer
- a packet of waterproof, adhesive plasters of different sizes
- sterile prepared dressings, consisting of pads attached to varying lengths of bandages which are quick and easy to put on
- triangular bandages to make slings or secure dressings
- two gauze (open-weave) bandages and several crêpe bandages
- a large packet of cotton wool
- calamine lotion, for soothing burns, stings, etc.
- tweezers, blunt ended scissors, safety-pins
- soluble aspirin or paracetamol.

Health and Safety at Work

Many workplaces are unhealthy and it is remarkable how people go on tolerating them. Some of the buildings where we work are the most poisonous of places. For instance, it is not uncommon for people working in offices to complain that they feel lethargic or drowsy and have flu-like symptoms such as a runny nose, watery eyes or a dry throat. This has been described as the 'sick building syndrome'. It is brought on by such things as poor ventilation, bad lighting, passive smoking, stressful, tiring or repetitive work and the use of potentially harmful chemicals. It has been found, however, that the worst cases of the sick building syndrome are found in sealed, air-conditioned buildings rather than naturally ventilated ones. If you work in an unhealthy place like that, obviously you must persuade your employer to improve working conditions – and the best way to do this is collectively with other employees and with the help of a trade union health and safety representative – or you must find another job in a healthier atmosphere.

We have already dealt with the damage that can be inflicted on the unborn child by tobacco (see Chapter 2). This is a hazard in many workplaces where cigarette smoke is a major source of air pollution. There is evidence that even low concentrations of cigarette smoke can contribute to building sickness. Passive smoking occurs frequently in open-plan offices.

There are other buildings that are not obviously poisonous, but they are not suitable places for women who are planning to become pregnant or men whose sperm count may be affected. These are places where chemicals are used which are known to be harmful to reproductive systems and to the fetus in the early stage of pregnancy (see pages 187–8). Even chemicals which do not affect your general health can damage your reproductive system. Do not wait until you actually become pregnant before changing your job or getting an employer to provide adequate protection against the ill effects of toxic chemicals because it is that crucial early stage of pregnancy, when the fetal central nervous system is developing, in which your baby could be harmed.

There are other workplaces which are not obviously unhealthy and although you cannot say you feel 100 per cent fit, you get used to them. You may not want to leave a job you enjoy or where you like the boss or the money is 'good'. So, no doubt you will say that the job matters more than the building. And, anyway, you can't see anything wrong with the place. There are hundreds of places a lot worse. Psychologists have a word for your state of mind – *scotomatization*, which means not seeing what you don't want to see or seeing only what you want to see. We all suffer from that sort of blindness at times.

So let us try to look at this problem of health and safety at work as objectively as we can. How do we know if it is damaging our health or our reproductive system (which is the effect of prolonged exposure to some chemicals) or the health of an unborn child? What features of the building, or aspects of the job, must we look at very carefully? In the following pages we give suggestions for combating what are generally considered the main health risks at the workplace. The things to look at in any job are: the toxicity of the materials you have to use – and, remember, all risks are relative; it is possible to poison yourself with pure water if you drink large quantities of it – the cleanliness of the workplace, the way various equipment is designed and organized for efficiency and comfort (ergonomics), the temperature, lighting, the quality of the air you have to breathe, the number of hours you spend at work, the number of breaks you have, the nature of the work – whether it is creative and enjoyable or repetitive and boring – the amount of standing or lifting you have to do, and the health of fellow-workers.

There are many industries and occupations today where the kind of work you do and the chemicals you use are potentially damaging to your reproductive system or can put a mother and her unborn baby at risk. Take the largest of our industries, which employs more women than any other, the National Health Service – is it a healthy place for a man or woman to work if he/she is planning to start a family? If, for example, you are a hospital nurse, should you go on working in a place where there is so much disease, stress, cytotoxic drugs, bacteria and X-ray equipment, if you are going to become pregnant? There are all kinds of health and safety fears expressed in connection with medical work. It has been suggested, for instance, that pregnant women who inhale small amounts of anaesthetic gases as part of their work run a risk of miscarriage. And how safe is it to lift heavy patients when you

MAJOR INDOOR AIR POLLUTANTS IN OFFICE BUILDINGS

Pollutant	Sources	Health Effects
Ammonia	Blueprint machines, cleaning solutions	Respiratory system, eye and skin irritation
Asbestos	Duct and pipe insulation, spackling compounds, insulation products, fire retardants, ceiling and floor tiles	Pulmonary (lung) fibrosis, cancer
Benzene	Synthetic fibres, plastics, cleaning solutions, tobacco smoke	Central nervous system damage, skin, respiratory system irritant. Possibly genetic damage
Carbon dioxide	Humans' exhaled air, combustion	Headache, nausea, dizziness
Carbon monoxide	Automobile exhaust, tobacco smoke, combustion	Headache, weakness, dizziness, nausea, long-term exposure related to heart disease
Ethanol	Duplicating fluids	Dermatitis, liver damage, intoxication
Fibreglass	Insulation material	Skin irritations, possible lung damage
Formaldehyde	Urea-formaldehyde foam insulation and urea-formaldehyde resin used to bind laminated wood products such as particle board and plywood; tobacco smoke	Respiratory system, eye and skin irritation, nausea, headache, fatigue, cancer (in exposed laboratory animals)
Methyl alcohol	Spirit duplicating machines	Respiratory system and skin irritation
Micro-organisms (such as viruses, bacteria and fungi)	Humidifying and air-conditioning systems, evaporative condensers, cooling towers, mildewed papers, old books, damp newsprint	Respiratory infection, allergic responses

Motor vehicle exhaust (carbon monoxide, nitrogen oxides, lead particulates, sulphur oxides)	Parking garages, outside traffic	Respiratory system and eye irritation, headache (see carbon monoxide), genetic damage
Nitrogen oxides	Gas stoves, combustion, motor vehicle exhaust, tobacco smoke	Respiratory system and eye irritation
Ozone	Photocopying and other electrical machines	Respiratory system and eye irritation, headache, genetic damage
Paint fumes (organics, lead, mercury)	Freshly painted surfaces	Respiratory system and eye irritation; neurological, kidney, and bone marrow damage at high levels of exposure
PCBs (polychlorinated biphenyls), dioxin, dibenzofuran	Electrical transformers	Sperm and fetal defects, skin rashes, liver and kidney damage, cancer
Pesticides	Spraying of plants, premises	Depending on chemical components: liver damage, cancer, neurological damage, skin, respiratory system and eye irritation
Radon and decay products	Building construction materials such as concrete and stone; basements	Ionizing radiation-related diseases such as genetic damage, cancer, fetal and sperm damage
Sterilant gases (such as ethylene oxide)	Systems to sterilize humidifying and air-conditioning systems	Depending on chemical components: respiratory system and eye irritation, genetic damage, cancer
Tobacco smoke (passive exposure to particulates, carbon monoxide, formaldehyde, coal tars, and nicotine)	Cigarettes, pipes, cigars	Respiratory system and eye irritation; may lead to diseases associated with smokers; low-birthweight babies; contributes to poor sperm count

Toluene	Rubber cement, cleaning fluids	Narcotic, skin irritant
Trichloroethane	Duplicating fluid, white-out liquids	Dizziness, headaches, possible liver damage; suspected carcinogen
Trichloroethylene	Stencil machines	Liver cancer, lung dysfunction; central nervous system damage
Trinitrofluorenone (TNF)	Photocopiers	Suspected mutagen (genetic damage)
Vinyl chloride	Plastic products: pipes, light fixtures, upholstery, carpets	Carcinogen, suspected mutagen, dermatitis, bronchitis

General, Municipal, Boilermakers and Allied Trades Union, *WORK HAZARDS*

are expecting a baby? On the other hand, it can be argued that if you are a nurse, you should surely know something about the risks you are taking in your job. Although the law clearly places the overwhelming responsibility for health and safety on the employer, there should be some sharing of responsibility; and you should be aware of what you can do to protect your own health. (Don't, however, accept this from an employer as an excuse for neglecting health and safety.) Most medical workers are, in fact, extremely careful about protecting themselves against infection or any other health risk, and there are those who go so far as to say that the only risk factor for a hospital nurse is anxiety. To the question about lifting, the answer NHS employers might give is that a nurse who is stupid enough to attempt to lift a heavy patient when she is pregnant is unfit to be a nurse. No responsible ward sister would require her to do any heavy lifting. The same goes for working with anaesthetic gases. A nurse usually has good advice near at hand or she is in a better position than many people to find answers to health problems.

On the other hand, nurses are often under extreme pressure to work unsparingly for patients. To refuse a job which is for the good of the patient, even if it puts their own health at risk, may be regarded as dereliction of duty. They may see the short-term need to help the patient as overriding their long-term concern for their own health, especially if there is no one else to help because of staff shortages. And it is often difficult for individuals to change conditions at the workplace – often only the collective efforts of the work-force can achieve improvements.

There are many places in hospitals where potentially dangerous chemicals are used by NHS staff, not only by doctors and nurses – such as in the laundry and central sterilization. The disposal of clinical waste can be poisonous, dangerous and offensive. Cancer-causing substances are used in various hospital laboratories. For example, Benzene, a known carcinogenic chemical, is used as a general solvent in automatic tissue-processing machines (histokinette) in dental, chemical and pathology laboratories as well as operating theatres.[3] Some hazardous chemicals used in hospitals can be replaced by others less hazardous, e.g. the hazardous pesticide Lindane can be replaced by sodium hypochlorite when ambulances have to be disinfected or 'de-bugged'. Benzene, which is used in laboratory tests, can be replaced by cyclohexane.

It should, however, be pointed out here that saying something is a hazard is not the same as saying it is a risk. The two words are often confused. A hazard is a potential cause of harm; a risk is the likelihood that some harm will come to you if you behave in a careless way or use a hazardous substance without protection or caution. You may be able to do something about a risk when you know what it is.

There are, in fact, many things everybody can do to try to minimize health risks at the workplace. You must, of course, observe health and safety regulations. If, however, there are occasions when you are required to take unnecessary risks, you should, as we have said, take the matter up with your health and safety representative. If your efforts at improving your conditions of work take too long or are blocked, then you have two possible courses of action: either you change your employment or you and your fellow-employees may have no alternative except to consider or threaten industrial action to get the conditions improved. Unfortunately, at present an employee has not the right (as he or she has in Canada, for instance) to refuse dangerous work even where the worker's health is at imminent risk and where there are reasonable grounds for holding this view.

Remember, though, that the law is on your side when you insist on knowing what the risks are and what the employer's safety policy is.

The Health and Safety at Work Act (Section 2 [3]) states that all employers who employ five or more people must:

- produce a written statement of the safety policy
- revise that safety policy 'as often as may be appropriate'
- give details of organization and arrangements for putting the policy into effect
- bring the written statement to the notice of all employees
- consult the safety representatives about the making and maintenance of arrangements for safety.

This statement should include identification of hazards and hazardous areas of work, systems and guidelines for these hazards and training procedures for both managers and employees.

HAZARDOUS CHEMICALS

Altogether there are about 60,000 chemicals in regular use in industry today, and many new ones are added every year. We do not know the health risks of many of these, but there are certainly a large number of commonly-used chemicals that we do know can damage your health if not handled with extreme caution. For instance, prolonged exposure to the chemical formaldehyde, which is used in eighty-five different industries, including cosmetics and furniture-making, can cause breathing difficulties, burning of the eyes, nose and throat, and nose bleeds.

Unfortunately, there are a great many hazardous substances used in industry that are exempt from the Notification of New Substances Regulations (1982). This means that there is no statutory system of pre-market testing, unlike food additives and drugs. The Chemical Industries Association admits that there is no toxicity information at all on 75 per cent of chemicals used at the workplace. In effect, workers and their families are guinea-pigs in one huge experiment with chemicals that may well be hazardous.

The new Control of Substances Hazardous to Health regulations (COSHH) introduced in October 1989 go some way towards rectifying this. These regulations make it mandatory for an employer to obey five basic principles of occupational hygiene:

1 Assess the risk to health arising from work and what precautions are needed.

2 Introduce appropriate measures to prevent or control the risk.

3 Ensure that control measures are used and that equipment is properly maintained and procedures observed.

4 Where necessary, monitor the exposure of the workers and carry out an appropriate form of surveillance of their health.

5 Inform, instruct and train employees about the risks and the precautions to be taken.

If you are planning a pregnancy, you should ask yourself if there could be a health risk in any of the chemicals in regular use at your workplace. Look at everything: pots or tubes of glue, cleaning

---

OCCUPATIONS/INDUSTRIES FOR WHICH THERE IS SOME EVIDENCE OF REPRODUCTIVE HAZARDS

Glue/adhesive users in offices, shops, factories, artists' studios, etc.
Rubber
Plastics
Viscose Rayon
Electronics
Soldering
Printing
Food
Motor vehicle repair
Hairdressing
Dry cleaning
Ore smelters
Painters
Potters
Machinists
Nurses, pharmacists, laboratory workers, and others working in hospitals (anaesthetic gases, solvents, hormone preparations, cytotoxic drugs)

Much of the evidence is inconclusive, but there is enough to warrant taking extra care in these occupations/industries.

The above is based on a list given in a current General, Municipal, Boilermakers and Allied Trades Union (GMB) guide, *Your Reproductive Health at Risk.*

---

liquids, liquids for erasing type – all the small things that look harmless, as well as the more obvious chemical hazards in factories, such as drums of poisonous or corrosive chemicals. A good rule is, if you can smell it, suspect it. Whatever you smell is being absorbed by your body and may be causing ill health, even damaging your reproductive system or, if you are pregnant, your unborn child. The embryo is very sensitive to hazardous chemicals between the 20th and 30th day after conception, when most women do not realize they are pregnant.

Toxic substances enter the body through the skin, mouth or nose. When working with poisonous chemicals you must be aware of these three routes of entry and take all necessary precautions to prevent absorption. A moment's carelessness could have unpleasant consequences. Items of protective clothing, such as gloves, overalls, face masks and safety goggles, are provided in some hazardous occupations and you can prevent ingestion, which occurs when chemicals get into food via the hands, by not eating snacks while working with chemicals, washing your hands thoroughly before meals and avoiding touching your mouth while working. Often, if the hazard is an everyday substance such as glue or a hairspray, very little protection is offered by an employer.

The law, as we have said, requires that an employer must supply his or her work-force with information about all known hazards and potential hazards at work. All containers of toxic substances must be clearly labelled. If you are unsure about a substance, you are entitled to see the manufacturer's data sheet, which should give you:

- what chemicals are in the substance and their proportions

- what the health hazards of these chemicals are (known and suspected)

- what precautions are required for safe working with the substance

- what first aid measures should be taken in case of an accident.

Unfortunately, information from a manufacturer is often misleading or completely inaccurate. If you suspect this, or if the data sheet does not give you all the information you require, you should ask your employer to get the manufacturer to provide fuller and more accurate information, with back-up evidence of the facts. Try to obtain a copy of the GMB leaflet, *Chemicals – Your Rights to Information*, which advises you what to ask for and how to tell if the information you are given is reliable. Your health and safety representative will take up any complaint you may have about exposure to toxic substances with your employer.

Remember, employees also have duties. You are, according to law, expected to take reasonable care of yourself at work and to avoid causing injury to others. A responsible attitude to your job and to others working with you is essential in avoiding risks to the health of yourself and your colleagues.

OCCUPATIONAL DERMATITIS

There are few things as depressing as a skin rash that will not go away. Some factory and office workers, and others in hazardous occupations, keep on getting troublesome skin conditions (occupational dermatitis) because of the chemicals they have to use. Any illness, even if it is only a mild rash, that causes stress will affect a pregnancy. It is therefore important to trace the irritant that is responsible for your rash and to take steps to avoid or reduce further exposure.

There are two categories of occupational dermatitis: (1) contact dermatitis; and (2) sensitization dermatitis.

Contact dermatitis is caused by substances called primary cutaneous irritants which attack the skin, causing tissue destruction. This occurs when there is sufficient concentration of the substances over a varying period of time. After removal from exposure recovery usually follows. Further exposure can often be tolerated without serious recurrence of the condition, so long as extra precautions are taken and there is limited contact.

Examples of primary cutaneous irritants:

- mineral oils
- greases
- solvents such as petrol, white spirit
- cement
- physical agents: heat, cold, radiation, friction.

Sensitization dermatitis is caused by substances called cutaneous sensitizers, which may not cause an inflammatory response on first contact, but may cause an allergic response in the metabolic reactions of the skin. Dermatitis occurs when the response has developed, which can take place over a period of days or months. The dermatitis will go after removal from the source of the irritant. However, the allergic response will remain and dermatitis will develop rapidly with very little additional exposure. Some people react to substances that are generally considered as primary irritants with an allergic dermatitic response after further exposure.

Examples of cutaneous sensitizers:

- photographic developers
- rubber additives
- methanol solutions
- wood dust – African (or Iroko) teak
- nickel compounds
- some hair dyes
- antibiotics, penicillin and streptomycin

In general, substances known to cause dermatitis in offices include:

- carbonless copying paper
- adhesives
- carbon and copy paper
- duplicating fluid
- duplicating materials
- indelible pencils
- cleaning fluid
- plastic
- synthetic detergents
- selenium (some photocopiers)
- photocopier toners
- inks

- ink remover
- rubber and synthetic rubber
- type cleaners
- waxes and polishes
- audio typists' earphones

An air-conditioned environment, which lowers indoor humidity, increases air movement and inhibits sweating, can lead to dehydration of the skin and damage to its protective barrier. These factors, combined with excessive use of hot water and soap, can cause itching and dermatitis. Make sure that the heating and ventilation systems are adequate and do not cause drowsiness.

LIFTING AND STANDING

Many injuries at work are the result of lifting heavy loads. Back injuries are the most common ranging from muscular tension which causes stiffness, aches and pains, to permanent deformity of the spine. Anything that goes wrong with the back can be a handicap for a woman during pregnancy, so do not do anything at work that could put a strain on the back muscles. Human evolutionary development to a standing position has not produced an efficient machine for lifting or carrying heavy loads. Tensions are created in the deep back muscles with reactions at the base of the spine when heavy weights are lifted. Mechanical means, such as two- and four-wheeled trucks and trolleys, should be used to lift and carry heavy loads. If you are required to carry anything heavy, you should make sure that it is well below the maximum permissible weight recommended by the International Labour Organization (ILO): Adult male – 40–45 kg (88–100 lb); Adult female – 15–20 kg (33–44 lb).

If you have to lift or carry anything within the permissible limit, you should always employ the 'kinetic' method (see illustration), which uses leg power rather than the more vulnerable back muscles and relies on the momentum generated by the whole body to carry a load.

Training yourself to lift properly is not the only way of avoiding back injuries. The best answer is to get rid of manual handling

CORRECT AND INCORRECT POSTURES FOR LIFTING AND CARRYING

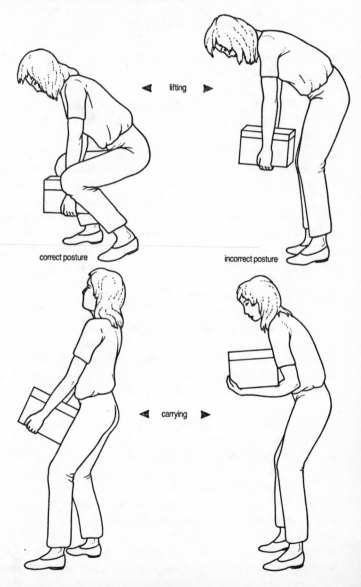

lifting

correct posture   incorrect posture

carrying

assume that lifting and carrying loads is inevitable in your job. There are two important questions you should ask yourself and put to an employer: can lifting and carrying be avoided – for example, by using trolleys or conveyer systems? Can systems of work be changed to remove the need for items to be carried from one place to another? Or, more broadly, can new machines, processes or systems of work be introduced to minimize manual handling?

According to a survey of 292 women attending antenatal clinics in North London by two nursing advisers to the Health and Safety Executive, standing and lifting are the greatest problems in pregnancy. It is advisable, therefore, before you become pregnant, to make sure that your job does not involve you in periods of continuous standing or too much lifting.

The types of occupations which involve women in a lot of lifting and standing include nursing, teaching, factory work, cooking, shop work, kitchen and canteen work, hairdressing, work behind pub and hotel bars, printing.

DUST AND FUMES

Inhaling toxic dusts and fumes can seriously damage your lungs. Some dusts, such as asbestos, are lethal. Others are classed as 'nuisance' dusts, but can still affect your health – for example, gypsum from plaster of Paris. People working in the plastics industry are particularly vulnerable. Dusts from PVC, pigments or fillers may cause breathing difficulties and lung disease. Fumes from heated plastic can be dangerous, for example carbon monoxide, hydrogen chloride (from PVC); styrene (from polystyrene); nitrogen compounds (from nylon and acrylonitrile). The control of hazardous dusts usually involves dust suppression and exhaust ventilation, but it may also be necessary in some situations to wear protective breathing equipment.

Flour and grain dust can cause asthma, so obviously if you work in a bakery you should make sure that your employer is taking all necessary precautions to keep working surfaces spotlessly clean and the working environment free of dust. You will not be accepted for work in a bakery if you have any respiratory problem. Besides dust, the heat in a bakery can be a hazard (see below). Several other dusts in the food industry can cause asthma. One survey of bakery workers who sprayed a mixture of egg white and water on meat rolls found that eight out of the thirteen had asthma believed to be caused by egg protein in the spray.

Workers who handle quantities of polyurethane (pu) foam are at risk of respiratory disorders. Those most affected are people who work in the manufacture of furniture, textiles, toys, household goods, bedding and cars. Cutting pu foam with hot wires can lead to the production of toxic isolyanate gases which can cause severe respiratory damage. Crumbling the pu foam can lead to hazards from inhaling dust particles.

Cement dust can cause long-term health problems, including bronchitis, emphysema, shortness of breath and other lung and chest problems. Dust generated at different stages of manufacture may contain crystalline silica (quartz), which can cause lung scarring. People who work in offices or canteens in the industry or who live in the vicinity, and wives of men who work in cement manufacturing plants, can be affected.

Under the new COSHH regulations an employer must evaluate the risk to health of any hazardous substance in the workplace. This includes dust. An employer is also obliged, under the Health and Safety at Work Act, to take a sample of the atmosphere for analysis (environmental monitoring) if there is any suspicion that dust is causing health problems. Besides harming the respiratory system, dust can, of course, also irritate the eyes.

Men working in occupations where a lot of dust is generated should pay special attention to genital cleanliness. Wives of men in jobs such as mining, quarrying, glass-making and pottery have higher rates of cervical cancer than other women. It is believed that dust under the foreskin could cause this.[4]

Men and women who work in a dusty environment can take hazardous chemical dust home in their overalls and clothing and in their hair. Asbestos is the obvious example. It has been demonstrated that the health of women who washed their husbands' overalls and children in the house were seriously affected by asbestos. An employer should be responsible for the cleaning of overalls and also provide showers for employees.

WORKING WITH SOLVENTS

Solvents – chemicals that are used to dissolve other substances to form a solution – that are commonly used in industry can disrupt or damage the reproductive systems of both men and women, and cause leukaemia and other cancers. A report in July 1989, prepared for the World Health Organization by the International Agency of Research into Cancer, established a clear link between various cancers and occupational painters. The report fuelled pressure on the paint industry to switch from solvent-based paints to safer, water-based paints. Working with solvents can cause irregular periods, miscarriages and infertility in women, and genetic damage and loss of sex drive (libido) in men. Hazardous solvents include degreasers, thinners, spirit or dry-cleaning agents, and those found in paints, pigments, lacquers, pesticides, glues and type-correction fluids. Even the so-called 'safer' solvents are poisonous.

The effects of inhaling some solvent vapours, even for a short time, can be serious. In one case a teenager working in a car-valeting business died after being overcome by the fumes when he was using a small amount of a solvent to remove marks from a car seat. Methelyne chloride, which is a solvent used in hairsprays and paint strippers, is suspected of causing cancer.

The short-term effects of using solvents are: headaches, dizziness, sickness, painful tingling of hands or feet, muscular weakness, drowsiness, lack of appetite, irritation to the eyes, irritation of the nose, throat or lungs. Long-term effects include damage to the brain and nervous system, lungs and kidneys. Avoid using solvents if you possibly can. If you must use them, do so sparingly and wear gloves. Men and women working in the dry-cleaning business and hairdressers are among those who should be specially careful. If you work where potentially dangerous solvents are in use ask if they really need to be used. For example, for cleaning is it possible to use steam or heated water jets? Make sure that levels of vapour are lower by about 50 per cent of the exposure limit. Your health and safety representative will advise you about this. Also make sure that protective equipment is good enough. For instance, gloves should be made of material which will prevent the penetration of a chemical.

HEAT STRESS

Working in high temperatures can damage your health and affect reproductive systems. Symptoms of heat stress include headaches, a rapid pulse and breathing rate, fatigue, cramps in muscles, dizziness, nausea and fainting. A person who works in hot conditions should take plenty of extra fluids and salt. If unchecked, heat stress can, in extreme conditions, lead to 'heat stroke' when the victim has a flushed face, a hot, dry skin, an oral temperature of 102°F (38.8°C) or higher and becomes confused or unconscious. Death will follow unless treatment is prompt. Treatment consists of removing all clothing, washing the victim with cold or tepid water and fanning, and wrapping the person in a cold damp cloth. Continuous work in hot conditions can also affect the heart. The body will also absorb more toxic chemicals at temperatures above 90°F (33°C), partly because liver function is impaired.

NOISE EXPOSURE

Prolonged exposure to high levels of noise can cause permanent hearing damage. You may get used to noise and may not be aware of the damage it is doing. Many people suffer from a loss of hearing sensitivity, called Temporary Threshold Shift (TTS), after a noisy car or train journey. When they arrive home they will turn up the volume of a radio or television, but later when they settle down to an evening's listening or viewing, they find the volume is too high and have to turn it down for comfort. They may also speak in a loud voice at first, because they have been shouting above the din of traffic and will miss some of the things said by someone who has had no need to shout to be heard.

The ability to regain sensitive hearing is lost by people who have been exposed to prolonged noise year after year, and a Permanent Threshold Shift (PTS) takes place. Young people who frequent discos, where noise levels are very high, put themselves at risk of permanent deafness. Noise exposure at discos has been quoted as being ten times the standard set for occupational exposure. But you have a choice in the disco: you can walk out if the noise is excessive. This is not true of all workplaces. Noise levels sometimes exceed safety levels.

An EEC directive, ignored in some workplaces, calls on employers to reduce noise levels, to provide adequate ear protectors (ear muffs), and to give employees adequate information and training on noise levels, risks to hearing and on statutory provisions that affect them, and to offer employees regular hearing checks when they work with noisy machinery. Employers must put up notices forbidding employees to enter noisy areas without wearing ear muffs.

The Health and Safety Commission (HSC) has produced draft noise regulations which become law in 1990. The commission recommends a noise level below 85 decibels (dBA). The HSC report states that about 11 per cent of workers exposed to between 85 and 90 dBA and 27 per cent of those exposed to 90–95 dBA for their working lifetime will suffer serious hearing loss.

LIGHTING

Poor lighting in offices, shops and factories can lead to various health problems, ranging from eye strain and headaches to postural problems, muscular strain and stress. Different tasks call for different lighting requirements. You should establish whether you are getting enough light for your particular job. If it involves close work such as drawing or proof-reading or reading photocopies or carbon copies, your light requirement will be at a higher level than if you are doing routine work such as filing or you work, say, as a porter or a commissionaire in a reception area where you are not required to do much reading. Make sure that there is no glare or reflection from unshielded lights or fluorescent tubes, VDU screens, bare windows. All light fittings should be glare-fitted. If there are problems about poor lighting conditions the Health and Safety Executive will be able to advise you on what action to take.

CANTEENS

Canteen food is often of a poor quality and the standard of hygiene often leaves a lot to be desired. Food is, as we have seen, most important in building health in the pre-pregnancy period. Nowadays with so many scares about listeria, salmonella and other bacteria getting into our food, you cannot be too careful about what you eat, particularly if you have not prepared the food yourself. Canteens tend to serve greasy food, dishes that have been reheated or left standing about in a warm atmosphere, and sandwiches made of white bread with fillings of soft cheese, pâté, and other suspect fillers. Efforts should be made by employees, through their health and safety representative, to make sure that their canteen observes the highest standard in quality of food and hygiene.

VDUs

VDUs are found in most offices nowadays and many of them are operated by women. It has been established that there is some kind of link between VDU usage and miscarriages and birth abnormalities, though it is not known what precisely that link is. It should be said, therefore, that in terms of scientific evidence it is quite a tenuous link. However, even the slightest possibility of a link should not be ignored and many women will want to give up working with VDUs during pregnancy or in the pre-pregnancy period, though explaining that to the boss may be difficult. Most people's fear concerns radiation, but it cannot be shown that there is any causal connection between low-dose radiation emitted by the normal VDU and pregnancy problems. There is, however, a theory that bad posture and stress precipitate a miscarriage.

The issue was first raised in 1979 when four out of seven pregnancies in the classified department of the *Toronto Star* newspaper in Canada resulted in babies being born with deformities; all these women used VDUs extensively in their work. Since then a number of other similar cases have been reported but most of them have been inconclusive as far as the effect of ionizing radiation is concerned. There are many variables in these studies, including radiation, posture, stress and personal medical history. There is also the fear that the electro-magnetic field of VDUs could interfere with biological systems but there is no conclusive evidence for this at present. What evidence there is comes from studies of electric power lines.

It does seem likely, however, that VDU workers will suffer ill health if they spend long hours exposed to the glare of a screen, sitting on poorly-designed chairs doing dull, repetitive work. A Canadian study found poor job design and dehumanizing working conditions among the main causes of ill health in VDU workers. Another study by the North East London Polytechnic came to a similar conclusion. They also found that over half of the heavy users in their study felt that the introduction of VDUs made their health worse.

The lessons are:

● If you are hoping to become pregnant or you are pregnant, the safest thing to do is to avoid VDU work or work in an area where VDUs are used. Try to persuade your employer to offer you other work or to send you on a training course to improve your skills.

● If, however, VDU work is unavoidable, make sure you have plenty of breaks – you should not work more than fifty minutes without a break – and take your ten to fifteen minute breaks away from the VDU. Don't just sit there nibbling chocolate. VDU use should be restricted to well below four hours per day, which is the limit recommended for normal work.

● Pay attention to your posture while working with a VDU. Insist on a well-designed chair that is fully and easily adjustable for height and backrest.

● If you have medical problems which you think may be caused by continued use of a VDU you should see your doctor and tell your employer about them.

● Many VDU users have eye and vision problems as a result of glare. Glare can in many cases be eliminated by repositioning the VDU in relation to light sources.

OVER-USE INJURIES

These are called Repetitive Strain Injuries (RSI), injuries caused by repetitive work, such as working with a VDU, in which a strain is put on particular muscles and tendons, often in the wrist, forearm and elbow, that can be quite painful and incapacitating. Injuries of

wrong   right

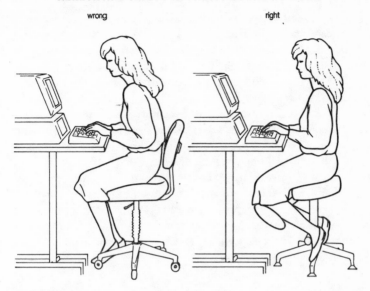

this kind include tennis elbow (epicondylitis), writer's cramp and Teno (tenosynovitis). If the symptoms are left too long, the injury may become difficult to treat. In their severe form, over-use injuries can make many daily tasks impossible or difficult to do. Holding or lifting a baby, for instance, might be very painful for someone with Teno, which causes inflammation of the tendon sheaths in the hand, wrist and arm.

More than 2,000 men and women get DSS compensation for their disability from Teno every year. The sort of work that causes Teno is typing, assembly work or packing. For example, two typists in a London solicitors' office hit the keys 30,000 times an hour. After a year and a half they had to leave because they were too disabled to do their jobs fast enough. Not only repetitive acts cause problems. Excessive force or bad posture are also involved, hence the alternative name, Cumulative Trauma Disorders (CTD).

If you think you are developing a condition of this kind go to your doctor immediately and let your employer know. Not many people, including employers, realize how damaging over-use injuries can be. People tend to put up with them as 'part of the job'. Obviously, this is something you must avoid if you are planning a family – and that applies to men as well as women. Pregnancy in itself can restrict your movements and your partner will need to help a lot with many jobs in the house. There was a case of a man who packed a thousand bobbins a shift in a textile plant. After two years he and two work-mates became disabled and were unable to continue with their work.

The only way to prevent over-use injuries is for the employer to install equipment and furniture that are designed for the job and to organize the workload so that there are adequate staff for repetitive work. If you are doing this kind of work, you should have frequent rest breaks – five minutes each half hour. Fast keyboard work should not exceed four hours a day. A good employer will welcome any suggestions for improving working conditions. Expert advice can be obtained from an ergonomist (see page 255 for address of Ergonomics Training Centre). Exercising at work can also help (see page below).

TENSION-RELEASING EXERCISES FOR COMPUTER OPERATORS

The following exercises are based on a set of exercises devised by Denise Katnich, a Los Angeles consultant to the President's Council on Physical Fitness and Sport and sponsored by Verbatim, a US manufacturer of floppy disks. They are designed to help computer and word-processor operators avoid the aches and pains caused by the kind of work they do. Select the exercises that fit your individual needs and do them during short and frequent breaks at work.

Shake up

To warm up and get the blood circulating, move your neck, shoulders, arms, thighs, legs and feet in quick succession, not spending more than a few seconds on each movement. Repeat the exercise several times.

Deep breathing

To help you relax, close your eyes and concentrate on your breathing. Inhale deeply through the nose and exhale forcefully out of the mouth. Repeat about six times.

Neck

Allow your head to drop slowly to the left, then to the right. Slowly drop your chin to your chest, then raise it as high as it will go. Turn your head as far as you can to the left, then to the right. This exercise will help to keep your neck muscles supple and prevent or alleviate a stiff neck.

Eye cupping

Your eyes may become tired at the computer, so now and again give them a rest. Close your eyes, cup your hands over them and lean forward with your eyes resting on your hands. Focus your attention on the eyes. Maintain this position for as long as possible and as often as possible. It will help to prevent eye strain.

Shoulder roll

Slowly roll your shoulders forwards
four or five times in a circular
motion. Then roll your shoulders
backwards in the same circular
motion. This will help to release
tension from the neck and
shoulders.

Arm circles

Raise your arms and stretch
them to the sides with your
elbows straight. Then slowly
rotate them in small circles
forwards and then backwards.
This will keep the joints in
your shoulders mobile.

Pectoral stretch

Grasp your hands behind your neck and press your elbows back as far as they will go. Allow your arms to fall limply at your sides; then repeat the exercise. It will stretch the front of your chest and help to correct a slouching position.

Upper arm stretch

Grasp hands behind your back. Straighten your elbows, then lift your arms as high as you can. This is helpful in preventing rounded shoulders, which may happen if you sit for hours bent over a desk.

Upper back stretch

Sit upright on your chair and place
your hands on your shoulders.
Push your elbows forwards, trying
to bring them in contact, so that
you feel the muscles of your upper
back stretching. Drop your hands
at your sides, relax, then repeat the
exercise. It helps to prevent any
stiffness in the upper back.

Side stretch

Interlace your fingers and lift your
arms up over your head keeping
your elbows straight. Push your
arms backwards as far as they will
go. Then slowly lean first to the
left, then to the right so that you
feel the side of your body
stretching. The exercise stretches
the muscles along the sides from
arm to hip.

Wrist flex

Put your right elbow on the table with your hand raised. With your other hand push the wrist backwards towards the top of your forearm. Then swivel the wrist rapidly six or seven times. Do the same with the opposite hand. This will help to prevent over-use injuries.

Five finger exercises

With palms of the hands down, spread your thumb and fingers as far apart as they will go. Hold for five seconds. Relax and repeat several times. Then pull each finger hard, trying to crack the knuckles. Finally, move the fingers up and down as if playing a piece on the piano in a fast tempo. These exercises will release the tension in your hands and fingers and help to prevent over-use injuries.

Legs and buttocks

Place hands on your chair, with the feet flat on the floor and lift up your hips and buttocks. Tighten your buttocks. Hold for the count of five. Then sit back on your chair and relax. Repeat twice. The exercise will strengthen legs and buttocks, which will tend to become flabby through sitting for long periods of time.

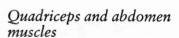

Quadriceps and abdomen muscles

Sitting straight up in your chair raise your legs to form an L-position with your body. Relax, then repeat the exercise. The exercise will strengthen the quadriceps and abdominal muscles.

Relaxing the back

Sitting in your chair, drop your neck, shoulders and arms. Let them go completely as if you were a floppy rag doll. Then bend down between your knees, as far as you can. Return to the upright position, straighten out and relax. The exercise will take the pressure off your lower back.

Trunk twists

Twist your trunk from the waist, three times to the left and right, turning your head in the same direction. Very good for trimming the waistline and improving flexibility.

Windmill

Sitting in your chair with your feet
apart on the floor, bend over and
place the fingers of your right hand
on your left foot with your left
hand extended up as in the yoga
triangle. Then repeat the exercise
with your left hand touching your
right foot. Keep doing this in a
continuous movement. Trims
your hips and waistline.

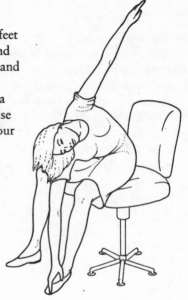

Knee kiss

Sitting in a chair, grasp your leg
with both hands and draw it up to
your chest, bending your head to
touch the knee. Repeat with the
opposite leg. Stretches the
hamstrings.

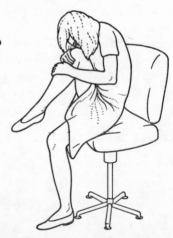

Arm muscles

Stretch your arms out parallel to
the floor. Then bend the elbows,
so that the hands, palms down, are
in front of the chest. Keeping the
arms straight push them back as
far as possible. Improves the arm
muscles.

Stretching the middle upper-back

Hold your right arm just above the
elbow with your left hand. Gently
pull your elbow towards your left
shoulder so that you feel the middle
upper-back stretching. Repeat the
exercise pulling the left arm to the
right shoulder. It will increase the
flexibility of the middle upper-
back.

Hugging yourself

Cross your arms in front of your chest, reaching the fingertips towards your shoulder blades. This relieves tension in the shoulders and upper back.

WHERE TO GET ADVICE

Doctors and nurses of the Health and Safety Executive's Employment Medical Advisory Service advise employers and employees on all aspects of health at work. You will find the telephone number of your local contact in the telephone directory under Health and Safety Executive. Other organizations which offer advice are the Health and Safety Advice Centre, Working Mothers' Association, the Maternity Alliance and the National Childbirth Trust. There are a number of trade union safety and health groups and resource centres in Birmingham, Hull, Newcastle on Tyne, Leicester and other provincial cities. The TUC has produced a *Noise at Work Handbook*. The General, Municipal, Boilermakers and Allied Trades Union (GMB) produce a number of leaflets and guides on health and safety at work, including a comprehensive guide on *Health and Safety for Women*, covering such subjects as VDUs, chemicals, laundries and dry-cleaning, lighting, noise, air-conditioning, and hazards in the health services. The London Food Commission publish a book (produced by GMB) on *Canteen Food*. City Centre provide information on VDU hazards including a 'factpack' on pregnancy (see page 246).

9

When a Baby is on the Way

When your plans have worked out and you discover a baby is on the way, you should, if you have been careful about your health, be mentally and physically prepared for the months ahead. There will be no need to change your lifestyle, you will already be doing everything possible to give your baby a good start in life. In fact, he will already have had quite a good start because he will probably be about eight weeks old in the womb when you discover he is there. And you will feel happy that he has come to no harm as the result of anything you have done.

How do you know you are pregnant? Well, your doctor will be able to determine pregnancy by a physical examination around the eighth week. Usually he or she sends a urine sample to a hospital and you will have to wait a few days before knowing the result.

On the other hand, you can buy a do-it-yourself kit from a chemist. This detects human chorionic gonadotrophin (HCG), a hormone which is produced in the developing placenta soon after conception. This occurs around the twenty-first day of pregnancy, counted from the first day of the last period, and its level rises until it reaches its maximum between the ninth and twelfth week. There is usually enough HCG in the urine to detect its presence around the sixth week of pregnancy when a period is overdue by about seven to fourteen days.

Manufacturers of these kits claim an accuracy of 98 per cent if instructions are followed correctly, but occasionally some women do get what is known as a 'false negative' when they are actually pregnant. This is probably the result of testing too early, before the

HCG has had a chance to build up. It would be wise to repeat the test if you still have not had a period a week later. Other possible causes of the false negative are too little urine or urine that is too diluted or has been kept too long before testing. When you are doing these tests it is best to use early morning urine, which is more concentrated than later in the day.

Learning to be Parents

Pregnancy, apart from everything else, is an opportunity to build on your relationship. It is also a time for learning to be parents. Try setting aside some time during the day to relax together and talk about the pregnancy. You might begin with relaxing exercises or massage. The months of carrying the baby will produce chemical and hormonal changes in the mother's body which will affect her moods. She might be depressed at times, over-emotional or exhausted. She might worry about her looks, and there will be times when she may hate herself and the idea of a baby and the whole business of being pregnant. There will be all sorts of swings of mood. So use the quiet time every day to talk together about these things: about your feelings, about the baby and life in general. Talk openly, freely, but try to avoid talk about medical or financial problems. This is no time for negative thoughts. When you start to feel the movements of the fetus, get your partner to place his hands on your abdomen, gently massaging the area, and feeling the strength of the new life that will bring you both so much joy. Talk about being a family and what that means for your future. What are your goals as a family?

Medical attitudes to pregnancy have placed too much emphasis on the physical aspects, and the things that can go wrong medically, and not enough attention has been paid to the burgeoning parent–child relationship that is actually a continuous process from pre-conceptual plans, through pregnancy to childbirth. But attitudes are changing. In recent years, since modern technology has enabled us to see the baby growing in the womb, the fetus has for many become 'the unborn child'. This is how the mother has always felt about her baby. 'Fetus' is the word the doctor uses – a word devoid of emotional content – but outside the surgery you never hear a mother referring to 'my embryo' or 'my fetus'. Usually she talks about 'my baby', and both partners sometimes playfully give him a nickname. At a conference on the theme 'Encounter with the Unborn' (in Badgastein, Austria, 1986) the Swedish gynaecologist Peter Fedor-Freybergh said: 'Generally, pregnant women show a high degree of sensitivity and sensibility toward their unborn child, which, by contrast, many professionals lack.' He went on to say that a mother–child dialogue begins on an unconscious level from the start of the unborn child's development. 'The dialogue becomes a reality,' he said, 'when the mother, consciously or unconsciously, changes her attitude and begins to experience the unborn "it" as an unborn "you".

The fetus has in the past been regarded by many as a passive and witless passenger in the womb, completely devoid of feeling. But we know now that this is the very opposite of the truth. As Professor A. W. Liley has pointed out, the fetus is the dominant partner in a pregnancy:

It is the fetus who guarantees the endocrine success of pregnancy and induces all manner of changes in maternal physiology to make her a suitable host. It is the fetus who, single-handed, solves the homograft problem – no mean feat when you reflect that, biologically, it is quite possible for a woman to bear more than her own body weight of babies, all immunological foreigners, during her reproductive career. It is the fetus who determines the duration of pregnancy. It is the fetus who decides which way he will present in labour. Even in labour the fetus is not entirely passive – neither the toothpaste in the tube nor the cork in the champagne bottle as required by the old hydraulic theories in the mechanics of labour.[1]

The gynaecologist Frank Hytten has also pointed out how ruthlessly selfish and active the fetus is in creating his own environment:

The fetus is an egoist, and by no means an endearing and helpless little dependant as his mother may fondly think. As soon as he has plugged himself into the uterus wall he sets out to make certain that his needs are served, regardless of any inconvenience he may cause. He does this by completely altering the mother's physiology, usually by fiddling with the control mechanisms.[2]

In the first half of pregnancy the fetus moves about with ease in the buoyant, amniotic fluid. When he rests he chooses the most comfortable position, sometimes with his chin resting on his chest and sometimes with his head tilted back. In the first half of pregnancy the uterine cavity is relatively large and globular, so movement is not difficult, but in the second half it becomes ovoid and the growing fetus feels cramped and uncomfortable. Usually he flexes his knees and this is normally achieved in the head-down position, but if he decides to extend his knees, which sometimes happens, he will fit in best in the reverse position which results in the so-called breech birth – that is, feet first.

It is remarkable how many couples do not share their feelings about the baby until just before the birth or even not until the baby is born. You can enjoy the baby before he is born. You can make plans for him, even talk to him. Though he will not of course, understand your words, he can certainly hear your voice along with all the other sounds that bombard him in the womb.

When does consciousness begin? How much is the fetus affected by the mother's emotions? How sensitive is the fetus to the changes that occur in her body, her swings of mood, which have a chemical or hormonal basis? These are among the questions asked and researched by the International Society for Prenatal and Perinatal Psychology and Medicine (ISPP), which was founded in 1971 and now has members drawn from different disciplines – gynaecology, endocrinology, psychology, paediatrics, anthropology and so on – and from many countries. Dr Peter Fedor-Freybergh, the gynaecologist quoted above, is their president. Their work is gradually becoming known and respected on the Continent and in the USA, but is hardly known at all in the UK, except for the occasional news item (mostly sceptical or derisory) or feature about such subjects as prenatal stimulation, pre-learning theory or prenatal therapy, which are not taken very seriously by the UK medical establishment. All this, however, represents only a part of ISPP research into medical and psychological aspects of pregnancy and childbirth. Their approach is 'holistic' and their broad aim is education for parenthood.

What do we know about the way the fetus responds to external stimuli? There is plenty of evidence now that the fetus is very sensitive to sound and touch. From the twentieth week of gestation the fetus responds to a wide range of sounds, some of them in frequencies so high or low that they cannot be heard by the adult ear. In late pregnancy a mother can sometimes feel the fetus jump when a door slams or a car backfires. The sleeping pattern of the fetus is the same as the mother's. Encephalograph (EEC) examinations have shown that during sleep the unborn child has phases of rapid eye movement (REM) which in the adult indicates dreaming. He is relaxed when the mother is relaxed and disturbed when she is. All the mother's behaviour, what she eats and drinks, how she lives, whether she is relaxed or distressed, will have some effect on the unborn baby, who has been known to kick furiously when the mother is smoking.

The psychoanalyst and paediatrician David Winnicott stressed the importance of a mother getting to know the fetus 'as a person' before birth if there is to be a 'good mother–child relationship after birth'.[3] A positive attitude to the unborn child will develop into a positive attitude at birth when you feel you already know your baby. Talking to mothers-to-be Winnicott said: 'I think the most important thing is that you feel your baby is worth getting to know as a person and worth getting to know from the earliest possible moment.' Knowing what is going on as a child develops in the womb, feeling his kicks and his responses to various sounds (according to Professor Liley, the fetus has been known to move rhythmically to certain kinds of music) is all part of the bonding process.

Winnicott did not mention the father; but it is just as important for him to get to know the baby, or to feel that the baby is as much his as his partner's right from the earliest moment. Feelings about the baby must be shared. A quiet time together every day will be very rewarding, particularly when the baby starts making his presence felt and a threesome becomes established.

As we saw earlier, the happiness of the expectant mother has a positive influence on the outcome of pregnancy. Dr Aidan Macfarlane in *The Psychology of Childbirth* writes about the clinics run in China 1,000 years ago 'not so much in the interest of physical well-being as to ensure the tranquillity of the mother and, through her, of the baby'. Whatever contributes to the happiness of both parents during the nine months of pregnancy is bound to have a beneficial effect on the child.

In the USA there is a growing interest in prenatal stimulation with organizations set up to promote pre-learning programmes. One such programme, 'Project Prelearn', launched in 1989 by Dr Brent Logan, director of the Prenatal and Infant Education Institute in Washington, claims that a child who is stimulated before birth is usually calmer and more attentive than other babies, and goes on to develop above-average learning skills and to do well educationally. The basis of this stimulation is patterned sound, which is similar in volume, tone and rhythm to sounds heard in the womb. These sounds are recorded on an audio-cassette and played to the fetus via transducers placed low on the mother's abdomen. Mothers are encouraged to sing to their unborn babies. For example, suitable songs are taught to expectant mothers at the Children's Hospital, Minnesota. It has at least been demonstrated that the same songs are recognized by the baby after birth and can have a calming effect on him. Music, especially singing, has been shown to benefit children who have been born prematurely. Music therapy is used at the Neonatal Intensive Care Unit, St Joseph's Hospital, Wisconsin, USA. The music they play to infants with respiratory distress helps them regulate their breathing. Pillow speakers and audio-cassette tape recorders are used to play prepared recordings of parents' voices talking, reading and singing.

Music therapy also has benefits for the mother during pregnancy. Singing, for instance, is a simple way of exercising the pregnant woman's diaphragm and teaches her to breathe out, which can help her relax during labour.

Whatever produces good feelings in parents and whatever relaxes the mother and, through her, the child should be encouraged. This positive approach satisfies what the humanistic psychologist, Abraham Maslow, called a 'being need', as distinct from a need to satisfy a hunger, which he called a 'deficiency need'. A 'being need', as Maslow describes it, 'presses toward fuller and fuller being, toward what most people would call good values: toward serenity, honesty, love and so on'. Maslow gave us 'self-actualization' which means becoming fully human, truly yourself; and 'the peak experience', which happens when you are fully functioning as a human being. Michel Odent, a pioneer of natural childbirth, believes this approach towards becoming 'fully functioning' as a

human being, is an essential condition of what he calls 'primal health', which is the shifting of emphasis from the prevention of illness to the *genesis* of good health. Good health for the baby starts with the positive feelings of a couple when they are planning for parenthood and continues throughout pregnancy to childbirth and infancy and through to adulthood.

Talking and singing to the child, talking about the child, knowing what is happening to him as he grows through the nine months of pregnancy, are bound to lead to a positive attitude and a warm attachment to the child by both parents after birth. It strengthens the emotional bonds between parents and child. The moments when you are together feeling the presence of the unborn child will remain with you for the rest of your life.

Antenatal Care

As soon as you know the baby is on the way you should take steps to ensure that for the next nine months you will get the best quality of medical care. You may feel that you can manage perfectly well on your own without doctors. You may object, as many women do, to medical intrusion by a male-dominated profession, particularly by male obstetricians and gynaecologists. But it is imperative to have regular checks during pregnancy to prevent any potential problems from developing.

The first step is to see your GP who will confirm your pregnancy and make arrangements for antenatal care. This can take several different forms. You may be looked after by the antenatal clinic at your local hospital, in which case all that your doctor will do is notify the clinic at the hospital. However, it is becoming more common nowadays for hospitals and GPs to share the responsibility of antenatal care ('shared care'). You will then be booked into hospital for the birth, to attend appointments for tests and to see specialists, but for most of the time you will be looked after by your own doctor with the help of the community midwife or practice nurse. The advantage of this is that you get more individual attention and are unlikely to feel that you are just one of many pregnant women on a production line – an impression often given in a crowded antenatal clinic. If you are lucky, you will see the same doctor every time (but it should be said that such good continuity of care is not common) and may get to know the midwife who will be coming to look after you after the birth. Also, waiting times at hospital antenatal clinics can be long and tiresome but are likely to be shorter in your own doctor's surgery.

If you prefer this more personal kind of antenatal care and your GP is not able to offer it, you are within your rights to ask to be transferred to a doctor who does practise shared care for the duration of your pregnancy. If you can arrange shared care, you will be given a co-operation card – a record of your notes – by the hospital clinic which you carry with you when you go to your doctor. You will almost certainly need to go to the antenatal clinic for a booking appointment around twelve weeks, when you will

WHEN A BABY IS ON THE WAY

probably meet other women at the same stage of pregnancy as yourself, whom you will have plenty of time to get to know during the waiting period. Take along a notebook containing questions you want to ask the obstetrician.

At the booking appointment the hospital will test your urine, take a sample of your blood to check on your health and monitor your blood pressure. There may be an internal examination (though some doctors try to avoid this because of the slight chance of miscarriage), and you might also see a community midwife and a health visitor who will explain their roles to you.

There are various kinds of antenatal classes available, but unfortunately there is not much of a choice outside London. The NHS run classes at local hospitals and clinics, but these are mostly for women only, though some hospitals run parental classes. The National Childbirth Trust, who pioneered the idea of breathing and relaxation techniques, run classes for couples. And the Active Birth Centre runs classes for those who favour the squatting or kneeling position when giving birth.

FATHERS

It is important for the prospective father to attend antenatal classes. Fathers who are prepared for the birth of their babies usually become much more involved in caring for them after birth than those who have had little or no preparation for the event.

An empirical study carried out by Drs H. Nickel and E. M. T. Kocher at the University of Trier in West Germany found that fathers who had taken part in antenatal preparation were more likely to do some of the so-called 'unpleasant' tasks like changing nappies, and they also had more confidence in taking over the care of the baby single-handed than fathers who had no preparation and sometimes felt estranged from their wives after delivery.[4] The fathers who had learned the skills of babycare enjoyed close contact with their babies, bathing and cuddling them and carrying them close to their bodies, and the children themselves benefited emotionally from this close contact. Couples who took part in the research described the baby's behaviour as 'more cheerful, more responsive, he/she has better vocalization' than the children of couples where the care of the baby was left mainly to the mother. Such behaviour could have important social benefits and could benefit child behaviour later on.

It has been suggested that there is a need for a training programme for expectant parents which would incorporate some of the psychological aspects of child development in the first year of life. A training programme of this kind should start before pregnancy. The couple themselves could follow such a programme before and during pregnancy and then continue it during the first year of the child's life. In fact, this learning process should continue right through to the child's school years. Parents should learn not to be so dependent on professional guidance and more willing to share their experiences with one another and with their children as they develop good family relationships.

For most fathers pregnancy is just a time of waiting. They watch, in a state of nervous anticipation, the gradual changes that take place in their partner's body. The mother feels the changes in her body, the father feels the changes in his mind – in his thinking and expectations. We heard of one father who put it this way: 'It took nine months for the baby to be born. And I had nine months to think him into existence.'

An expectant father sometimes has physical symptoms similar to those of the mother. Pregnancy for him may be a time of stress, he may feel neglected and may experience feelings of helplessness which can sometimes lead to aggression or escaping from the situation and finding solace elsewhere. A father should not keep these things to himself. Unfortunately, the father's experience of pregnancy is largely ignored by the medical profession, and the father may feel that he would prefer to keep his problems to himself when his partner needs all his support. This will not help anyone: pregnancy must be a shared experience.

The father who has played his part in planning the pregnancy and sharing it throughout the nine months is unlikely to find it so stressful and should have no difficulty in expressing his feelings when he is depressed or 'turned off' by his partner's pregnancy, which sometimes happens. The whole object of pre-conceptual care is to prepare both parents for whatever problems may occur in pregnancy, whether they are emotional or physical. The main problem for some couples is knowing what the problem is. Solutions become obvious when problems are identified.

Sex in Pregnancy

Most couples continue to enjoy sex during pregnancy. Some women may say that the way their bodies change increases their sensitivity and pleasure. Pregnancy can cause a pelvic tension that is similar to sexual excitement and this may be the reason why there are those who say that they experience an orgasm for the first time during pregnancy or others who say that they come to orgasm more quickly.

Men may need reassurance that their partner really enjoys sex at this time, and that no damage is being inflicted on the developing child. There will, of course, be times when the pregnant woman is feeling tired and under the weather and not up to intercourse. It is important at these times for the woman to let her partner know just how she is feeling and to reassure him that he is still loved.

If there is any bleeding during pregnancy, it would be advisable to abstain from sex for up to two weeks after the bleeding. Many couples continue to enjoy sex to the end. In fact, intercourse can be an efficient way of bringing a pregnancy to an end. A hormone in the male sperm – prostaglandin – helps to induce labour, but only when the woman is ready. Prostaglandin will not trigger off an early labour or cause a miscarriage. However, some obstetricians recommend that women who have had a miscarriage should abstain from intercourse during the first three months of pregnancy.

Sexual problems unrelated to pregnancy itself should be sorted out before conception. If the pregnancy is planned and both partners have enjoyed a close sexual relationship, then the changes that occur during pregnancy should only involve changes in technique and timing. For instance, the man on top may be too uncomfortable for the woman and another position will be preferred. It is important to recognize the role of sexual intimacy in maintaining a close bond during pregnancy. Otherwise, if sexual problems are not dealt with before conception, they can lead to frustration and conflict during pregnancy, a deterioration of the sexual relationship, and what some call 'disbonding' – a weakening of the family bond.

Prevention and Treatment of Illness in the Unborn Child

Caring for the pregnant woman is, of course, of paramount import-ance, but it must never be forgotten that there is another life there in the womb from the moment of conception. There are two people to be cared for: mother and child. The New Zealand gynaecologist Albert Liley says that he always treats mother and child as two patients. The unborn child can be ill in different ways from the mother, though the cause may lie in some kind of mineral or vitamin deficiency or toxin in the mother. The child in the womb can be neglected, though mainly out of ignorance, and in less obvious or culpable ways than the neglected infant. Some potential illnesses can be prevented before conception, or, if they do occur during pregnancy, they can sometimes be diagnosed and treated in the womb. Enzyme deficiencies in the unborn child and other abnormalities of metabolism, growth or development, can be treated through a diet that puts back the missing nutrients or hormones or prevents toxins from being absorbed.

Following the thalidomide tragedy many experiments were carried out on animals to try to find ways of combating potentially toxic drugs. It was found, for instance, that when thalidomide was given to rats, the well-nourished rats had undamaged babies, but the off-spring of the poorly-nourished rats had deformities similar to those found in humans who were exposed to the drug. Our knowledge of the effect of diet on health has made it possible to prevent various abnormalities from occurring during pregnancy. It is for this reason that it is so important to establish a healthy diet before conception.

FETOSCOPY

Thanks to the development of fetoscopy, or the examination of the fetus through the uterine wall, a more direct approach to treatment of the unborn child is possible. Using a fetoscope, an artery or vein in the umbilical cord can be punctured and pure fetal blood drawn off for analysis. In the same way, repeated fetal blood transfusions have been successfully carried out in the second three months of pregnancy to treat anaemia in the unborn child.

There are a number of exciting developments in the treatment of deformities. For example, fetoscopy has been used to heal or repair facial deformities including hare lip and cleft palate.

Fetoscopy can also be used in the identification of disorders such as thalassaemia, where carrier parents have a one in four chance of producing a child with this frequently fatal haemoglobin disorder (found chiefly in children of Mediterranean stock) or Duchenne's muscular dystrophy which is linked to the x-chromosome (the female determining factor carried in the sperm and ovum).

There are risks in the use of fetoscopy, which include leakage of amniotic fluid during the later months of pregnancy and bleeding. There is also the possibility that the fibriotic light in the fetoscope could damage the baby's eyes. One advantage, however, is that fetoscopy and other investigative procedures are alerting obstetricians to the sensitivity of the tiny human being in the womb. One obstetrician who was examining an unborn baby's eyes with the help of fetoscopy, said: 'I had a blood vessel lined up and was just about to strike when out of nowhere came this hand to knock away the needle. I think it was coincidental, but who knows?'

ULTRASOUND

An ultrasound is a routine procedure in most hospitals to check developmental dates and to examine the fetus for congenital abnormalities. These machines give very precise images and it is possible to examine the heart and its four chambers when it is only 1cm in diameter and the unborn child is only eighteen weeks old. It is a thrill for parents to be able to see their child on the screen some time before birth, though the picture to them may not seem as precise as it does to the operator and they will probably need an interpretation of what they see. A scan can detect multiple pregnancies, measure the size of the fetal head (to determine the gestational age of the baby, so that you can work out the date of birth), ascertain the position and health of the placenta, and detect a number of congenital abnormalities. It can also determine the sex of the baby in late pregnancy.

For an early ultrasound you are asked to attend with a full bladder. You lie on a couch or examining table, oil is rubbed on your stomach, and a probe is moved to and fro over your abdomen.

Because of the fears about X-rays, ultrasound was welcomed as a safer investigative instrument. But even so, it is generally used with caution, because of the possibility of inflicting damage on rapidly growing cells. At present most research does not suggest that any great harm is done by ultrasound, but it must be said that alarm bells have been ringing for some time. There is the suspicion that cell chemicals may be damaged during cell production by ultrasound. For example, a paper in the *Lancet* in 1983 described experiments on rats which showed that exposure to ultrasound delayed neuromuscular development and reduced the effectiveness of the body's immune system. And remember, there was a time when the fluoroscope used by every shoe salesman was not considered harmful. It was fun to look at your toes on an X-ray machine in a shop, but no one would submit themselves to such a risky examination today. In 1984 a National Institutes of Health report stated that ultrasound was not essential in any condition and went on to say that the use of ultrasound should be discouraged as a means of merely looking at the unborn baby or determining its sex (*Medical World News*, 1984). In the UK, where there is legal abortion, ultrasound is offered for the detection of neural tube defects in the case of women at risk, who would consider an abortion if the test proved positive (see below). There are sometimes psychological gains in the use of ultrasound which many consider outweigh the possible, but unproven, biological risks. The pregnant woman who has fears about her baby is reassured when she sees the tiny fetus on the screen and is told all is well. Ultrasound can arouse very positive feelings for the unborn child in the parents.

AMNIOCENTESIS AND BLOOD TESTS FOR DOWN'S SYNDROME AND NEURAL TUBE DEFECTS

Amniocentesis is a test carried out between fourteen and twenty weeks of pregnancy to establish whether your baby has any chromosomal disorder. Analysis of fetal cells found in the amniotic fluid around the baby will reveal whether or not there is an abnormal number of chromosomes. This is a characteristic of Down's syndrome and the main reason why a test may be carried out on women aged over thirty-five who have an increased risk of carrying a Down's syndrome baby.

Recently, however, a blood test in early pregnancy has been developed by the Department of Environmental and Preventive Medicine at St Bartholomew's Medical College, London, which identifies women with an increased risk of Down's syndrome or neural tube defects so that they can decide whether or not to have an amniocentesis (in the case of Down's syndrome) or a detailed ultrasound scan as well as an amniocentesis (in the case of neural tube defects). The result of the blood test is reported as either 'screen negative' or 'screen positive'. The test is usually carried out at sixteen weeks of pregnancy.

Every pregnant woman has a risk of having a baby with Down's syndrome. The risk increases as a woman becomes older. About one in 1,000 women who are twenty-eight years old will give birth to a baby with Down's syndrome, but a woman who is thirty-eight years old has about a one in 200 risk. Until recently it was thought that a woman's age was the only way to tell what her risk would be. Now levels of certain substances in the blood – alpha-fetoprotein (AFP), unconjugated oestriol (uE3) and human chorionic gonadotropin (hCG) – are measured and taken into account as well as age to determine the risk.

A screen-positive test does not mean that there is an abnormality in your baby. Most women with positive tests will have normal healthy babies, but what the test shows is that the risk of having a Down's syndrome baby is one in 250. If the test is positive, you will be offered an ultrasound scan to determine if your dates are correct: levels of AFP, uE3 and hCG vary as a pregnancy advances, and if it is found that you are not as far or further along than you thought, the screening test will have to be reinterpreted and may no longer be regarded as positive. If the ultrasound shows that your dates are correct, you will be offered an amniocentesis.

If the risk of Down's syndrome is found to be less than one in 250, and the AFP level is not high, the result is termed 'screen negative'. Nine out of ten women have a negative result.

In the case of neural tube defects 'screen positive' indicates that there is more than two and a half times the normal level of AFP in the mother's blood, which is considered a risk.

Leaflets explaining the blood test are available from the Department of Environmental and Preventive Medicine, St Bartholomew's Hospital Medical College.

The amniocentesis procedure is carried out under a local anaesthetic. A needle is inserted in the abdominal wall and a sample of amniotic fluid is drawn off. Ultrasound is used to make sure the needle is inserted in the right place and does not harm the baby or placenta.

Many women are grateful for amniocentesis. If there is no sign of abnormality in the fetus, which is the usual result, the woman will feel less troubled for the rest of the pregnancy. There is, however, a slight risk of miscarriage, estimated at little more than one per cent. There is also a 15 per cent chance that the test will be unsatisfactory. In the first place, it is not easy to obtain a sample of fluid, and more than one attempt may have to be made. Even then, there is a slight chance that the test may go wrong in the laboratory and false results will be obtained. The test for Down's syndrome takes around three to four weeks to complete, so you are 19 to 20 weeks into your pregnancy before you know the result. There are parents who would regard this as too late for an abortion, and some of them are now being offered another simple test which can be carried out at an earlier stage of pregnancy.

CVS

This test is called chorion villus biopsy, but is more usually known as CVS (chorion villus sampling), in which a small sample of the developing placenta is removed for analysis. The test can be carried out in the tenth week of pregnancy. Here again there is a slight chance of miscarriage, estimated at one to four per cent.

It must be remembered that terminating a pregnancy, even as early as ten weeks, can be a traumatic experience. For those who are carrying a child with some chromosomal abnormality, the decision to abort will be very painful. There are some doctors who say you should not have a CVS or amniocentesis unless you are prepared to go through with a termination.

Some doctors find it easy to say to an older woman, 'Don't worry, your child will probably be normal, but if we do find some abnormality, it's a simple matter nowadays to terminate a pregnancy.' It is never a simple matter. That is why it is so important to do everything possible to prevent things from going wrong, or at least to be fully aware of the risks before conception. Good pre-conceptual care is the best insurance against abortion.

If you accept the offer of CVS, the possibility of a termination must be weighed against the possibility of a lifetime spent caring for a severely handicapped child. However, what happens in most cases, as we have said, is the tremendous relief, after a diagnostic test of this kind, of finding that your child is normal.

'The test was over before I knew it,' said Sue Bookman who, after much soul-searching, decided she didn't want an amniocentesis and was offered the CVS test at King's College Hospital (*Mother*, October 1987). 'It took ten minutes from start to finish. I remember saying, "Is that really all there is to it?" It appeared that was all there was and after a couple of minutes' rest I was allowed to go. The consultant warned that I might feel a bit of a dull "period" pain a little later on, but I didn't.'

The wait afterwards can be agonizing. The woman quoted above had to wait fifteen days. 'But it was truly the most wonderful news in the world,' she said, 'when we heard our baby was normal.'

If you consider yourself to be at risk, you should discuss the possibility of undergoing a CVS or amniocentesis and make a hospital appointment as soon as possible. There will be little problem in arranging an amniocentesis but as yet CVS is not widely available.

WHERE TO GET HELP
If you are unfortunate enough to be carrying a handicapped child,

before you make the agonizing decision about whether or not to have an abortion you can get help and advice from one of the societies that deal with individual handicaps, such as the Down's Children's Association or the Association for Spina Bifida and Hydrocephalus, and they can put you in touch with other parents who have had to face the same dilemma. Other organizations which can help are the Women's Health and Reproductive Rights Information Centre, which publishes a range of information on relevant subjects, including abortion, and The National Abortion Campaign, which produces a quarterly magazine, a wide range of information material and an extensive publications list. A very helpful leaflet, *Abortion*

FETOSCOPY

Diagram of 18–20 weeks pregnancy: fine fetoscopy needle has been positioned, by direct vision through fetoscope [not shown], for withdrawing small sample from a blood vessel in umbilical cord. In amniocentesis the needle (cannula), which is not so fine, draws a small amount of fluid for analysis from the amniotic sac.

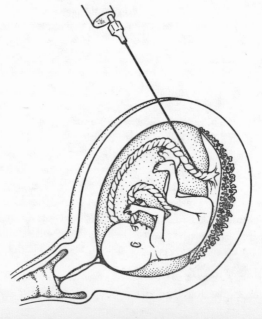

CVS

A small sample of the chorion villus (developing placenta) is removed for analysis. To avoid infection, the needle is sometimes inserted through the abdominal wall, as in amniocentesis.

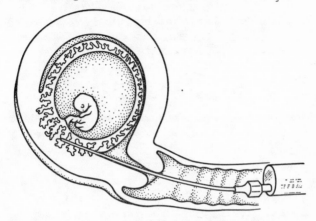

Questions and Answers is available from Marie Stopes House (see 'Further Information' for addresses and telephone numbers).

Everything depends on the severity of the handicap and the degree of suffering it will cause the parents and their child. But how is one to define and measure suffering? Many so-called handicapped children are able to enjoy life. Again and again one hears about the gentle nature, the patience and courage of many such children. A Down's syndrome child, for instance, is usually very lovable and easy to manage and may well live a reasonable life for many years. There are other children such as those suffering from cystic fibrosis or haemophilia who, with care, are able to live full lives and take part in many everyday activities.

Melanie Phillips and John Dawson describe the two extreme attitudes to abortion:

For those with absolute views there is no problem. For Roman Catholics, for example, abortion can never be permitted because since a human person with its immortal soul is formed at conception, any destruction of the conceptus is murder. A parallel, if antithetical, certainly characterises those who believe that a woman has an absolute right over her body, and since a fetus is merely a part of the body, it is a woman's right to choose whether a pregnancy should continue or be terminated.

The attitude embodied by the law, and accepted by the majority of doctors, falls between these two extreme positions. It does not place an absolute value on human life so that a fetus has to be saved at all cost. But it places a very high value upon human life, so that any destruction of the fetus has to be capable of justification . . . It is not considered justifiable to abort a fetus for social convenience . . . but only if the birth presents a threat to the physical or mental health of the mother, or if there is a risk that the child, if born, will suffer serious physical or mental handicap.[5]

The important word in this context is 'serious'. The difficulty may lie in defining what is serious. Is Down's syndrome serious? It is, of course, serious in the sense that it is life-threatening, but is it serious enough to justify an abortion? The quality of life, not the length, is for many the most important factor in deciding whether an unborn child shall live or die.

These are disturbing questions and there are no easy answers. In the end it is the parents who must make the agonizing decision.

Parents who are at risk of bearing a handicapped child should get their GP or obstetrician to refer them to a genetic counsellor before they decide on having a baby. It is best to face this problem before conception rather than afterwards when you may live in dread of giving birth to a deformed or sick child. (For more about genetic counselling, see Chapter 5.)

Minor Complaints in Pregnancy

For most couples the only problems, we hope, will be the fairly common ones such as morning sickness, backache or heartburn. If you have followed a fitness for pregnancy programme you will find that you do not suffer as much as many other pregnant women who have not prepared for pregnancy. If you are healthy at the start you should remain healthy throughout but do not expect to be completely free from all of the irritations of pregnancy, because they are sometimes caused by hormonal changes. You may find that you will suffer from some of the following minor complaints.

MORNING SICKNESS

This is one of the most distressing and infuriating problems of early pregnancy. It can start as early as the first week after conception or may not occur until eight weeks later. For those who have taken care of themselves and follow a healthy diet it may not happen at all, but there is no guarantee of that. The fact that it is so common does not make it feel any better. The trouble is, it is taken for granted. No one really knows the cause, but it is believed to arise because of hormonal changes in the body combined with blood pressure changes that occur in the early weeks. Nausea and vomiting occur at any time of the day, but are most distressing when they happen first thing in the morning. It is best to take your time getting up. Do everything slowly after that. Many women find that nibbling some dry toast and drinking a cup of tea before getting up helps. Do not eat fatty foods during the day. Frequent snacks of carbohydrate foods and eating dry biscuits before going to bed may also be helpful. You can also try taking a small dose of vitamin B6 combined with vitamin C and zinc sulphate which you can buy from the chemist without a prescription. The problem usually goes away in the thirteenth or fourteenth week.

HEARTBURN

This is an unpleasant burning pain in the chest and upper abdomen, often accompanied by an acid taste in the mouth and belching. In spite of the name, it has nothing to do with the heart. The cause of heartburn is the muscle at the top of the stomach becoming lax during pregnancy so that it cannot prevent digestive acid from the stomach entering the oesophagus and irritating its sensitive lining. Heartburn is usually a symptom of late pregnancy when the baby fills the abdomen but can occur at any time. It is best to have frequent snacks to soak up the acid. Do not eat fatty or spicy food. In fact, go on eating the kind of food you ate before pregnancy.

CONSTIPATION

This is a common complaint in pregnancy and is caused by hormonal changes, but if you eat plenty of fresh fruit and some raw vegetables during the day it should not bother you unduly. Exercise can help. In fact, if you continue with your yoga exercises, adapting them slightly for pregnancy, and eat the sort of food you ate in your 'getting fit for pregnancy' programme you will find that constipation is not a problem. Diet and exercise will also help to prevent piles (haemorrhoids) which are associated with constipation.

STRETCH MARKS

These are caused by a high level of progesterone produced in pregnancy and – more significantly – weight gain. Stretch marks usually appear on the abdomen, but may appear on breasts and thighs as well. They first appear as purple lines but gradually fade to a silvery white. Unfortunately, once you get them you will not be able to get rid of them. Oiling the skin will not prevent stretch marks, but the skin does tend to become dry and a good moisturizer will make it feel less itchy.

BACKACHE

This is another common complaint that can make pregnancy really miserable. It is caused by progesterone softening the muscles and ligaments around the back as the body prepares itself for birth, plus the strain of carrying the baby. The best way to prevent this is by exercising the back muscles before pregnancy, so that they are strong and supple. Swimming or yoga exercises are good ways of doing this and it is useful to have some training in posture, such as the Alexander Technique which will teach you to stand and sit straight (see Chapter 4). If you do suffer from backache in spite of all your exercising, a hot-water bottle will relieve the pain, and massage by your partner can help both physically and emotionally if you are feeling thoroughly fed up. Getting down on all fours can also help because it takes the strain off the spine.

Sacro-iliac pain at the base of the spine can be agonizing. If backache becomes a serious problem, see your doctor or a chiropractor or osteopath. Backache may also be a symptom of a urine infection.

TIREDNESS

A complete sapping of energy is one of the first symptoms of pregnancy and can be very depressing. Three o'clock feels like nine o'clock, some women say. It is fairly common for a pregnant woman to feel that if this happens so early in pregnancy, then she is not going to cope and, if she is at work she may feel like giving up her job. The best solution is not to fight the tiredness, but to get more sleep. You could make things easier for yourself, if you are still at work, by taking regular breaks and having forty winks in the rest room or some other quiet place. Rest after the midday meal. Try to change your hours of work and avoid rush hours in the morning and evening. Do not do so much housework. Your partner can take over more of these chores.

The tiredness tends to go in the middle months, but returns towards the end when the physical demands are great and discomfort at night prevents you from getting enough sleep. Some women find that taking oil of Evening Primrose at night helps to relax them. The tiredness may be exacerbated by stress, so a relaxation exercise at the end of the day (see Chapter 4) may help to reduce tension felt in the muscles.

INSOMNIA

This is almost as common as tiredness, particularly late in pregnancy when you may have to get up several times at night to empty your bladder, or you may feel too hot, or you may be wakened by your baby's movements. Try going to bed as soon as you feel tired, and do not wait until you are exhausted. A deep, warm bath before going to bed will help. Make sure that you get into a warm bed. Put some pillows underneath the bulge. Relaxation exercises may also help. Try camomile or a herbal tea before going to bed.

MUSCLE CRAMPS

These sharp and sudden pains in the legs are quite common in pregnancy, especially at night. The best treatment, if you are in bed, is to get up and vigorously massage the area around the affected muscle. Or get your partner to do this for you. (Involve your partner as much as possible in everything that happens to you in pregnancy; he should be prepared for this and his involvement will make all the aches and pains more tolerable.)

Some people believe that cramp may be the result of calcium deficiency. It is important to have an adequate intake of this mineral which is found in dairy products, nuts and canned sardines (see page 63).

SWELLING OF THE FEET AND ANKLES

Your feet and ankles are under increased pressure during pregnancy and they may cause you some trouble. The swelling will probably be at its worst late in the day. High-heeled shoes may exacerbate the problem. Make sure that your shoes are low- or flat-heeled. The problem can be relieved by raising your feet whenever possible when sitting or lying down. Swelling is not serious in itself – it is quite common and usually nothing to worry about – but it could conceivably be a symptom of a serious condition and should be reported to your doctor or midwife especially if your fingers are swelling as well.

VARICOSE VEINS

These can be quite painful, causing your legs to ache and throb. As the womb grows in pregnancy the pressure within the veins of the legs is increased, so they become enlarged and worm-like. Some doctors will provide you with support stockings on prescription. These should always be put on before you get out of bed. Otherwise put your legs up as often as possible in such a way that your heels are higher than your hips.

Choices

There are movements such as the Radical Midwives Association, the Association for Improvements in Maternity Services (AIMS) and the Active Birth Centre, which are doing their best to improve conditions for the pregnant woman and the mother in labour. They insist that women should not accept their pregnancy passively as their destiny, submitting themselves to the ministrations of doctors, midwives and obstetricians. They object to pregnant women being treated as patients with some kind of illness and having to go into hospital to have their baby.

Their argument is that the whole ethos of hospital treatment involves intervention; and once you find yourself in hospital it will be difficult to prevent doctors from interfering with natural processes. Hospitals, they say, are places for sick people, and anyone who occupies a hospital bed is likely to be treated as if she were sick. She will have needles stuck into her, be told to provide urine samples for testing, be given pills, have her blood pressure taken, be investigated by male doctors and will have to submit herself to all kinds of high-tech procedures which might not be absolutely necessary. She may feel sometimes that her body is no longer her own. Her sense of her own uniqueness as a person and her self-esteem may be gradually eroded.

These are very common criticisms today. They arise because of a changing view of health and disease, and a suspicion of high-tech medicine and the way the medical profession seems to compound any problem of illness by its zeal for gadgetry, machinery and powerful drugs. Many people feel that high-tech procedures divert doctors' attention from the lives and struggles and anxieties of their patients. There is a longing for more gentle ways of dealing with health problems and a suspicion of orthodoxy and authoritarianism. Orthodox medicine is fine in an emergency or for a serious illness, it could be argued, but a more gentle approach in pregnancy and labour is preferable. There is no doubt that there is some truth in these complaints. Couples should be prepared for a rough ride if they start insisting on being told more about what's happening to them. Whatever happens to the pregnant woman is also happening to her partner and their unborn child because it affects their future. Therefore it is a couple's right to ask obstetricians why certain procedures are being followed, if they are absolutely necessary and why they are not being given choices which might include some form of alternative medicine.

An increasing number of mothers nowadays are insisting on

playing an active part in their pregnancy and the birth of their child. The more active a woman is, both physically and in the way she lives her life and makes decisions, the more likely she is to be active and positive in her approach to labour. The more passive she is, the less prepared she will be for the active work of labour. The active approach is not just something acquired during pregnancy. The way we should approach childbirth is the way we should live our lives.

To be fair, the picture we have painted of hospitals may be true of some but not of all. And even though going to hospital for a birth may seem unnatural and a bit daunting to some, there are many hospitals that provide a first-rate service and allow the mother to make choices and reassure her that it is a safe place to have her baby. There are doctors who insist that the safety and happiness of the unborn child are as important as those of the mother; and that home births involve certain risks. Lives are sometimes lost, they say, because of the absence of life-saving equipment in the home. Others would dispute this. Some respected studies suggest that the home is a safer place to have your baby than a hospital. Things go wrong in hospitals as well as in the home.

In recent years there have been improvements in hospital maternity services. In most hospitals now there is a recognition that the husband has a right to be present at the birth of the child. There are many obstetricians who are aware of current criticisms and are much more sensitive than they used to be to the needs and fears of pregnant women. They are more willing to explain exactly what is happening to them and will offer them certain choices. We are moving gradually away from authoritarianism in medicine towards a general acceptance of the right of patients to participate in their own treatments.

ASSERTIVENESS TRAINING

Assertiveness training is becoming popular for women and would be very helpful when they feel at their most vulnerable during pregnancy. It is of course difficult to assert yourself when lying on a couch with your knickers off while you are being examined by a male gynaecologist. Saying no and being assertive is for some women very difficult at the best of times: they have become so accustomed to being compliant. What makes it even more difficult is the attitude of some old-fashioned doctors who believe they always know what is best for pregnant women, and will not allow them an opinion of their own. Assertiveness skills will be very useful in some awkward encounters with the medical profession and will enable you to say no without giving offence. Many further education establishments now run classes on assertiveness training and it might be a good idea for women, who have difficulties in asserting themselves, to take part in this kind of training before they become pregnant. Their partners might also benefit from these classes. Men may tend to collude with doctors in getting their wives through the pregnancy with the minimum of fuss: which means, of course, doing what they are told to do without asking questions.

WHERE TO HAVE YOUR BABY

Couples who would like to have their baby at home must be prepared to fight for their right to choose a home birth. If your own GP is unwilling to provide medical care for a home delivery, or cannot recommend someone who will, you should write to the Director of Nursing Services (Midwifery) of your District Health Authority, saying that you want a home birth and that your own doctor will not provide medical care.

If you can afford between £700 and £1,000 for a home confinement, the Independent Midwives Association may be able to help. They are, however, still a small organization, consisting of about thirty-five midwives, mostly working in the London area. They work in teams of two or more, providing continuity of care – antenatal, birth and postnatal care. But the same care should be available on the NHS.

In case of difficulty you will find support and encouragement from the Society to Support Home Confinement or the Association for the Improvement of Maternity Services (AIMS). But if you are not absolutely sure about where you want to have your baby and you have established a good relationship with your midwife, you will probably feel inclined to accept her advice, and she may very well recommend a hospital birth. Any wishes you may have about the way you would like to bring your baby into the world should be mentioned to your GP or whoever sees you at the antenatal clinic. If you are hoping to manage with a minimum of drugs, you should say so. Any drug you use will to some extent interfere with the natural process of birth. Gas and air may be preferred to pethidine because you can control the amount you have and when you remove your mask the gas soon clears from the system. Pethidine, which is an injection usually given in the buttocks, stays in the system for some time and affects the baby, who is dopey at birth, slower to suck, and may have breathing difficulties. These side-effects can to a large extent be alleviated by injecting the baby with another drug, nalaxone (Narcan). Even so, the baby usually remains sleepy until it has worked the drug out of its system. Pethidine is a useful relaxant for those mothers whose tension may be slowing down labour. It is sometimes given with other drugs to reduce the vomiting it can cause. However, some of these anti-emetics have the unfortunate side-effect of making you forget the birth altogether. The usual dose of pethidine is between 100 and 200 mg but if you feel you don't want so much, but certainly need something to help you relax, you could try a lower dose of 50–75 mg, which has been found to work just as well for some women.

Many hospitals offer an epidural anaesthetic. This is an injection in the epidural space around the spinal cord. It has the effect of removing all sensation from the uterus but leaving some feeling in the legs. It is extremely helpful and welcomed by mothers in long and difficult labours and when the baby is delivered by caesarean section, but if the injection is given too late in the first stage of labour, the mother may not be able to push the baby out and a forceps delivery, with all its risks, will then be necessary.

The ability to work with pain in labour is something you can acquire and is taught at active birth classes. Breathing is important; so the exercises you started before pregnancy should be helpful during labour. Mothers talk about how they 'breathed' through the contractions. What they mean by this is that the breathing and the contraction became, as it were, one and the same movement.

Their breathing did not eliminate the pain but it helped them to 'ride' a contraction.

Pain is felt by different women in different degrees of intensity. Some fortunate women only feel the odd twinge, while others are flat out for twenty-four hours. Some find singing or playing their favourite music helpful. The important thing is to try to go along with whatever happens, riding the storm, or tornado, as someone once described it. It has been found that the women who do best are those without any definite expectations, apart from the fact that they are going to feel some degree of pain. There is no doubt the intensity of pain depends to a great extent on your mental attitude: if you are anxious and tense, you will feel pain more acutely.

Doctors tend to talk of the hard work and discomfort of labour and do not prepare a woman for honest-to-goodness pain. If you are able to accept pain as healthy and normal during labour and can cope with it, you are likely to be the sort of person who will be in charge of your life and able to cope with the problems and pains that are a part of living. Labour pain is a positive experience – and, remember, there is a reward for your pain when it is all over.

When it is all over you will be glad that you and your partner are still fit, as you probably will be, to go on coping together and enjoying your new responsibility. Pre-pregnancy preparation is not only a preparation for the powerful moment of giving birth; it is a preparation for life, for all the years of bringing up your child or children and creating a positive attitude to family life with all its pleasures and pains.

References

1
Timing the Birth

1 D. H. Stott, 'Children in the Womb: The Effects of Stress', *New Society*, 19 May 1977, pp. 329–31.
2 Monika Lukesch, 'Psychologie Faktorem der Schwangershaft', Dissertation, University of Salzburg, 1975.
3 J. K. Russell, 'Early Teenage Pregnancy', in T. Lind (ed.), *Current Review in Obstetrics and Gynaecology*, Churchill Livingstone, 1978.
4 Zena Stein, *Journal of Epidemiology*, 121, 1985, pp. 327–39.
5 Bruno Bettelheim, *A Good Enough Parent*, Thames and Hudson, 1987.
6 Sheila Kitzinger, *Birth Over Thirty*, Sheldon Press, 1982.

2
Environmental Hazards

1 Claire Patterson, quoted in Des Wilson, *The Lead Scandal*, Heinemann, 1983.
2 C. N. Martyn, 'Geographical Relations between Alzheimer's Disease and Aluminium in Drinking Water', *Lancet*, 14 January 1989.
3 Ann Striessguth, 'Prenatal Effects of Alcohol Abuse in Humans and Laboratory Animals', in Tissin and Begleiter (eds.), *The Pathogenesis of Alcoholism*, vol. 7, Phenum Press, 1983.
4 May Holland, 'Alcohol and the Unborn Child', in *Guidelines for Future Parents*, Foresight, 1986.
5 Nabeel D. Sulaiman et al., 'Alcohol Consumption in Dundee, Prima-

gravidas and its Effects on Outcome of Pregnancy', *British Medical Journal*, 28 May 1988.
6 Vernon Coleman in *Guidelines for Future Parents*, Foresight, 1986.
7 Aubrey Milunsky, *How to Have the Healthiest Baby You Can*, Simon and Schuster, 1987.
8 T. Sazonova, 'A Physiological Assessment of the Work Conditions in 400 Kilovolt and 500 Kilovolt Open Switch Yards', in *Scientific Deliberations of the Soviet Institute of Lubow*, 46, 1966.

4
Exercising for Fitness at Conception

1 Judith Lumley in Geoffrey Chamberlain, *Pregnancy Care: A Manual for Practice*, John Wiley, 1986. This book, written for professionals, deals with various aspects of pre-conceptual care.
2 H. B. Valman and J. F. Pearson, 'What the Fetus Feels', *British Medical Journal*, 26 January 1980.
3 Dahong Zhuo, *The Chinese Exercise Book*, Thorsons, 1986.

6
Difficulties of Conceiving and Miscarriage

1 Joseph Bellina and Josleen Wilson, *The Fertility Handbook*, Penguin, 1986.
2 Margaret Leroy, *Miscarriage*, Optima/Miscarriage Association, 1988.
3. H. J. Huisjes, *Spontaneous Abortion*, Churchill Livingstone, 1984.
4. Cited in *The Fertility Handbook*, see note 1, above.

8
Health and Safety in the Home and at Work

1. Editorial, 'Listeriosis', *Lancet*, 14 January 1989.
2. *Which?*, August 1989.

3 Health and Safety Executive, *Pilot Study of Working Conditions in the Medical Service*, 1978.
4 J. Robinson, *Cancer of the Cervix – Occupational Risks of Husbands and Wives and Possible Preventive Strategies*, 1982.

9
When a Baby is on the Way

1 A. W. Liley, 'The Personality of the Fetus', *Self and Society*, June 1977.
2 Frank Hytten in Aidan Macfarlane, *The Psychology of Childbirth*, Harvard University Press, 1977.
3 David Winnicott, *Mother and Child: A Primer of First Relationships*, Basic Books, 1957. See also Roy Ridgway, *The Unborn Child*, Wildwood House, 1987.
4 H. Nickel and E. M. T. Kocher, 'The Role of the Father in Care-Giving and in the Development of the Infant', *Prenatal and Perinatal Psychology and Medicine*, Parthenon Publishing, 1988. This book contains a wide range of papers dealing with various aspects of the work of the International Society for Prenatal and Perinatal Psychology and Medicine.
5 Melanie Phillips and John Dawson, *Doctors' Dilemmas*, Harvester Press, 1985.

Further Information

1
Timing the Birth

The Maternity Alliance 59–61 Camden High Street, London NW1 7JL. Tel: 071-837 1265.

An independent national organization campaigning for improvements in rights and services for mothers, fathers and babies. They have compiled a bibliography on health before pregnancy.

Women's Health and Reproductive Rights Information Centre 52 Featherstone Street, London EC1Y 8RT. Tel: 071-251 6332.

Provides information on all aspects of women's health. It has approximately 3,000 names and addresses of groups and specialists in women's health-care.

The Parent Network 44–46 Caversham Road, London NW5 2DS. Tel: 071-485 8535.

A peer group which can help you prepare for parenthood. It provides training in communications skills and mutual support for single parents and others involved in child care.

National Childbirth Trust 9 Queensborough Terrace, London W2 3TB. Tel: 071-221 3833.

An organization devoted to education for pregnancy, birth and parenthood. They do not cover pre-conceptual care, but have much to offer couples before conception: e.g. assertiveness in pregnancy is taught by NCT teachers. There are over 300 branches and groups in the UK. For details of local branches ring or write, enclosing SAE.

HELP: Thames Television 149 Tottenham Court Road, London W1P 9LL. Tel: 071-387 9494.

Publishes eight fact sheets on pregnancy, including one on pre-conception. Send SAE for details.

2
Environmental Hazards

ASH (Action on Smoking and Health) 5–11 Mortimer Street, London W1N 7RH. Tel: 071-637 9843.

For information about smoking and health, including the damage smoking can do to the reproductive system.

Alcoholics Anonymous PO Box 514, 11 Redcliffe Gardens, London SW10 9BG. Tel: (help line) 071-352 3001.

Offers help and advice for people with alcohol problems and will put you in touch with your nearest branch.

Foresight (Association for the Promotion of Pre-conceptual Care) The Old Vicarage, Church Lane, Witley, Godalming, Surrey GU8 5PN. Tel: 042874 500 (between 9.30 am and 7.30 pm).

Publishes pamphlets and books relating to pre-conceptual care and provides a counselling service for couples with fertility problems. There are over forty Foresight clinics in Britain which offer advice on a healthy diet and lifestyle before pregnancy. *The Foresight Wholefood Cookbook* is designed to help you plan a balanced diet and contains many delicious recipes. There are suggestions for those with special dietary problems.

Health Education Authority Hamilton House, Mapleton Place, London WC1H 9TX. Tel: 071-631 0930.

Publishes a number of useful information leaflets including *Facts about Alcohol; How to Stop Smoking – for You and Your Baby; Vaginal Health and Discomfort; Cystitis; An Important Message for Women of Child-bearing Age* (rubella vaccinations).

3
Eating for Health before Pregnancy

The Institute for Optimum Nutrition 5 Jerdan Place, London SW6 1BE. Tel: 071-385 7984.

Offers a personal health programme to help you maintain an ideal weight and to keep you mentally alert and physically toned. It has a clinic, library, health-food and book shop.

The Soil Association 86 Colston Street, Bristol B31 5BB. Tel: 0272 290661.

Established in 1946, this organization sets the standards for organic agriculture, which they describe as 'an environmentally friendly way of producing high quality, healthy food by crop rotation and natural inputs, whilst treating farm animals with real concern for their well-being'. The Association campaigns for unadulterated food, including 'healthy meat' and has produced a ten-point plan for cleaning up our food, which includes the withdrawal of the most hazardous pesticides and the labelling of fruit and vegetables with pesticides used during growth and harvest. Approved growers and farmers display the Soil Association's symbol. The Association publishes national and regional lists of approved growers and farmers.

London Food Commission PO Box 291, London N5 1DU. Tel: 071-633 5782.

Campaigns for improved nutrition and better access to healthy food. Publishes *Food Magazine* which gives detailed information about pesticides.

Friends of the Earth 26–28 Underwood Street, London N1 7JQ. Tel: 071-490 1555.

Consistently draws attention to health risks arising from pesticide residues and the contamination of water supplies. Publishes pesticide incident reports.

The Trade Union Pesticide Group Transport and General Workers Union, Transport House, Smith Square, London SW1P 3HZ. Tel: 071-828 7788.

Co-ordinates the work of trade unionists concerned with pesticide use and abuse. It has lobbied for improved safety for workers using pesticides and fought to get improved data sheets from the manufacturers.

The Vegetarian Society 53 Marloes Road, Kensington, London W8 6LA. Tel: 071-937 7739.

Provides information about a vegetarian diet and its health benefits.

The Vegan Society 9 Mawddwy Cottages, Minllyn, Dinas Mawddwy, Machynlleth SY20 9LW. Tel: 06504 255.

Provides information on vegan diets and experiences of vegan mothers.

Action Against Allergy 23–4 George Street, Richmond, Surrey TW9 1JY. No telephone.

Campaigns for diagnosis and treatment through NHS doctors, hospitals and clinics. It can supply sufferers from allergic conditions with information and guidance on sources of medical help. Please send SAE.

4
Exercising for Fitness at Conception

Yoga for Health Foundation Ickwell Bury, Biggleswade, Bedfordshire SG18 9EF. Tel: 076 727 271.

Residential courses using the yoga approach in the control of chronic disorders such as diabetes. Simple physical work combined with mental techniques is now being used increasingly for a large number of chronic disorders. Ickwell Bury is a delightful country mansion, set in a 300-year-old walled garden.

Yoga Biomedical Trust PO Box 140, Cambridge, CB1 1PU. Tel: 0223 67301.

A charitable trust investigating the health benefits of yoga. YBT has a computerized file of over 2,000 yoga teachers from all the main yoga organizations in the UK. It can provide inquirers with the names and addresses of local yoga teachers to suit their needs. It can also provide yoga teachers with lists of sympathetic doctors and therapists in their localities. It has a bibliography of research literature on yoga and meditation, comprising about 1,600 references to papers, books, symposia and other reports.

The Alexander Institute 16 Balderton Street, London, W1Y 1TF. Tel: 071-408 2384.

The Institute was established in 1965 as a centre of excellence to 'teach and propagate the Alexander Principle'. It encourages teachers, students and the general public to use the centre for regular contact with what they call 'an Alexander environment'. It will provide the names and addresses of local teachers of the Alexander Technique.

Transcendental Meditation (TM) Freepost, London SW1P 4YY. Tel: 0800 269 303.

TM is taught at eighty centres around the country. The course consists of seven systematic steps, the first two being introductory presentations which are free. The full course costs £165 or £85 if you are a student or unemployed. Leaflets about TM and the address of your nearest centre can be obtained from the above address.

Relaxation for Living Dunesk, 29 Burwood Park Road, Walton-on-Thames, Surrey KT12 5LH. Tel: 09322 27826.

Provides information about relaxation techniques, including a reading list. Send SAE.

5
Infections, Illnesses and Genetic Disorders

Association for Spina Bifida and Hydrocephalus 22 Upper Woburn Place, London WC1H 0EP. Tel: 071-388 1382.

Support for couples offered termination after amniocentesis.

Association to Combat Huntington's Chorea Borough House, 34a Station Road, Hinckley, Leicestershire LE10 1AP. Tel: 0455 615558.

Offers support and advice to families with a history of Huntington's Chorea.

British Diabetic Association 10 Queen Anne Street, London W1M 0BD. Tel: 071-323 1531.

Helps diabetics to understand fully the implications of the disease and how to cope with it. The Association publishes a *Pregnancy Pack*, full of useful advice on how to keep your diabetes under control from the moment of conception. Other publications include *The Edinburgh Pre-pregnancy Clinic* and *Can I Marry? Of Course!* The association also publishes a number of diet and recipe books for diabetics, including *Vegetarians on a Diet*, a wholefood vegetarian cookbook.

British Epilepsy Association Crowthorne House, New Wokingham Road, Wokingham, Berkshire RG11 8AY. Tel: 0532 439 393.

Offers advice to mothers with epilepsy. Among its publications are *Epilepsy and the Family* and *The Epilepsy Handbook*.

Cystic Fibrosis Research Trust Alexander House, 5 Blyth Road, Bromley, Kent BR1 3RS. Tel: 081-464 7211.

A charitable trust helping all those who are suffering from CF and their families. Through its journal it keeps families informed about the latest treatments and research. Among its publications is *Fertility, Pregnancy and Conception in CF*, a well-informed and frank discussion of many of the problems facing the young CF adult.

Down's Children's Association 4 Oxford Street, London W1N 9FL. Tel: 071-720 0008.

Publishes *The Genetics of Down's Syndrome: an Account for Parents*.

The Haemophilia Society 123 Westminster Bridge Road, London SE1 7HR. Tel: 071-928 2020.

Provides help and advice for haemophiliacs and their families. The Society keeps members up to date on developments in treatment and care: this applies especially to AIDS.

Endometriosis Society 65 Holmdene Avenue, London SE14 9LD. Tel: 071-737 4764.

Support and advice for women suffering from endometriosis.

PID Support Group c/o Jessica Pickard, 61 Jenner Road, Stoke Newington, London N16 7RB. Tel: 081-806 6073.

Support and advice for women suffering from Pelvic Inflammatory Disease (PID).

Pre-Eclamptic Toxaemia Society (PETS) c/o Dawn James, 88 Plumberow, Lee Chapel North, Basildon, Essex SS15 5LP. No telephone.

Provides information and advice and publishes a regular newsletter. It also has a library service.

6
Difficulties of Conceiving and Miscarriage

Tambrands Dunsbury Way, Havant, Hants, PO9 5DG. Tel: 0800 525 522.

Tambrands, the makers of Tampax, market a simple-to-use ovulation prediction test kit called *First Response*. It identifies the day a woman is most likely to conceive. Tambrands have produced a video and free booklet on the various causes of infertility.

The Medical Education Trust 79 St Mary's Road, Huyton, Liverpool L36 5SR. Tel: 051-489 5996.

Publishes a pamphlet, *The Pill and Sex: Risks to Health and Fertility*, a basic guide for parents and teenagers.

Impotence Information Centre Freepost, Staines House, 158–162 High Street, Staines TW18 1BR. No telephone.

Provides information about recent developments in the treatment of male sexual dysfunction.

The Miscarriage Association 18 Stoneybrook Close, West Bretton, Wakefield, West Yorkshire WF4 4TP. Tel: 0924 85515.

Information and counselling for women who have had miscarriages and their families. They will also help those who, though they have not had a miscarriage, may have anxieties about losing their baby before birth. They run self-help groups throughout the country. Enclose SAE when writing.

Child 367 Wandsworth Road, London SW8 2JJ. Tel: 071-486 4289.

Self-help for couples with fertility problems, and a miscarriage support line.

Association of Sexual and Marital Therapists P O Box 62, Sheffield S10 3TS. No telephone.

A professional organization providing a forum for the exchange of information and experience in sexual and marital therapy.

7
Contraception

Family Planning Information Service 27–35 Mortimer Street, London W1N 7RJ. Tel: 071-636 7866.

Publishes leaflets on methods of birth control and sexually transmitted infections. You can phone or write for details of NHS or fee-paying family planning clinics.

Marie Stopes House, The Well Woman Centre 108 Whitfield Street, London W1P 6BE. Tel: 071-388 0662. Branches in Leeds and Manchester.

Offers advice and assistance (e.g. fitting the cap) with all aspects of family planning. Will also advise on abortion. They may be able to help you get an NHS abortion; otherwise, they will arrange a private abortion as cheaply as possible.

Natural Family Planning (NFP) Centre Birmingham Maternity Hospital, Edgbaston, Birmingham B15 2TG. Tel: 021-472 1377 Ext. 4219.

Training and research centre for natural family planning. Write to them for the name and address of a qualified NFP teacher in your area.

Other centres and co-ordinators include:

LONDON/SURREY/HANTS Mrs R. D. M. Byrne, 51 Ditton Road, Surbiton, Surrey KT6 6RF. Tel: 081-399 4789; *and* NFP Centre, Clitherow House, 1 Blythe Mews, Blythe Road, London W14 0NW. Tel. 071-371 1341.

LIVERPOOL Mrs Wyn Worthington, 26 Dooley Drive, Netherton, Merseyside L30 8RS. Tel. 0222 754 629.

BRISTOL NFP CENTRE NFP Centre, Room 8, Central Health Clinic, Room 54m, Tower Hill, Bristol BS2 0JD. Tel. 0272 291010 Ext. 223.

CARDIFF Mrs Colleen Norman, 218 Heathwood Road, Heath, Cardiff CF4 4BS. Tel: 0222 754 628.

NOTTINGHAM Mrs C. Orger, 10 Buckingham Road, Woodthorpe, Nottingham NG5 4GE. Tel: 0602 262684.

YORKSHIRE Mrs S. Cronin, 4 Cornborough Avenue, Haworth, W. Yorks YO3 0SH. Tel: 0904 424015.

SCOTLAND Dr John Dunn, 45 Queen Mary Avenue, Glasgow G42. Tel: 041-424 4364.

The Natural Family Planning Service, Catholic Marriage Advisory Council 1 Blythe Mews, Blythe Road, London W14 0NW. Tel. 071-371 1341

Offers teaching service and advice free of charge. A charge is made for ovulation thermometers and charts which, however, should be available free under the NHS from family planning clinics and family doctors.

8
Health and Safety
in the Home and at Work

VDU Workers Rights Campaign City Centre, 32–35 Featherstone Street, London EC1Y 8QX. Tel: 071-608 1388.

Offers information and advice for VDU workers.

Health and Safety Executive Library and information services: Broad Lane, Sheffield S3 7HQ. Tel: 0742 752 539; *and* St Hugh's House, Stanley Precinct, Bootle, Merseyside L20 3QY. Tel: 051-951 4381; *and* Baynard's House, 1 Chepstow House, Westbourne Grove, London W2 4TF. Tel: 071-221 0870.

Guidance concerning the health and safety of men and women at work. Publishes a leaflet *Pregnancy at Work*.

Working Mothers' Association 3 Webbs Road, London SW11 6RU. Tel: 071-700 5771.

Self-help organization for working parents and their children. Through a network of local groups they provide an informal support system. On a national level, WMA offers information and advice representing members' views to interested organizations, policy-makers and employers.

British Society for Social Responsibility in Science 28 Horsell Road, London N5 1XL. Tel. 071-607 9615.

Publishes *Hazards Bulletin* and *Measuring Chemicals at Work*.

General and Municipal Boilermakers and Allied Trades Union (GMB) Thorne House, Ruxley Ridge, Claygate, Esher, Surrey KT10 0TL. Tel: 0372 62081.

Publishes guides and leaflets on most aspects of health and safety at work, including *Health and Safety for Women*, *Chemicals at Work* and *Hazards Information Pack*. Ask for their health and safety publications list.

Trades Union Congress (TUC) Congress House, Great Russell Street, London WC1B 3LS. Tel: 071-636 4030.

Publishes a number of guides on health and safety at work, including *Women's Health at Risk*, *TUC Handbook on Dust at Work*, *Health and Safety in the Office*, *Health and Safety at Work: Know your Rights*, *TUC Guidelines on Visual Display Units* and *TUC Guidelines on Noise at Work*.

Ergonomics Training Centre Suite 9, Museum House, Museum Street, London WC1A 1JT. Tel: 071-636 5912.

Provides training and consultancy in ergonomics and other human aspects of systems, especially office systems. Its courses include 'Understanding Ergonomics' and 'Visual Display Terminals Ergonomics'. It advises on safe systems of work, including fire precautions, accident procedures and occupational health cover.

9
When a Baby is on the Way

Active Birth Centre 55 Dartmouth Park Road, London NW5 1SL. Tel: 071-286 9655 or 071-267 3006.

Organizes classes for women who wish to give birth as naturally as possible, with the minimum of medical intervention.

Independent Midwives Association (Melody Weig) 65 Mount Nod Road, London SW16 2LP. No telephone.

A group of independent midwives offering antenatal care, birth and postnatal care in the home. Their fees vary between £700 and £1,000. They can help women who have a preference for natural birth.

Association for Improvements in the Maternity Services (AIMS) 163 Liverpool Road, London N1 0RF. No telephone.

A voluntary group offering support and advice to parents about their choices in maternity care. The group campaigns for improving maternity services.

Society to Support Home Confinements Lydgate, Lydgate Lane, Wolsingham, Bishops Auckland, Co. Durham DL13 3HA. Tel: 0386 528 044.

Offers advice to couples who want to arrange a home birth.

Pregnancy sickness: a telephone counselling service on 0943 609209 (Barbara Pickard) or 0274 551 309 (Marie Lewis).

Prelearning Broadvale Association, 17 Market Place, Brentford, Middlesex TW8 8EG. Tel: 081 568 7331.

UK distributors of prelearning programme developed by Dr Brent Logan to stimulate the unborn child, from the sixth month of pregnancy, by gentle sounds based on the maternal heartbeat.

Index

Sazonova, T. (on electro-magnetic fields), 48

Sedgwick, James (on alcohol and pregnancy), 32

selenium, 65

slimming, 50, 54

smoking
how to stop, 41
low birthweight and, 39
miscarriage and, 40, 150
passive exposure to, 104
smoker's placenta, 39

spina bifida, 128–9

Stein, Dr Zena (on deferred childbearing), 8

Stott, Dr D. H. (on stress in child handicap), 4

stress
heat, 197
infertility and, 19
maternal, effect on unborn child, 3–5
meditation, breathing exercises and, 91–9

Striessguth, Dr Ann (on FAS), 32

syphilis, 110

systemic lupus erythematosus (SLE), 122

Ta'i Chi Chuan, 87–91

Teno (tenosynovitis), 200–201

Thompson, Dr Elizabeth (on genetic counselling), 123

thrush (*Candida albicans*), 107

thyroid disease
hypothyroidism, 119
hyperthyroidism, 120

toxocariasis, 104

toxoplasmosis, 103

Trowell, Dr Hugh (on high fibre and diabetes), 117

tyramine, 24

urethritis, 107

Valman, Dr H. B. (on effect of maternal anxiety on fetus), 92

VDUs, *see under* radiation

vegetarians, 57, 58

vitamins
ascorbic acid (C), 62
choline, 62
cynocobalain (B12), 61
folic acid, 61
nicotinic acid, 61
pyridoxine (B 6), 60
riboflavin (B 2), 60
thiamine (B 1), 60
vitamin A, 60
vitamin B, 59

walking, 75–8

water safety, 171–2

weight
ideal before pregnancy, 69–70

X-rays, *see under* radiation

yoga
breathing, 95–8
exercises, 80–87

zinc, 25, 31, 57